Tell Them to Get Lost

Travels with the Lonely Planet guidebook that started it all

Brian Thacker

WILLIAM HEINEMANN

A William Heinemann book
Published by Random House Australia Pty Ltd
Level 3, 100 Pacific Highway, North Sydney NSW 2060
www.randomhouse.com.au

First published by William Heinemann in 2011

Addresses for companies within the Random House Group can be found at
www.randomhouse.com.au/offices.

National Library of Australia
Cataloguing-in-Publication Entry
Thacker, Brian, 1962–
Tell them to get lost / Brian Thacker.
ISBN 978 1 74275 195 5 (pbk.)
Southeast Asia – Description and travel.
915.90453

Cover photographs from stck.xchng (crocodile: carollam; goat: zirak; rat:
puellakas; snake: stylesr1)
Cover design by Design by Committee
Internal design by Midland Typesetters, Australia
Typeset in Palatino 11/16 pt by Midland Typesetters, Australia

10 9 8 7 6 5 4 3 2

Printed and bound by The SOS Print + Media Group

The paper this book is printed on is certified by
the ©1996 Forest Stewardship Council A.C.
(FSC). SOS Print + Media Group holds FSC
chain of custody certification
(Cert no. SGS-COC-3047).

FSC promotes environmentally responsible,
socially beneficial and economically viable
management of the world's forests.

FSC
www.fsc.org
MIX
Paper from responsible
sources
FSC® C011217

To my sweet, darling Beth

Contents

Introduction

'The town was full of drunk tourists staggering around singing football chants, but the guidebook described it as a sleepy fishing village with only one place to stay,' I pointed out to Lonely Planet's founder, Tony Wheeler.

Tony and I were sitting side by side at a book signing after sharing a panel at the Melbourne Writers Festival. There was a long queue of people in the bookshop waiting for their books to be signed, but they just didn't happen to be any of *our* books. (The queue of mostly old ladies were all waiting to see some American author with a beard who wrote detective/thriller/love stories – or something similar.) I'd been telling Tony about when I had travelled around the Greek island of Corfu on a scooter using a 1971 guidebook that I had picked up at a boot sale in London for 50 pence. Although it had only been 16 years after the book was published, Corfu had been an entirely different place. Those once-quiet fishing villages had all been transformed into colossal resorts and the 'delightfully empty beaches' now had wall-to-wall sunburned bodies.

Suddenly an idea occurred to me.

'Has anyone ever attempted to travel with the first Lonely Planet On a Shoestring guidebook?' I asked the guru himself.

'No, I've never heard of anyone doing it,' Tony said with a shrug.

I thought about it for a minute. 'Would you have a copy of your first guidebook that I could have?'

A few minutes later, I was planning a trip around South-East Asia following Tony and Maureen's footsteps through Portuguese Timor, Indonesia, Malaysia, Thailand, Laos, Burma and Singapore, but with a catch – I would use the original 1975 Lonely Planet *South east Asia on a shoestring* as my only guidebook.

This was exactly the next great adventure I was looking for. After 25 years of gallivanting around the globe, I was always on the lookout for alternative ways to see and experience the world. Though I still travelled the, you might say, conventional way, I found it so much more exciting when I could delve deep into a culture through the eyes of a local or explore without any preconceived ideas of what a place was like. My somewhat unconventional travels had included a couch-surfing jaunt across every continent, a tour of the world's wackiest festivals ⁿd a journey without a guidebook to countries I knew ˡutely nothing about.

Introduction

I'd only seen a small slice of South-East Asia (a bit of Thailand and Singapore), so this trip would give me a chance to discover what the region was like through the eyes of a backpacker traipsing through Asia in the 1970s. I was intrigued to find out what had changed and what was still around since the Wheelers rode through steamy jungles on a clapped-out Yamaha motorcycle wearing bell-bottom pants.

Back then, Asia was the new frontier for young travellers who journeyed overland from Europe to Australia, on what would become known as the Hippie Trail. The hippies were the real trailblazers through South-East Asia. Their parents weren't interested in exploring the region – particularly Australians whose perception of Asia had more to do with the horrors of war than the wonders of ancient civilisations.

The overland travellers of the '60s and '70s had many reasons for going to Asia: some sought spiritual enlightenment, some were seeking freedom from the moral and social restraints of home and some just wanted to drop out. Or just take lots of drugs. The hippie hot spots on the overland route were full of cheap guesthouses that were in turn filled with the sweet smell of marijuana. By the time the Wheelers published *South east Asia on a shoestring*, young Australians were beginning to head over to Asia in droves.

A few weeks after the book signing, I met up with Tony at the Lonely Planet office in the working-class Melbourne suburb of Footscray to pick up his slightly battered copy of the 1975 *South east Asia on a shoestring*, otherwise known as The Yellow Bible.

'That hotel is still there,' Tony exclaimed, as he flicked through the old guidebook. 'And so is that one.' I was quite surprised to discover how thin the book was – in size as well as content. At only 148 pages, it dwarfed in comparison to the current 15th edition of the guide-book, which was more than 1000 pages long and weighed almost as much as my luggage.

Of course, some things had changed since the first edition. For a start, the current edition had a few more country additions. Missing in action from the original guidebook was Vietnam (at the tail end of the Vietnam War), the Philippines (Ferdinand Marcos had declared martial law) and Cambodia (Pol Pot and the Khmer Rouge had seized power). But they weren't the only polit-ically unstable countries. Only a few short months after the launch of the original guidebook, East Timor (which was then Portuguese Timor) was invaded by Indonesia and didn't gain independence until 2002. Laos had been taken over by the communist Pathet Lao at the same time Indonesia was storming into Timor and tourists weren't welcome back into the country for decades. In 1974, Burma had already been suffering under a military dictatorship and sadly, almost 40 years later, there is just a different maniacal general running and ruining the country. Some countries have flourished, however. Thailand has become one of the world's biggest tourist ~~as~~. Singapore has become richer and cleaner, and

Malaysia is even more westernised and shiny. Indonesia has gained substantial economic growth, but along the way has dealt with bombings, tsunamis, earthquakes and millions of Australians taking over Kuta Beach.

After handing over his copy of the old guidebook, Tony took me on a tour of the Lonely Planet office. 'There are four hundred staff in this office alone,' he explained, as we shuffled past an army of mostly young folk with their heads lost behind computer screens. Lonely Planet has marketed some 650 titles in 118 countries, with annual sales of more than six million guidebooks – making it the world's largest publisher of travel guides. They also offer TV programs, magazines, mobile phone applications and an online community of over 700,000 travellers.

We ended the tour in Tony's office, which he shared with his wife Maureen. They travelled together, lived together and worked together. The couple had met on a London park bench in 1970, when Tony noticed Maureen reading Tolstoy's *Childhood, Boyhood, and Youth*. Maureen, who had grown up in Belfast, had only moved to London at the age of 20, the week before. Not long after meeting, the two were off across Asia's Hippie Trail in a decrepit 1964 Austin mini-van. After nine months of meandering, the Wheelers ended up in Sydney with only 27 cents to their name. Because they were asked so many questions about where they went and how they did it, the Wheelers decided to self-publish *Across Asia on the Cheap*. The 94-page pamphlet, which Tony had written at their kitchen table, sold 8500 copies in Australian bookstores. 'It took off because, in the 1970s, the first generation of baby boomers began to travel,' Tony said. 'It all came together for us.'

It was those baby boomers, who were beginning to travel extensively through South-East Asia, that inspired Tony and Maureen to travel again and write a guidebook about the region. So, in early 1974, the Wheelers set off from Melbourne and up the coast to Darwin. From there, they flew to Baucau in former Portuguese Timor, then spent the next year travelling through the region collecting information.

In the old guidebook's introduction, Tony wrote that South-East Asia offered 'cheap and interesting travel without the constantly oppressing misery of some of the less fortunate parts of Asia'. Certain 'hotspots' in the region attracted the 'tourist crowds', but there were also many 'untouched places that only the people who are willing to put in a little effort and withstand some discomfort will really appreciate'.

The book's introduction also offered some helpful health advice, such as 'catching malaria is not a good idea' and if you 'happen to get a stomach bug then starving the buggers out is a good solution'. He also added that 'to avoid stomach problems in the first place stay away from dubious looking places'.

In the 'Money' section, Tony provided this piece of sage wisdom: 'Bring plenty of this fine stuff.' However, in the 'What to Take' section, he advised: 'As little as possible is the answer, but not so little that you become a scrounge off other people as some of the "super light-weight" travellers do.' When it came to visas, Tony wasn't a big fan. 'My number one Asia hate is visas and the rubber stamp craziness that seems to pervade the whole area,' he wrote. 'Visas are an annoying, time-consuming, unnecessary hassle that only serves to keep a lot of paper pushers in work.'

The visa situation was one of the very few things that I did check into before I left. As far as the rest, I would be putting my faith in a 35-year-old guidebook. Since I didn't want to wear the same underpants for 12 months as the Wheelers may have in 1974, I would be racing through the region in 12 weeks. The way we travel around South-East Asia would have undoubt-edly changed since 1974, and now I would find out how much was still the same. Were Indonesia's tourist offices still 'bloody useless'? Did the Malaysian border patrol still stamp 'suspected hippy' on your passport? Was Patong still a 'freak centre with fruit salad on the menus'? And, more importantly, do restaurants on Kuta Beach still have the funkiest funghi in South-East Asia? Or what if everything had become one big highway overpass?

Luckily, I was reassured by the founder of Lonely Planet himself.

'Some things never change.'

Portuguese
Timor

1

Dili

There's a good tourist office in Dili.
South east Asia on a shoestring, 1st edition, 1975

As yet there's no tourist office in Dili.
Southeast Asia on a Shoestring, 15th edition, 2010

'How much for a taxi into Dili?'

'Ten dollars.'

'But it says here that it is only one dollar,' I said, showing the taxi driver my 35-year-old guidebook.

'Okay . . . five dollars.' He shrugged.

I grinned and threw my backpack into the back seat of his old beaten-up Toyota. 'Do you know the Beach House?' I asked.

He stared at the book's hand-drawn map of Dili for a minute before turning it upside down then sideways. 'Ah, yes,' he said. His big smile revealed teeth that looked as though they hadn't been brushed since 1974.

There was only one Dili hotel listed in the guide-book. At the Beach House, or the 'aptly dubbed Hippie Hilton', you could 'unroll your sleeping bag on a concrete floor for $US1 and stay as long as you like'. It seemed unrolling sleeping bags on floors was quite popular in East Timor back then. The book noted that there were only a few hotels in all of Timor, but that if you asked nicely you may be allowed to unroll your sleeping bag on a lounge room floor. There was also another alternative on offer – one you didn't really have to ask nicely about. According to the guidebook, local jails provided 'emergency accommodation for the intrepid traveller from time to time'. Who needed an emergency? Just throw a rock through a shop window and you'd get a whole bunch of free nights' accommo-dation. And even a few bowls of gruel thrown in for good measure.

My guess was that the Beach House was probably no longer called the 'Hippie Hilton'. All those free-spirited, free-loving hippies had long gone home – and more than likely got themselves nice, sensible jobs and now lived in nice, sensible homes and wore nice, sensible clothes.

The outskirts of Dili certainly didn't look very free-spirited or free-loving. Burned-out and abandoned buildings dotted the dusty landscape, while the large potholes in the road looked like the aftermath of a bomb-ing raid frenzy. Since 1974, East Timor – or Portuguese Timor as it was known then – had been burdened by tragedy. The old guidebook proclaimed the Portuguese

4

colony was a 'beautiful unspoilt country with a rare opportunity to see an old fashioned colony'. There was an inkling of change mentioned, but the description made it sound all so innocent: 'In late '74, noises were being made about cutting Timor loose or turning it over to Indonesia.' The Portuguese had indeed cut Timor loose, but there had been no handing over. In late 1975, East Timor had declared its independence, only to be invaded and barbarously occupied by Indonesia a week later. What followed was decades of hardline rule with over 180,000 civilian deaths and a long, traumatic fight to regain independence. In 1999, a huge majority of East Timorese voted in favour of independence. The vast army of Indonesian troops deployed in Timor decided that if the Timorese wanted their country back then they would make sure there wasn't much of a country left for them. On their way out, they ripped the country apart – destroying homes, shops, government buildings, roads and powerlines and even poured cement into the water pipes. The East Timorese were left with a broken country that wouldn't be easy to fix.

Dili looked like a city in transition. You just didn't know if that transition was that of a city being built or a city falling apart. There were some signs of modernity, however. Standing out in the midst of the dusty, bedraggled buildings stood a brand-new, shiny car dealership with brand-new, shiny Toyota 4WDs on show. It was probably there because every second car on the road was a UN vehicle. And every one of them seemed to be in a hurry to get somewhere. And hopefully not somewhere that involved rioting locals.

I admit that I had a touch of trepidation about coming to East Timor. On the Australian government Department of Foreign Affairs and Trade (DFAT) Smartraveller website, they warned travellers to reconsider their need to travel to East Timor because of the fragile security situation and the risk of violent civil unrest. 'The situation could deteriorate without warning,' the site continued. 'Violence could occur anywhere at any time in East Timor.' The government recommends taking 'particular care to avoid demonstrations, street rallies and public gatherings' which 'may turn violent'. And according to DFAT, there is a history of gang-related violence, robbery, arson and vandalism in Dili: 'Rocks have been thrown at vehicles, particularly during the early evening and at night. You should avoid armed groups of people, including martial arts groups.'

Then again, that didn't sound too bad. Although I would be taking very particular care to avoid gang-related violence, robbery, arson and vandalism, I would have to scratch my plan to hang out with a martial arts group.

When I was there, at least East Timor was only on the list of destinations for which DFAT advises you to 'reconsider your need to travel' and not on the 'do not travel' list, which includes Afghanistan, Burundi, Central African Republic, Chad, Georgia, Iraq, Somalia, Sudan and New Zealand. Okay, New Zealand didn't really make the list. But the Smartraveller website did warn about 'black ice' while driving in winter and that you should also be aware that, 'Not all railway crossings have barriers, particularly in country areas.'

East Timor had more than black ice to deal with. The Smartraveller website warned that, 'Driving conditions are frequently hazardous due to poor road quality, poor signage and a lack of street lighting.' At least Dili had roads. In fact, in 1974, Dili had the only paved road in the whole country, according to the guidebook. Mind you, getting around wouldn't have been easy, anyway. There were only two petrol stations in the entire colony. So those UN vehicles must have used a lot of gas, because the driver and I passed four petrol stations before reaching Dili.

I wasn't surprised to see some serious loitering among the locals when we hit the city, but I *was* surprised to see pigs wandering down the footpath on their way to the shops. While the hogs browsed the store windows, men squatted on their haunches in doorways and under the shade of frangipani trees and small groups of young women wearing tight jeans and bright T-shirts strutted down the street arm in arm. The people looked more Pacific Islander than Asian, with their dark skin and black curly hair.

The pigs, with their little piglets in tow, also strolled along the black sand beach, which was described in the old guidebook as 'fairly dismal'. Now we were driving along the oceanfront, past large and grandiose homes

– except that they weren't homes. These were the consulates of the much more fortunate. On the beach side of the tree-lined esplanade, rows of vendors in tin shacks sold coconuts, tropical fruit, fish and mobile-phone cards.

After cruising along the waterfront for some time, my driver stopped and pointed towards a couple of wooden tables piled high with fish. 'Beach House,' he announced. I couldn't see anything that resembled a Beach House or a Hilton – hippie or otherwise. 'Beach House is here.' He gestured wildly beyond the smelly fish.

The Beach House was there. Or what was left of it, at least. A large concrete slab punctuated the centre of the scruffy beach. It was the same piece of concrete where you could unroll your sleeping bag for a dollar and stay for as long as you liked. Except there were no walls or roof. My driver had only been excited because he knew where the Beach House *used* to be. I stood on the slab and surveyed my surroundings. Right, so now where do I stay? I wondered. My taxi driver had already skedaddled and there were only a couple of pigs on the beach to ask where I might find a cheap but pleasant lounge room floor for the night. I walked back past the fish sellers and noticed a hotel across the road overlooking the beach. The Hotel Turismo looked decidedly dishevelled, but at least it had walls. It could have been around since before 1974, but it was hard to tell if it was old or just very dusty.

I walked through the garden of bright pink oleanders into a hot and stuffy reception where the cheerful girl at the desk quoted me a ridiculous price for a room. I wasn't expecting to pay a dollar and stay as long as I liked, but $US50 was a bit steep for a basic and, if the outside was anything to go by, run-down room. In 1974, the currency in Timor had been Portuguese escudos, then the Indonesian rupiah. It was now US dollars – although they had absolutely nothing to do with the US, which was 14,000 kilometres away.

While I was filling out the ludicrously detailed registration card (Why did they need to know my favourite colour?), I asked the receptionist if she knew what year the hotel had opened. As she shrugged, a little voice behind me said, 'The hotel opened on the twenty-fourth of April, 1967.' The little voice belonged to the very little Joaquim Calluto, the hotel janitor. Joaquim, clad in faded overalls and carrying a light bulb in one hand and a broom in the other, not only knew when the hotel had been built; he had helped build it with the Portuguese owner – who had fled the colony when the Indonesians invaded.

Joaquim's eyes lit up when he started talking about the hotel's 'grand opening'. 'The restaurant was full of people dressed in suits and evening dresses,' he gushed. 'The owner imported a whole crate of champagne and the corks exploded when you opened them. We'd never seen anything like it.'

Joaquim remembered the hippies 'over on the beach' in the '70s, but said that not many had stayed at the Turismo. Instead, 'There were many spies staying here.'

His voice was hushed, as though they were still listening somewhere. The hotel had also been the favoured place to stay among foreign journalists.

'The Balibo Five also stayed here and one slept in your room,' Joaquim said. 'Do you know much of them?'

'Yes, of course,' I said. Most Australians know much of them.

Not long after the old guidebook came out, an Australian news crew set out from the hotel for the town of Balibo. Although they were heading to the town to report on the anticipated attack from the Indonesian army, they thought that, as journalists, they would be protected. But the Indonesians didn't want any news of their aggressive attack getting out, so as soon as the journalists arrived they were fired upon by the invading troops. Four were killed on the spot and the fifth Balibo victim was stabbed to death after he attempted to hide in a bathroom.

As Joaquim escorted me to my room, I asked him whether life was better during Portuguese rule, Indonesian rule or independence. Joaquim stopped and looked at me for a moment. 'It is hard now,' he admitted. 'But it is much better. We have our country back.'

My room wasn't as run-down or as dusty as I'd predicted, but the bars on the window were a bit of a concern. Were they there to keep people in or to keep people out? Before I went out, I made sure to check the room for bugs. Both the creepy-crawly variety and the creepy-spy variety.

The old guidebook map of Dili was pretty much impossible to follow. Not only were there no street names, but I couldn't get my bearings because most of the places listed weren't there anymore. There was no tourist office or TAT office (a now-defunct French airline) and the mention of only one bank didn't help when there was now one on just about every block. It wasn't until I happened upon the surviving government building that I finally figured out where I was on the map. I gasped, for this was quite a milestone. This was the first place listed in the old guidebook that I'd found. The creatively named 'Government Building' was described as 'quite impressive, with a couple of fierce looking Timorese guards at the door'. The building was quite impressive in that none of the paint was peeling off, and there were still a couple of Timorese guards (although probably not the same ones), but they looked far from threatening. One was snoring away while the other was too busy picking his nose to look 'fierce'. And the building wasn't that 'impressive' – although I found it quite impressive that it was still standing long after the Indonesian army had run amok.

On the way back to the hotel – well, with that old map I could have been heading anywhere but my hotel – I passed the Resistance Museum, which was housed in the suitably grand Old Portuguese Court of Justice building. The museum had opened in December 2005 to document East Timor's arduous journey to freedom. My one-dollar entrance fee got me two rooms full of exhibits I didn't understand because the descriptions were in Portuguese, though I did comprehend all the guns on display. The only thing in English was a time chart of East Timor's road to independence. The last panel read, 'East Timor. The world's newest country.'

East Timor was just one of 39 'new' countries that have graced the world map since the old guidebook came out in 1975. Some have flourished, like Slovenia, Antigua and Barbuda, Seychelles, Vanuatu and Estonia, while others, like East Timor, have struggled, including Angola, Eritrea, Djibouti, Moldova and Kirabati. East Timor possibly had the most difficult struggle of all, with the time chart chock-full of events that involved either civil unrest or Indonesian-led violence.

One of the most infamous incidents was the Santa Cruz Massacre. On 12 November 1991, a memorial march to Santa Cruz Cemetery was turned into a blood-bath when Indonesian soldiers opened fire inside the cemetery killing more than 270 East Timorese. This was just one of many brutal massacres in East Timor during Indonesian occupation, but this atrocity was caught on film and the subsequent fallout brought world attention to the conflict and led the way to independence.

I asked the fellow at the front desk to show me where the Santa Cruz Cemetery was on my map. He stared at it for about two minutes before shaking his head and drawing his own representation on a scrap piece of paper. I asked him if he remembered the day of the massacre. 'Yes, we all remember it,' he said.

In the infamous video of the shootings, the cemetery oozed an eerie and frightening atmosphere. But as I wandered into the quiet graveyard, it couldn't have been more different. The cemetery was bursting with flowering frangipani trees and the blossoms' sweet, melancholy fragrance hung heavily between the white and pale blue graves. It's almost impossible to fathom such cold-blooded violence when you are surrounded by such peace and beauty. I'd felt the same way while standing on the pristine green pastures in the battle-fields of Somme and in the neat and pretty Hiroshima Peace Memorial Park.

I didn't stay long. A cemetery was creepy enough without the shadow of an atrocious past hanging over it. As I walked out, I passed a couple on their way in. They gave me such a sweet smile as if to say that every-thing was all right. Things really were better. These warm-hearted folk had their country back.

There were three restaurants recommended in the old guidebook. My taxi driver hadn't heard of any of them. But then again, my taxi driver Castro was only 20 years old. I wondered if he at least did know whether to duck to avoid any rocks that may be thrown at vehicles, particularly during the early evening and at night, as the Smartraveller website warns.

Castro's taxi, like many taxis driven by young folk in the city, was hotted up. Or as hotted up as you can get with limited funds. The most prized addition to a taxi in Dili appeared to be a novelty horn. Every couple of minutes, Castro would pass another taxi and exchange novelty horn blasts. Novelty headlights were also popular. As in headlights of all different colours. Castro's headlights were purple. Like a lot of the taxis, though, he didn't have them on. This saved on petrol, Castro explained, and he also drove incredibly slowly for the same reason.

When it came to eating out, the old guidebook praised the Restaurant Baucau, where everyone met for 'excellent Chinese food'. Not anymore they didn't. We pulled up in front of where the restaurant was supposed to be and it was now a rather gloomy and dusty shop selling rusted car parts.

Next on the list was the Tropical Snack Bar, where 'reasonably priced western food can be found'. Five minutes later, we pulled up in front of the City Cafe.

'This is the Tropical Snack Bar,' Castro announced.

'Um, it has three signs saying City Cafe,' I said.

'Yes,' he said, before dumping me on the street.

I stepped inside the restaurant and asked a waitress, 'Is this the Tropical Snack Bar?'

'Yes,' she said, nodding to the potted palms in the corner.

I sat outside on the terrace, which was packed with UN types, international aid types and human rights organisation types. While the book suggested I drink Mozambique beer or Portuguese wine in East Timor, I didn't see any Mozambique beer on the menu – only Australian beer with a choice of Victoria Bitter,

Melbourne Bitter and Foster's. I decided on a glass of Portuguese wine – though I think Mozambique wine would have tasted better.

As I was ordering my meal, a UN car pulled up to the front. I watched as a fellow rushed in and came out with a sixpack of VB. Over the course of my meal, I noticed a steady stream of UN folk buying large quantities of beer. Must be hard at work protecting the country, I thought. Hopefully there wouldn't be any violent civil unrest while I was there, or the UN soldiers would have all turned up a bit tipsy.

For my 'reasonably priced western food', I ordered the grilled fish and vegetables – with a black hair for garnish. At ten US dollars, I supposed it was reasonably priced, but it wasn't reasonably edible. It was more like garlic with a side dish of fish and vegetables. I couldn't even see the type of fish under the piles of garlic. That made me an easy target for the gangs of robbers, arsonists and vandals on the walk back to the hotel – they'd be able to smell me a mile off. The streets were gloomy and the smiling locals now appeared as dark, threatening figures hiding in doorways. I couldn't see their faces. Or their machetes, for that matter.

On the way back to the Hotel Turismo, I stopped for one more drink at the One More Bar to try to drown away the overpowering taste of garlic. The big-screen TV in the upstairs bar showed Australian Rules football, while Midnight Oil blared from the sound system. The bar was full of Australian UN personnel drinking

Foster's and eating Aussie pizzas that cost more than they did in Australia.

I sat down at the bar next to Craig, a UN police officer. He looked surprised, even shocked, when I told him that I was a tourist. He insisted he had not seen a single tourist since he had been in East Timor. 'At these prices, I'm not surprised,' I told him. I only stayed for one more drink because I would be getting up early to catch a bus to Baucau. (I'd pretty much seen all of Dili in one afternoon.)

'Do you know of any nice lounge room floors to stay on in Baucau?' I asked Craig before I got up to leave.

2

Baucau

Bus: Dili – Baucau US$3.
South east Asia on a shoestring, 1st edition, 1975

Bus: Dili – Baucau US$2.
Southeast Asia on a Shoestring, 15th edition, 2010

The price of the bus from Dili to Baucau had gone down since 1974. That said something, though probably not something very good. Had the roads gotten even worse? In the original guidebook, the map of East Timor illustrated solid lines for 'bad roads' and dotted lines for 'worse roads'. The road to Baucau was only a 'bad road', but after 35 years I couldn't help but wonder if it had turned into a 'worse road' or perhaps even the 'worst road'. The old book observed that all roads in Timor ranged from 'bad to indescribable'. The road to Baucau was probably now indescribable, I imagined, and if I couldn't even describe a road, then how would I be able to write about it?

The cheaper price may have also had something to do with the fact that the bus might simply fall apart – while you're having your bag stolen. The Smartraveller website warned, 'Take care if using buses, microlets or trucks used as public transport due to the poor condition of many of these vehicles and poor driving standards. There is also an increased risk of robbery.'

I took the Mobile Disco Bus to Baucau. It reminded me of a packed, smoky nightclub. Inside the microlet (or minibus), mind-numbingly loud disco music blasted out of giant speakers while everyone smoked (as in *everyone* smoked) and screamed at each other over the music. There was no booze, however – although I saw a girl mysteriously throw up, later in the trip. And there wasn't much room to dance, either. The 16-seat bus jammed 30 locals inside, plus a few dozen large bags of rice piled high in the aisle. Some sat on the rice with their heads squashed up against the roof, while others hung out the open door clinging on with the tips of their fingers. The fellow sitting next to me, whose concern for personal hygiene was somewhat lacking, may as well have been sitting on my lap. And I only had six hours of this.

The road climbed out of Dili into dry, barren mountains and small villages made up of mostly burned-out shacks. In the middle of one of these tiny villages, I noticed a not-so-burned-out church in pastel shades of lemon and pink. As we descended the range on the other side, the rugged mountain spurs appeared to tumble right down to the sea. The road had at least been upgraded to bitumen since 1974, although I think this bitumen was made with papier-mâché and treacle. Where the road had broken up, it had simply been tarred over with more treacle. Needless to say, the bumpy roads meant a bumpy ride, which made everyone look as if they were rocking out to the music. The 'conductor', on the other hand, was doing a bit of crowd-surfing as he clambered over people to sell tickets. At one point, he stopped the bus in order to step outside and sell tickets to the daredevils hanging off the bus.

The old guidebook described the next part of the journey as 'quite a spectacular trip, particularly after Manatuto as the road runs right along the cliff edge'. That cliff edge was still there and the road did run right along it, but I wasn't sure if it was still spectacular. That's because I kept my eyes closed for most of it. The road twisted and turned upon itself like an itchy snake, with yawning, unfenced precipices falling away to either side of the road. Those lunatic passengers hanging precariously out the door were literally dangling over the edge with nothing between them but air and a dramatic drop. One slip and that would have been the last we'd ever see of them. Ah, so that's why the conductor made sure he got his ticket sales in early, I thought.

After a few more stops in tiny villages – where five people would get off and seven people would get on – we pulled up in the middle of a small but busy market. Suddenly, every single person in the bus exited. While I sat waiting for the bus to refill again, the driver motioned for me to get off, too. 'No, I'm going to Baucau!' I screamed over the thumping music.

'Baucau,' he said, pointing outside.

'Baucau!' I repeated.

'Baucau!' he said, pointing to the other side of the bus.

This went on for a few minutes until I came to the conclusion that this was, in fact, Baucau. The reason I was so confused was because it had been less than three hours since we'd left Dili, and yet the old guidebook indicated that the trip would last six hours. Not only was the bus ride cheaper than it was in 1974, but it now took half the time.

The scruffy, down-at-heel town didn't look anything like the 'main entry point into Portuguese Timor'. Back in 1974, Baucau had been home to Timor's main port and the international airport. Tony and Maureen had begun their one-year journey here after they'd flown in from Darwin (with motorbike in tow). The Wheelers would have arrived on one of the three TAA flights each week from Darwin, which would have cost them $AUD73. I had taken one of the six flights now offered per week with Airnorth from Darwin to Dili, which cost me substantially more at $AUD650.

Baucau, even more so than the rest of East Timor, had taken the brunt of the terror inflicted by the Indonesians. When John Martinkus, author of *A Dirty Little War*, had visited the town in 1995, he reported that:

At night in Baucau the streets are deserted. The only movement comes from a tightly knit band of police outside their sandbagged post. For Timorese youth to move in the streets after dark is extremely dangerous. If detected, the result is likely arrest, torture and, for some, death.

It all went off with a big bang in 1999. Following the announcement of the 'yes' vote for independence in early September, the pro-Indonesia militia went on a rampage. By the end of September, Alan Matthews, who had headed the British government's emergency logistics team, called Baucau 'the first place that I've seen that is almost totally destroyed. Hardly any buildings are untouched. There is no power and no water.'

I hoped at least one of the two hotels listed in the old book hadn't been totally destroyed. And some power and water would be nice, too, I reckoned. The two hotels listed were the 'popular and cheap' Perola Oriental, which 'usually cannot cope with all the travellers passing through so doubles often become quadruples or even sextuples – so long as no government officials are looking', and the Hotel Baucau, where 'the bar is nice'. When I asked around the market for the Perola Oriental, the response was a whole lot of blank looks. I had a lot more luck with the Hotel Baucau, in the form of a big smile and directions pointing right around the corner.

I couldn't miss the hotel. It looked like a big peach. And the words 'Hotel Baucau' jumped out of the brilliant blue tiles on the pavement. Except it was no longer called the Hotel Baucau. The sign on the gate read 'Welcome to the Pousada de Baucau'. The hotel, which retained its colonial charm, had wide, sweeping steps (all peach-pink, of course) that led up to a wide verandah decorated with rattan furniture. It looked like the perfect place to don a Panama hat and sip a G & T. Even the airy and neat foyer looked perfectly inviting, so I immediately booked in for two nights. I had no trouble getting a room because it seemed that I was the only guest. As I made my way to my room, I didn't see a single person except the small army of staff who all looked far too young even to have been born when the old guidebook came out.

The pink theme carried through to my room, with its hot-pink shower, pink sink and tulip-pink toilet paper. In the corner sat an old writing desk and views over the old town and the ocean far below.

On the way out for an amble about town, I met the manager, Francisco Antonio Correia, who had the biggest, bushiest moustache that I'd ever seen. Francisco told me that the hotel had been built by the Portuguese in the 1950s and was then called the Hotel Flamboyant. There was nothing flamboyant about the hotel after the Indonesians took over, however. The hotel had been used by the Indonesian military to imprison and torture dissidents. After independence in 2002, the hotel had been renovated and converted into the lavish pink Pousada de Baucau. My room had clearly been nicely renovated, but it was a little disconcerting to think that the Indonesians may have used my room to string up dissidents by their testicles.

According to the old guidebook, Baucau had little to see – apart from the 'colourful market on Thursday and Sunday'. The only other sight mentioned was the old market building, or the Municipal Mercado, which had been 'bombed out during World War II and never repaired'. Thirty-five years later, it still hadn't been repaired – or protected from a few more bombings from the Indonesians. The formerly grand, and now grandly derelict, Municipal Mercado looked like a Roman forum on stilts. Inside the market, it felt more like the Municipal Banheiro (the Municipal Toilet). A strong stench of urine permeated the empty market. Mind you, that didn't seem to deter the locals who had strung up neat lines of washing across the main courtyard.

Walking the streets of Baucau wasn't easy. The footpath was so torn up in parts that it felt like a game of daredevil hopscotch. As I weaved my way through the rubble, I jumped at a horrendous noise coming from inside a large abandoned hall. Sticking my head through a small gap in the door, I discovered the horrendous noise was actually a thrash-metal band rehearsing. And although it was a big hall, the band was squeezed into a cramped, murky corridor at the back of the building. The lead singer motioned for me to come in, then shut the door behind me. The room was so pitch black, I couldn't even see the drummer. Two colossal amps blasted a song that I think was called 'Distortion in the Key of E'. And like every band practice session the world over, the lead singer kept telling the lead guitarist to turn his amp down, and the drummer kept banging away between songs while the rest of the band were trying to talk.

After I'd shattered one of my eardrums, I departed for the 'colourful market'. The market, which had stalls on either side of the busy road, was made up of small, open wooden shacks. In each shack was a crude wooden counter with tiny but neatly piled pyramids of food that looked as if they had been styled for a photo shoot. Most of the stalls seemed to be selling exactly the same thing: tomatoes, peppers, potatoes and garlic. Lots of garlic. And most of it, headed to the City Cafe in Dili, I imagined.

In the 'Shopping' section of the Portuguese Timor chapter, the old guidebook recommended buying 'wood-carvings, rather crude buffalo horn carvings and very nice blankets'. Tony Wheeler's favourite market goods, however, had been 'gift wrapped pigs' that were 'tightly bound in palm leaves for easy transport'.

Gift-wrapped pigs would have turned me off my lunch, but all those neat piles of brightly coloured food were making me hungry, and even though it was only 11.40, I was ready to eat. Again I asked around the market for the Perola Oriental, which 'turns out very good food', according to the old guidebook. But again, I received the same blank stares. I ended up at the Restaurant Amalia instead, after noticing a couple of UN soldiers walking in. If they were going there, then it must be okay, I thought. Unless they were about to raid the place for insurgents and I'd be caught in the middle of a nasty shootout.

I climbed down a series of steep steps to the restaurant, which opened out onto a wide terrace under the shade of a giant banyan tree. I was shown to a table with views of the old market and a soothing cool breeze. And what made the breeze even lovelier was that it was blowing the urine smell the opposite way. I asked the waiter if they had any Timorese food on the menu. 'Yes, we have satay chicken,' he replied. I didn't have the heart to break the news to him that satay was the national dish of their former oppressors.

After lunch, I decided to do what any good investigative and inquisitive writer would do – I lounged by the pool for most of the afternoon. In my defence, that's what the old guidebook suggested: 'When you have tired wandering the town, you can retire to the Hotel Baucau's swimming pool for five escudos.' And even better, it was now free. The pool sat across from the hotel, on the road down to the beach. It was Olympic sized, fed with fresh spring water and full of smiley, happy local kids splashing around. It wasn't very relaxing, though. Every single kid wanted a photo taken with the funny-looking, pasty-white guy.

Back at the hotel, I wandered around poking my nose into rooms that I probably shouldn't have been poking my nose into. I checked out the staffroom, the manager's office and even the broom closet. After closely inspecting the mops and buckets, I spent quite a bit of time in the reading room. Among the Dan Brown and John Grisham novels in Portuguese was an entire volume of encyclopedias from 1975. What a stroke of luck, I thought. The first thing I looked up was the entry on East Timor. Back then, the population was 650,000 (it was now around two million), while the capital, Dili, only had 25,000 (it had now jumped to 150,000). There was also an inkling of drama to come: 'The eastern half of Timor was a Portuguese colony, but following civil unrest is aiming to gain independence. The status is unclear and is likely to cause some tension in the future.'

Even those free-loving but not free-spending hippies received a mention: 'The benefits for the local tourism industry were disappointing – over half the visitors were "drifters" travelling on limited funds between Australia and Indonesia.' There were, however, high hopes for a burgeoning tourism industry: 'The island is developing a tourist program,' the encyclopedia said, 'and an Australian company is planning to build five hotels in East Timor to increase the present intake of 5000 tourists a year.' The numbers had actually decreased since then. In 2009, only 1500 tourists visited East Timor. Make that 1501.

I had been doing a bit of similar research from some old books back at home. Before I left for my trip, I ordered a bunch of books about South-East Asia (for historical, political, economic and environmental information) that were published between 1973 and 1975. The only problem about buying books on Amazon.com without a description, though, is that there is always a chance you'll get a dud. Three of the books I purchased did provide interesting facts, but I struggled to find anything worth using from *Southeast Asia* by EHG Dobby. The entire book was about soil dispersion – or something similar. Then again, maybe some would have been riveted by chapters with titles along the lines of 'The Development of Concave Profiles Typical of the Sunda Platform in the Bentong Valley' or 'A Physiographic Sketch of Mean Annual Rainfall in Goenong Oengaran'.

When I'd had enough of my literary sojourn in the reading room, I retired to the verandah for a G & T (minus the Panama hat). Even though no one else was staying in the hotel, it took 15 minutes to get a drink. I had dinner in the sunlit, but empty, dining pavilion, with its beautifully displayed wines and linen place settings. All of that linen felt a bit posh for this on-the-cheap backpacker, however, so I ordered the least expensive thing on the menu: soup. The suitably dapper waiter wasn't too happy when I kept asking him to refill the bread basket.

After dinner, I went for a walk to the night market. And I mean 'night market', as in it was totally dark. I couldn't even see the people manning the stalls, let alone any of the food on display. Some stalls had candles casting a weak pool of light on their piles of garlic, but the rest were cloaked in darkness. At least the UN troops would have been able to shop. All they had to do was slip on their night-vision goggles.

'Unfortunately, the beautiful beaches are 5 km sharply downhill from the town,' the old guidebook warned. But fortunately for me, the walk down, the next morning, was rather pleasant and mostly shaded by gargantuan banyan trees and towering palms. It also gave me the perfect opportunity to see village life up close. Not far down the road, I passed a small cluster of thatched huts where well-dressed locals were getting ready for a wedding. The blushing bride, in her crisp, clean white wedding dress, was standing in the dirt while the beaming flower girls knelt by her side, dusting off her high heels. Further down the road, men in suits were dusting off an old Toyota as the groom stood by, looking very sweaty. He could have been perspiring because he was extremely nervous, but more likely it was because he was wearing a three-piece suit under the hot Baucau sun. The groom and his groomsmen greeted me with warm smiles and a cheerful 'bom dia' (good morning in Portuguese).

Outside the village, the road snaked down into a series of long, lazy S-bends. Soon, the jungle gave way to rice terraces dotted with palm trees. Boys carrying long poles draped with fish on their shoulders and girls and women with sacks of potatoes and vegetables on their heads shuffled past me up the steep hill on their way to the market. Where were all the men? I wondered.

An hour later, I found out. I reached a fine sand lagoon where a rainbow of fishing boats rode at anchor in clear, turquoise waters. At the end of the beach stood a small fishing village, although there didn't seem to be much fishing going on. All the men folk were lounging in wooden shelters nestled under the palm trees. Just off the beach, I spotted a small sign for Baucau Beach Bungalows and wandered in for a look. I was greeted by the owner, José Maria Borges, and purchased a drink from his tiny (as in the size of a toilet) shop – which saved me from having to break open some coconuts. For the old guidebook suggested: 'If you are thirsty there are always plenty of coconuts lying around.'

José told me that in 1974, he was 28. Since then, he'd had ten children and built some bungalows – though there was only one of them left (that's bungalows, not children). José took me on a tour of that one and only bungalow. 'The others were burnt down earlier this year during the incident,' José observed drily.

'Why did they do it?' I asked him, as we gazed over at the concrete blocks and burnt remains of the three former bungalows.

José shrugged. 'After the incident, not many tourists come.'

I wasn't sure exactly what 'incident' he was talking about. Sadly, East Timor had endured its fair share of incidents in its recent past.

'I'll show you the good bungalow,' José smiled. He looked as though he smiled a lot.

The remaining bungalow was a simple, thatched hut overlooking a private and pristine beach. Without even seeing the inside, I asked if I could book it for the following night. Though the room was simple, it did have three beds (two doubles and a single), a bathroom, shower and even a flushing toilet. 'When I have more money, I will fix the other bungalows,' José assured me. 'More tourists will come when it's . . . um, quieter.'

'When do you think that will be?' I asked.

José beamed. 'Maybe next year.'

I asked José about the Perola Oriental and was happy to hear that it wasn't just a figment of Tony Wheeler's imagination. 'Yes, Mr Wu, the owner, was my friend.' Peter Wu had even received a mention in the old guidebook as the 'man in the know in Baucau'. Not anymore, however. 'Mr Wu left when the Indonesians came.' José bowed his head. 'Most of the Chinese people left.' Even Tony Wheeler had predicted such an occurrence. He wrote: 'The 10,000 or so Chinese who control the economy now fear for their lives.'

Before I headed back up to the hotel, I decided to go for a swim at my very own private beach. Well, not quite private – I shared it with a goat tethered to a palm tree next to the water. The water was perfectly clear and warm. Had I discovered paradise? No, I hadn't. I later found out that the Baucau Beach Bungalows were listed in the current *Southeast Asia on a Shoestring* and described as 'a little slice of paradise down by the beach'.

Because I wasn't looking forward to the long steep slog back up the hill, I strolled back through the village until I spotted a motorbike. 'Whose bike is this?' I asked a group of men lounging lazily under a tree. One of them pointed to a fellow sprawled out asleep on the sand. After I subtly nudged him awake with my foot, we began a game of charades. And even then, I couldn't get him to understand that I wanted a lift into town. As soon as I flashed some cash at him, however, he suddenly understood. Though his two-dollar fee was the same as the three-hour bus fare from Dili, I did need to get back in a hurry: the Australian Rules Grand Final in Melbourne was about to start.

When I'd asked the young man at reception if there was anywhere that might be playing the game on TV, he replied, 'There is an Australian army base up in the mountains. They might know it.' If the Australian army were anywhere near as accommodating as the Portuguese army, I might even get a floor for the night, for, according to the old guidebook, the 'Portuguese army can be very helpful; we had the floor of the officer's mess on one occasion'.

The fellow at reception escorted me onto the microlet (a minibus) and muttered some directions to the driver. I sat next to a man with a large machete in his lap and wondered if he was also going to watch the game. At a speed of about ten kilometres an hour, we jounced and clanged through an uninhabited and ragged countryside, a place as beautiful as it was forbidding.

Suddenly, in the middle of barren and dry nothingness, we stopped next to an abandoned building surrounded by goats and vicious dogs (mind you, all dogs look vicious to me). The driver pointed up to a dirt track that seemed to lead to nowhere at all. I shuffled nervously over a rise and came upon a tiny, open tin shack baking in the hot sun. Beyond it sloped a field of brown dust, and beyond that was a series of army barracks. As I approached the tin shack, I noticed a serious-looking guard sitting with a very serious gun. 'Halt, who goes there?' he barked. 'Don't move or I'll shoot!' Okay, he didn't really say that, but I did greet him with, 'G'day, mate,' just to make it clear straight up that I was a fellow Aussie and not a sympathising insurgent rebel. 'They wouldn't be playing the AFL Grand Final here, would they?' I asked.

'Yes, but I don't think you'll be allowed in,' he said with an apologetic grin.

I sighed. 'Oh, well.'

'Wait, I'll ask anyway,' he said, reaching for his walkie-talkie.

After he mentioned someone called 'Roger', he turned and gave me the thumbs up. 'Yeah, no worries, someone will escort you in.' That someone was a Herculean soldier carrying a Rambolean gun. I was escorted into the barracks, as in the room where the soldiers all slept. And some were still sleeping. At the end of the long bunk room, strapping young chaps in camouflage fatigues were sitting back watching the game on a huge plasma TV. As I took a seat, a couple of beefy soldiers smiled at me, while the rest eyed me suspiciously. No one spoke to me and I didn't know what to say to them: 'So, have you shot any insurgents lately?' The game was in full swing and most of the lads were screaming at the TV. I just hoped that someone didn't get too upset if their team lost – a few of them were cradling large guns in their laps. No one offered me a drink (even though there was a large fridge full of bottled water and Coke) and I spent the whole game sitting quietly, so I wouldn't offend any of the opposing supporters with large guns.

After the game finished, I snuck out (on the off chance they decided to use the skinny guy for bayonet practice) and made my way back to the main road without any idea of how to get back to Baucau. This might take a while, I thought. Just as the sweat from my underpants reached my boots, a UN vehicle drove past, then turned around and picked me up. 'What the hell are you doing wandering around here?' the driver asked as I jumped in. Noel was an Australian working for the UN and had been staying in Baucau for the past two months.

'Is there much trouble here?' I asked.

'Not really,' he said brightly. 'Sometimes there's a fight over a delivery of rice and they kill each other, but that's about it.'

I had dinner in the hotel restaurant again, but this time it was so full that I had to share a table with Johnno from Brisbane. Johnno was working as an NGO for the East Timor Ministry of Finance. 'Are you UN or an NGO?' Johnno asked.

'Um, neither – I'm a tourist.'

'A tourist? Wow!'

Johnno told me that on the weekends, the hotel was full of UN staff and NGOs from Dili. I have something to confess. I didn't know what NGO stood for. I'd always thought it was something that I should have known, so I was too embarrassed to ask. I finally looked up 'NGO' when I got home. It stood for Non-Government Organisation. But you probably already knew that, didn't you? Wait, there's more. According to Wikipedia, there are also BINGOs, short for Business International Non-Government Organisations, and QUANGOs, Quasi Autonomous Non-Government Organisations. Plus there are GONGOs, Government-Operated NGOs; TANGOs, Technical Assistance NGOs and MANGOs, Market Advocacy NGOs. I wondered, though, how many people openly admitted that they were DONGOs – Donor Organised NGOs.

Johnno had been in East Timor for three months. A week before he left Australia he had been lying in bed and couldn't sleep because he was so worried about how dangerous and how primitive East Timor was going to be. On his first night in Dili, he ended up sitting at a lovely restaurant on the beach, drinking Australian wine and eating lobster. 'It was nothing like I imagined,' he said. 'It really was . . . just idyllic.'

*

The fishermen, and I use that word loosely, were still loafing about when I arrived at the beach in the morning. 'There's not many fish at the moment,' José told me, as I checked into my bungalow. To be honest, I wasn't really that interested in fish. But I was interested in cocks. I asked José if there was still cockfighting on Sundays. Said the old guidebook: 'Every Sunday afternoon in every Timorese town and village the male population turns out for the national sport – cock fighting.' Though cockfighting received a quarter-page write-up in the old guidebook, this 'event of the week' didn't even get a mention in the current edition.

'Yes, it is on today,' José said. 'Would you like to go? My son can take you.'

I'd already lost my WWF and Greenpeace member-ships after eating whale in Iceland, so I might as well lose my Gould League membership as well, I decided. I should emphasise that I don't condone cockfighting in any way, but as José said, 'It's the biggest thing in Timor. You can't miss it.'

Before I went to watch a bit of gratuitous violence, I spent a lazy morning ambling from one perfectly picturesque, empty cove to another and swimming in warm, clear waters. Why was no one else here? I pondered. I found my answer when I spotted a yellow sign with a message in Timorese on a pole in the middle of a white-sand beach. I didn't know what the words '*Cuidado Nani Iha Nee*' meant, but I did know what the picture of a nasty-looking crocodile with nasty-looking teeth meant.

Back at the Baucau Beach Bungalows, I bumped into Jose's 28-year-old son, Nino. 'No, there are no crocodiles,' he said. 'Oh, except for one big one, but it's okay. We are trying to catch it.' Then I remembered seeing the goat tethered to a palm tree on the water's edge the day before and realised it must have been the bait. The goat had now gone. Either it had been chomped by the croc or moved because they now had me as bait splashing happily around in the water. Funny, I *had* noticed a few locals giving me a pitiful smile as I headed down the beach for a swim.

I had lunch at my own private dining table by the water's edge in front of my bungalow. Two women came down from the main house with trays filled with plates of food. Were other guests joining me? No, it was all for me. There was rice, grilled vegetables, boiled eggs (as in an entire plate full of boiled eggs), salad and fried chicken from KFC – or at least that's what it looked like. Even though I could barely get out of my seat from having eaten too much, I decided to go for a quick swim afterwards. I was very cautious, though. I only went in up to my knees. And, even then, whenever I saw a dark shape (probably more of the rock or seaweed variety), in the water, I jumped out, squealing like a little girl.

I got a ride to the cockfighting on the back of Nino's motorcycle. 'I like to practise my English,' Nino bellowed over the not-quite-tuned engine. 'Portuguese is no good.

Indonesian is no good.' Nino was a schoolteacher in the middle of a government-enforced three-month school holiday, so teachers could learn Portuguese to then teach the children. 'Kids don't want to learn Portuguese,' he told me. 'They want to learn English, so they can sing along to hip-hop music.'

The cockfighting 'arena' was located down a narrow dirt track not far from the Pousada de Baucau. I could hear the crowing before we even got there. We pulled up next to a dusty clearing between wooden shacks as groups of men arrived on motorbikes, packed microlets and on foot. We stood out from the crowd because we were the only ones without a rooster under our arms. The cockpit, which was under the shade of a towering tamarind tree, was fenced off with scrap bits of corrugated tin and surrounded by a row of rough wooden benches. Men stood around the clearing, sizing up each other's cocks. (Now, now, get your mind out of the gutter.) It was an all-male show – in both respects. The men looked pensive, shuffling nervously on the spot, while the roosters, who were happily clucking away, looked rather unruffled by the whole thing. Nino, who must have had a Gould League membership, ended up going shopping, so I was left alone with all the cocks. From the detailed spiel in the old guidebook, I did learn that 'an owner may have up to a dozen birds, usually of as many colours as possible as popular superstition holds that different colours are more likely to win at certain times of the day'. East Timor must be short on roosters nowadays, because most of the men only had one each.

While the men attended to their cocks (no, not in that way), groups of kids scuttled about selling pre-match snacks, cakes and drinks. They didn't have any hot dogs – but possibly they'd have some chicken strips later on. Before any fighting could begin, men were thrusting their cocks at each other to get them excited. (Oh dear, that really doesn't sound good.)

There was no pre-match entertainment or national anthem. The first two roosters that were suitably fired up were rushed into the cockpit, followed by a very restless crowd jostling for the best position. Two men, with their prized birds in hand, stroked them as they tugged off the leather sheath from the back of their feet to reveal a razor-sharp spike. The crowd began screaming as handfuls of cash were exchanged with the bookie in the pit. When the roosters were finally let loose, the shouting was deafening.

It was over in a few seconds. The swirling roosters raised clouds of dust before a bird was knocked down. The crowd cleared and I stood back. That was enough for me. I was interested in the spectacle, the tradition and the energy, but not the death. I wandered around snapping a few photos and when I stopped to look at my shots on the camera a quietly spoken man sat down next to me. 'Can I look, please?' he asked shyly. When I got to the shots from the fight, he said, 'That's mine.' He was the losing 'coach'. He looked at me sadly. 'My bird is dead.'

'What do you do with the bird?' I asked.

He shrugged. 'We eat it.'

I told you – chicken strips.

When Nino returned from the market, I was ready to go. The cockfights would go on into the evening. There would have been at least 50 cockerels – tied to motor scooters, trees or cradled in arms – waiting for their turn in the ring.

Dinner at my bungalow involved more plates of food, possibly beef or goat or perhaps even crocodile. I watched the sun sink and melt like orange sherbet into the ocean from my dinner table. By 7.30 it was dark. I guessed that there wouldn't be many nightclubs in the fishing village and, with nothing else to do, I was in bed by 7.45. As I lay reading, with the sound of the waves crashing at my door, I looked up at the mosquito net above my bed. It was totally covered in all sorts of strange and frightening-looking insects. The potentially bloodsucking (and perhaps even life-sucking) insects were the least of my worries, however. I sprung awake a few times during the night to the sound of gunshots. Were the sympathising insurgent rebels attacking? No – it was falling coconuts. It still scared the hell out of me every time, though. And that wasn't the only thing I could hear. Scampering and munching noises pervaded the room throughout the night, and I did my very best to ignore them. I figured it was either rats or baby crocodiles but thought it best that I didn't find out.

I awoke early (like four-o'clock-in-the-morning early) to the sound of exuberant crowing. The roosters were either jubilant from their win the night before or just plain happy to be alive. I had a bus to catch back to Dili, so I'd organised Nino to take me up to the bus station, in the dark. Sadly, I didn't have any breakfast. That was because I lost an entire packet of biscuits that I'd been planning to eat for breakfast. Well, I didn't actually lose the biscuits – the rats or the baby crocodiles in the room ate them all.

3

West Timor

The roads are so terrible that bus operators don't even
run services along this route.
South east Asia on a shoestring, 1st edition, 1975

Frequent buses run along the smooth main road that
follows the coast.
Southeast Asia on a Shoestring, 15th edition, 2010

I checked into the East Timor Backpackers Hostel when
I got back into Dili, where Johnno had told me I 'might
find a backpacker or two'. It was just like backpacker
hostels the world over: the dorm smelt like old socks
and there were five beds jammed into a room that would
barely fit a double bed. But thankfully, it did have air
conditioning – all those smelly socks would have grown
and bred in the stifling heat. I imagined there wouldn't
have been many air conditioners around in 1974, which
would have also meant lots of sweaty cheesecloth
underpants (or whatever hippies wore).

There was all of three backpackers sitting in the bar-cum-restaurant having breakfast when I arrived. And all three of them – a New Zealander, a Welshman and a Swede – had a copy of *Southeast Asia on a Shoestring* sitting on the table in front of them (the current edition, of course).

Two of the guys were in the process of doing a 'visa run'. They had popped over to East Timor for a few days because their three-month Indonesian visa was about to run out. Then they would head back to Bali for another three months. Tobias, the Swede, was working in East Timor. Well, when I say working in East Timor, he was actually working remotely for his clients in Sweden. As a graphic designer, he would receive a brief via email then do the project on his laptop, whether that was on a beach in Vietnam, in the hills of northern Thailand or sitting at a backpackers in Dili.

I got excited when Tobias told me that the hostel had scooters for hire. During this trip, I wanted to ride as much as I could in order to at least try to emulate Tony and Maureen's journey. Except that they rode the entire way across South-East Asia on a 250cc Yamaha trail bike, while I was about to ride a scooter that in its former life pottered around the suburbs of Australia delivering mail. The scooters for hire were retired 89.5cc Australia Post scooters. And while I headed out with only a small daypack, the Wheelers carried what Tony described as 'our whole world strapped to that motor-cycle'. They had a large container bolted to the side of the bike, another box on the back piled with more bags and a tent strapped to the handlebars.

Following the same route that the Wheelers took, I headed west out of Dili towards the Indonesian border. The hand-drawn map in the old book indicated that the road was merely a 'bad' road, and only went as far as the town of Maubara. The 'highway' out of Dili hugged the coast and had long ago fallen into a state of disrepair. Thankfully there was hardly any traffic, so I didn't have to dodge oncoming cars. I just had to negotiate the odd hole in the road – as in holes so large that you (along with your bike or car) would disappear right into them. I noticed that the most cavernous of holes had palm fronds shoved into them, just in case you didn't notice a mini Grand Canyon smack in the middle of the road. At certain points, the road felt so close to the sea that I could almost reach out and touch the fishermen who were casting their nets into the shallows. The local kids, on the other hand, wanted to reach out and touch mine. As I passed groups of children walking along the side of the road, they stretched out their hands to give me a high five. This wasn't such a good idea, however. My riding skills lacked so much in the skill department that at one point, I lost concentration and rode into a ditch. Oh, and I also knocked two kids over – or more like softly bumped them over, because I was riding so slowly.

The first major town I happened upon was Liquiça. All the old guidebook told me about Liquiça was that it was 'where an early world circumnavigator dropped in for lunch in 1522'. Okay, it didn't say that he dropped in for lunch, but that's what I did. Mostly because the Restaurant Liquiça was the first restaurant that I'd seen out of Dili.

'You work here in Timor?' the waitress asked as I sat down in the empty restaurant.

'No, I'm a tourist.'

'A tourist?' she exclaimed. She grabbed my hand and began shaking it vigorously. 'Thank you.'

I ordered the grilled chicken and rice, although the pork would have been a lot fresher. Later, I couldn't see the waitress to pay the bill, so I got up to find her. Then I heard a sickening squeal coming from the kitchen. I stuck my head around the corner of the open-sided outdoor kitchen to see a huge pig being slaughtered. A teenage boy had a long knife buried into its guts while blood gushed out all over the kitchen floor. A group of locals were all sitting around watching and laughing. This is what happens when you don't have TV. I scuttled off rather quickly – though I'm a big gore and guts horror-movie fan, this was just a little too real for me.

I didn't quite make it to Maubara. Even though the gauge indicated there was plenty of fuel, I ran out of petrol a few kilometres short of the town. I hitched a lift on the back of a motorbike, but as we approached the town of Maubara, we turned down a nondescript and non-petrol-station-looking side street. Then down a dirt lane past rusted tin shacks. Oh, no, this is where

I get lynched, I thought. We pulled up in front of a ramshackle house and the driver motioned for me to get off. 'Petrol,' he said with a big grin, pointing to a table by the front fence. On the table sat a row of one-litre Pepsi bottles filled with petrol. He beeped his horn and the proprietor, a ten-year-old boy, came rushing out of the house. Phew, that was lucky. Without any petrol, I could have been stuck in the middle of nowhere.

Thirty minutes later, I *was* stuck in the middle of nowhere. With a flat tyre. I didn't know how far it was to Liquiça, so I started walking the bike back to Maubara. I got about 50 metres and there, on the side of the road next to barren and parched fields, was a tyre repair shop. Or more like a tyre repair tin shack. Seven people worked on my tyre to the amusement of a group of onlookers and a couple of chickens (TV must be really bad in East Timor). Three of them got to work using an ancient, large steel clamp to take the whole back wheel off, while another two proceeded to set fire to the tyre. Or to the rubber patches on the tyre, at least. The patches didn't stop the leak, so two other staff members raced off on a scooter and came back 20 minutes later with a brand-new inner tube. Two hours later, the tyre was fixed. 'How much?' I asked, fearing the worst.

'One dollar,' he said nervously, as if he was charging me too much.

I got back to Dili just before the evening gloom descended. And just in time to see one very obvious new sight that wasn't in the 1975 guidebook. Just out of town and perched high on a limestone cliff top stood a massive statue of Christ with his arms outstretched. Looking nearly identical to the Christobal statue in Rio, the statue had been built in 1996 by the Indonesian colonial administration in an effort to win over the people of East Timor.

Not far out of Dili, the black sand and rubbish made way for a clean and empty (besides the odd wandering piglet or goat) white-sand beach. The old guidebook had mentioned these beaches, specifically the 'free use of beach huts'. I didn't see any beach huts, but I did pass at least 20 beach restaurants of all cuisines, including Thai, Indonesian, Japanese, Indian, and even a 'Hotel California' restaurant (where I imagine they had mirrors on the ceiling and pink champagne on ice). Fleets of UN cars filled the parking spaces at the front, while waitresses scurried across the road with trays of brightly coloured cocktails to tables on the beach. This was a very different world to Dili.

The huge car park below the Christ statue was empty, so I was the only person climbing up the steep, wide steps to the top. The long, hot climb was worth it and I was afforded gorgeous views of tall, arid hills and sparkling blue sea in all directions.

On the way back into town, I stopped at Caz Bar for dinner (Johnno's favourite place in Dili). The tables on the beach were full of Australian mums and dads sipping cocktails while their kids played in the sand.

When the UN eventually pull out of East Timor, this restaurant and beach will be one of the places where the new tourists will come. The country may be dishevelled and downtrodden, but the populace have pride in their 'new' country. What I liked about East Timor was its innocence. Yes, I can see the irony of that statement in regard to such a troubled place, but this new country was rebuilding itself from a ruined past and looking, perhaps tentatively at times, towards the future. As the sun set dramatically over the water and I ate my spicy coconut prawns and drank my chilled glass of Australian wine, I thought Johnno was right. It really was . . . just idyllic.

Indonesia

Image: Poppies Bali

4

Denpasar and Kuta

Denpasar is a fine alternative to Kuta and there are
some excellent hotels.
South east Asia on a shoestring, 1st edition, 1975

Denpasar has become such a congested, noisy hellhole
it's hard to imagine anybody staying there of their
own free will.
Southeast Asia on a Shoestring, 15th edition, 2010

I flew to Bali from Dili on Merpati Airlines. Back in
1974, the only way to get to Bali from Australia was
one or two Merpati flights per week from Darwin
'depending on mood'. There are now more than 20
flights a day from every major city in Australia to Bali.
Merpati no longer flies from Australia, but at least it
is still around. Out of the six recommended airlines
in the Indonesian chapter of the old guidebook, only
three are still flying. I'm guessing that the three that
aren't – Sempati, Zamrud and Bouraq – simply ran out

of planes. Indonesia ranks as one of the worst countries for air-safety records. In 2008, they were second behind the Democratic Republic of Congo for fatal crashes and an aircraft 'incident' was recorded in Indonesia every nine to ten days. Even their national carrier, Garuda, has one of the world's worst safety records among national carriers, with 14 fatal accidents since 1950. There were certainly enough opportunities to crash back in 1974 as well, according to the old guidebook: 'For a third world country, Indonesia has an amazing number of airlines and flying can still be a real experience in this dull Jumbo age.' Although, personally, I'm not sure I'd consider crashing to a horrible death as a 'real experience'.

One of the now-disbanded airlines did sound like a lot of fun, however:

> Zamrud is a real character airline. What other airline would take a vote on whether the passengers want to fly along the coast or over the mountains in Timor? And when opinion is split offer to zig-zag? Or make a low pass over Kuta beach for a look-see before landing in Bali?

Three airlines may have dropped off the radar (so to speak) since 1974, but in recent years Indonesia has gained a whole lot more new airlines to potentially drop out of the sky. There are now 39 airlines, including the tongue-twisting Sabang Merauke Raya Air and the somewhat dubious-sounding Batvia Air Wings. (You'd hope they would have wings.)

Yes, there is a good chance that your plane might crash to the earth in a ball of flames, but golly gee, the flights are cheap in Indonesia. When I arrived at Denpasar Airport, I booked all my internal flights in Indonesia, including a flight from Denpasar to Yogya-karta, with that well-known airline, Mandala, for only $49. I also booked flights with Garuda (I figured that they'd just had a major crash, so they wouldn't be due for one for a little while), Air Asia and Lion Air. I'm pretty much happy to fly with anyone – I figure if you're gonna go, you're gonna go. Then again, from just the name of some other airlines, I might have second thoughts. There is just something that doesn't breed confidence when an airline has a name such as Jubba Airways (Somalia), Aerotaxi (Cuba), Samaritan Tree's Air (Haiti), Lucky Air (China), Sky Horse Airlines (Mongolia) or Yak Air (Russia).

'I want to go to Denpasar,' I told the taxi driver in front of the terminal building.

'Denpasar?' he asked. 'Are you sure? You want to go to Kuta?'

'No, Denpasar.'

The road out of the airport was bumper to bumper with taxis most likely heading to Kuta, which was the main reason why I hadn't been to Bali before. I'd always steered clear of the 'Island of the Gods' because I thought it was more like the 'Island of the Yobs'. I imagined Bali to be full of seriously inebriated Aussies in Bintang singlets, staggering from the Aussie Koala Bar to the Aussie Kangaroo Bar.

There were no inebriated Aussies staggering through the streets of Denpasar, though. In fact, there seemed to be no tourists at all – which was surprising, when the city had 'surely the best known cheap hotel in all Indonesia if not all of South East Asia', as the old guidebook boasted. My thrill of discovering that the Adi Yasa Hotel was still there, however, was quashed when we pulled up in front. A 'FULL' sign was dangling from the front gate. When I enquired at reception if there were any spare rooms, I was told I could have any of the rooms. Because I was the only guest. The sign on the front gate had just flipped over in the breeze.

The reception was located in the middle of the hotel's courtyard, once surrounded by 'super beautiful gardens' and now super dusty and somewhat run-down gardens. When Tony had given me the old guidebook back at the Lonely Planet office, his face lit up when he came to the section on Denpasar. 'We spent so much time in the courtyard of the Adi Yasa,' Tony told me. 'It was always full and every night was a party. I remember we had a Goodbye Nixon Party in August 1974. We watched President Nixon's resignation speech and him leaving the White House.' It was also the place where Maureen had got stoned for the first time, Tony revealed. I could just imagine the courtyard jam-packed with long hair, thick sideburns and flared pants in a haze of marijuana smoke. The hippies hadn't been popular with many of the locals, though. In the book *Bali and Beyond: Explorations in the Anthropology of Tourism*, the author Shinji Yamashita described the 'hippy problem' and how this community was an unwelcome presence in the eyes of the Balinese. The hippies also had a bad reputation for not paying in restaurants, at tourist performances, for woodcarvings or for staying in hotels. In their peculiar way of thinking, the hippies idealised Bali. They did not think of the Balinese as dancing for financial reasons, but rather for religious or aesthetic reasons, so they thought there was no need to pay to see the performances.

The Indonesian government also did not care for our long-haired friends and did their best to get rid of them. They tried to hike up the price of losmens (guesthouses) from 35 cents to three dollars. In fact, the bureaucrats in Jakarta had been so appalled by the expanding 'tourist ghetto' and young 'underdressed hippies' of Kuta that they considered razing the entire area.

I looked around and found no sign of any hippies in the forlorn courtyard. 'Before the bomb, there were many guests,' Rai, the manager, explained. 'We had a restaurant and people even slept outside, it was so busy.'

'So it's not, um . . . very busy now?' I asked.

'No people come stay here now,' Rai mused. 'Maybe next year we get guests.'

I asked Rai about Adi, the 'delightful owner' mentioned in the old guidebook. 'He is my uncle,' Rai said, with a big smile. 'But he is dead from a car crash.' The car crash happened only a month after the original guidebook was published. 'He was a little drunk, maybe,' Rai continued. 'He crashed into a tree. You know, like a big tree on the side of the road.'

I dumped my bag in the formerly 'simple room', which was now just simply stained. Mind you, I didn't know what was more stained – the walls or the bedsheets. But for five dollars a night, I couldn't really complain.

I went for a wander around town among the 'cacoph-onous' traffic. It was now even more cacophonous with so much traffic that it took me ten minutes (and ten years off my life) just to cross the road. One of Tony Wheeler's favourite places was the market, and I was delighted to see that it hadn't changed since 1974. In fact, I wouldn't have been surprised if the old women in brightly coloured sarongs crouching next to giant baskets filled with flowers, bananas, papayas and mangoes were in exactly the same spot as they had been in 1974. The market housed stalls with neat piles of yellow saffron, rice, fish and raw meat festering nicely in the hot sun. And best of all, there wasn't a tourist trinket in sight or anyone hassling me: 'For you, special price.'

Just outside the market, however, it jumped very much into the future. Hip-looking teenagers with mobile phones stuck to their ears were performing tricks on skateboards. No matter where I travelled in the world, all teenagers looked the same: product-saturated hair, Yankees baseball caps and jeans halfway down their bum, with their underpants showing. It wouldn't have been like this in 1974 – I doubt the local teens were all wearing flared pants and platform shoes. They'd fall off their skateboards for a start.

Back at the guesthouse, I enjoyed a beer in the court-yard with Rai and Agus, Adi's 37-year-old grandson, who ran a painting and T-shirt shop out the front of the hotel. 'It's still the same furniture,' Rai told me, as I took a seat in the somewhat ratty rattan chair. 'When did the hotel open?' I asked.

'Uncle Adi opened Adi Yasa in 1962,' Rai said. 'And during the first few years, he ran the hotel then left to play guitar at the Bali Hotel every night.' The Bali Hotel, in Denpasar, opened in 1928; it was the first hotel on the island. Rai also worked at the Bali Hotel from 1966. 'And when Adi died, I took over the Adi Yasa.'

I was a little puzzled; Rai looked too young to have been working in 1966. 'If you don't mind me asking, how old are you?' I asked.

Rai smiled proudly. 'I'm sixty-four.'

He looked good: with hardly any wrinkles and only a sprinkling of grey hair, I'd thought he was around the same age as me. 'I was born in 1945,' Rai continued, 'in the same month that Soekarno declared independence from the Dutch.'

Agus, now 37, had only been four years old when his grandfather Adi died. 'I remember the funeral, though,' he said. 'It felt like the entire island came to it.' The old guidebook described Balinese funerals as 'fun', where bodies were 'cremated to release the soul so that it can go to its after life'. Agus politely excused himself then came back a few minutes later with a framed photograph of his dad. Agus was a carbon copy of his smiling grandfather. Both wore their long dark hair tied back into a ponytail, and shared that kind and genuinely warm smile that immediately made you feel like a friend. Adi looked about 30 in the photo, although he was probably around 60.

'Many people come to stay here because of Uncle Adi,' Rai said, looking at the photo with admiration. 'He was a very kind and gentle man.'

Along with the framed photograph, Agus also had returned with the eldest of his three young sons hanging onto his leg. 'When my son is old enough, he will take over the hotel,' Agus said as he ruffled the four-year-old's hair. 'Maybe there will be lots of people then.'

I showed Rai the old guidebook to see if he recognised any of the restaurants. Denpasar had 'all sorts of goodies', said the old guidebook – a stark contrast to the opinion of the current edition: 'Denpasar is no culinary Mecca.' First on the list was the 'delightful' Three Sisters Warung, which had been a regular dinner destination with 'some of the cheapest pseudo western food in Bali'.

'It closed after the bombing in 2002,' Rai explained. He lowered his head. 'Many restaurants closed.'

At the mention of every restaurant on the list, Rai shook his head sadly. Even the Delicious Restaurant had folded, which was a pity, because it probably would have been, well, delicious. I ended up having dinner across the road in a tiny hawkers' market. It was so tiny that it only had three restaurants. And they were all empty, except the one I chose. It had customers – all two of them. Tony recommended in the old guidebook that you couldn't go wrong with nasi goreng, so I had the nasi goreng. And away from the tourist hordes in Kuta, it cost me an almost-1974 price of under a dollar.

After the quiet, dusty backstreets of Denpasar, Kuta was a culture shock – or more like a lack-of-culture shock. On our way to Bemo Corner, we passed rows of tattoo and piercing parlours (I wondered why tourists were so inspired to get a tattoo when they were drunk), novelty T-shirt and junky art shops. Art shops had also decorated the streets of Kuta back in 1974, but the trouble then, according to Tony, was that there was just too much pushed out onto undiscerning tourists. 'Beware of the mundane and the overpriced,' the old guidebook said. Not much had changed: the trashy art shops near Bemo Corner were piled with more mundane clichéd art than you could poke a paintbrush at. Kuta had also been the place for custom-made clothing, including 'flour bag clothes', the specialty (which look as ugly as they sound – clothes made from old flour sacks). The specialty now was custom-made T-shirts. Or you could just buy one of the many novelty shirts with such classic lines as, 'Osama doesn't surf'(well, he certainly doesn't any longer), and the poignant and very clever 'Fucking Fucked Fuck'. My personal favourite, however, was a sale-priced tee onto which the Dunkin' Donuts logo had been changed into 'Fuckin Donuts'.

Using my 1974 map of Kuta, I headed towards Poppies Gang (a *gang* being a street) to find somewhere to stay. Even back then, Kuta had provided plenty of options: 'At last count, there were over 100 places to stay,' noted Tony, 'and, except for a few flash ones, all cheap ones.' Kuta was 'the world's number one cheap traveller's centre' back in 1974. Today, the narrow lanes overflowed with tourists chugging Bintangs in bars, buying 'McShit' T-shirts or skyping and updating their Facebook statuses in internet cafes: 'I'm sitting in an internet cafe in Kuta.' Back in the pre-computer days of 1974, there had been only one telephone in Denpasar (and another at the airport). If you wanted to stay in touch with your folks, you either queued for hours for a crackling phone line that sounded like your relatives were under the sea, or you diligently turned up to a post office hoping for some 'poste restante' mail. Even in Europe during the late '80s, I had kept in touch with my family through the post office. But the news was often old because I would pick up letters about three months later than I'd planned. And I only rang my parents once after I'd been away for five months – which, I confess, was because I'd wanted them to send me some money. Back in the '70s, travellers often had to carry large wads of cash around with them. Those untouched paradises didn't have many places to change traveller's cheques. And when travellers ran out of cash, they would spend weeks or even months hanging around waiting for money transfers.

After East Timor and Denpasar, there seemed to be so many tourists in Kuta. So many, in fact, that I couldn't find a room. I tried eight different places that were all full. The old guidebook had suggested to 'look around, you can't go wrong. The losmen "guesthouse" are like peas in a pod.' After two hours of trudging around losing my body weight in sweat, I finally discovered a small, cheap 'pea pod' down a side lane. Most rooms in Kuta were simply furnished with a communal *mandi* (basically a big bucket of water and a plastic scoop to pour water over your head), the old guidebook had said. In my case, the guidebook was dead on. But thankfully it did have a western-style air conditioner and a flushing toilet. In 1974, only a couple of the more expensive places had western-style toilets, Tony had pointed out.

That afternoon, I prepared myself to get hopelessly lost – my 1974 map of Kuta had only illustrated Poppies Gang and a few surrounding streets. I made my best guess towards the village of Legian which, back in the '70s, involved a 'quiet walk through the jungle along a dirt track lined with coconut palms'. It *was* still a jungle, but it was now just a jungle of pumping bars, nightclubs, restaurants, tattoo parlours and surfwear shops. Kuta felt as raffish, rowdy and as Australian as I thought it would. It was perhaps the only foreign place I'd been to where Australian pop culture seemed more potent than American. The street stalls were selling Australian music CDs and Australian newspapers to shirtless, bronzed Aussies who lurched through the streets with more than a few Bintangs under their belts. And it was only three o'clock in the afternoon.

Legian was described in the old guidebook as a 'mushroom village', but Kuta could very well have been known as a 'magic mushroom village'. At many of the restaurants, you could order the 'special pizza with the "special" ingredient being mushrooms'. Tony had also kindly advised his readers to 'get in early because there is quite a rush on them at mid-afternoon to ensure a good high by sunset time'. Tony wasn't the only guidebook writer extolling the high life in Bali. Another popular guidebook was the *Indonesia Handbook* written by Bill Dalton, who founded Moon Publications in a youth hostel in Queensland in 1973. During the past 30 years, Dalton has explored over 100 of Indonesia's 17,000 islands, visiting the country more than 50 times and amassing a total of six years in the islands. He described going to Bali as like 'stepping on a giant tab of LSD'. Dalton then went on to give advice on where to buy drugs: 'have boys pick magic mushrooms for you or pick them yourself beyond the village.' Scoring grass wasn't a problem, either. Dalton suggested that you simply go to the beach and look out for the freaks.

Although he did go on to warn that raids and busts did occur and you could be put in prison for '35 days with 20 Indonesians all in the same cell for an ounce of dope. And you only get visits on Sunday afternoons.' He also offered this sage advice: 'Naturally there is far more to Indonesia than dope and you miss a lot if you see every-thing from 9 miles up. On the other hand if it's cheap, good and easy . . .'

I thought it would be nice to see the beach at sunset (minus the tripping-out part), so I headed down to the famous, or infamous depending on which way you look at it, Kuta Beach. In all my travels, I'd never seen such a jam-packed beach. Walls and walls of bodies walked, sat, laid and squished together on the sand. In 1974, around 50,000 tourists had visited Bali. There were now more than two million a year. And most of those two million, it seemed, were on Kuta Beach. It wasn't long before I was accosted with offers.

'You want massage?'

'You want facial?'

'You want pedicure?'

'You want hair braiding?' ('You need hair for that,' I countered.)

'You want corn on the cob/satay stick/fruit juice/cocktail/beer?'

I was so exhausted from all the hassling that I finally succumbed to an overly friendly vendor and ordered a bottle of Bintang. Included in my somewhat inflated price was a chair on the beach with a terrific view of the sunset (and the masses of bodies in front of it). My chair was plopped down next to a Canadian couple who laughed when I asked if I was intruding on their romantic moment. 'Not with these crowds,' the man chuckled.

'Is it always this busy?' I asked him.

'No, it's Ramadan holiday. Half of Jakarta is here.'

After the sun dropped majestically into the crowds of people, I headed back into the hordes that jammed the footpaths. The old guidebook had listed quite a few dining options for Kuta, and the closest was the Mandara Guest House, known for its 'magnificent roast piglet feast'. The only problem – there were no street numbers listed in the book. It could have been either a Ralph Lauren store or a tattoo parlour now, and I'd never know the difference. I had better luck with Mama's, which the old guidebook called 'a long standing bargain for smorgasbord where you get as much food and fruit salad as you can manage'. In Bill Dalton's *Indonesian Handbook* he suggested that you 'sit out front and take in street life, check tourists out as they are driven from the airport craning their necks to look at filthy hippies'.

I asked a Balinese painting shop owner for directions to Mama's and he pointed down Legian Road. I was sure his directions had sent me too far, but then another local sent me further down the road. Mama's must have moved, I decided, because half an hour later, I found it. Except there was no smorgasbord. Or Mama.

It was now a German restaurant and the German owner hadn't even heard of the original Mama's. Needless to say, I passed on the sauerkraut and strudel and headed back along the beachfront.

Next up was the East West Restaurant, known for its 'expensive but irresistible' desserts of banana, pineapple and apple cake. At least this eatery would be easy to find, I figured, because it was supposedly located on the corner of the beach road and Poppies Gang. As I walked along, head buried in my map, I nearly bumped into a small sign for Poppies Gang. And there it was, in all its neon glory: not the East West Restaurant, but a monumentally monstrous McDonald's. As I stood there, deflating, a smiling local sidled up beside me. He handed me a small envelope, containing a letter that read: 'CONGRATULATIONS you have won a video camera. And one week's accommodation.' Ah, a timeshare. That about summed up how sad Kuta had become, I thought. McDonald's and timeshares.

I was running very short on dining options, but just up Poppies Gang was Poppies, a restaurant that Tony Wheeler had recommended as a place for a 'flash occasion'. After 35 years, it can't still be that flash, I thought. That's if it was still there, of course – or had not moved to Legian and become a Hungarian restaurant. To my surprise, it *was* still there and it *was* still flash (they even had a security guard at the entrance). It even had the same 'romantic garden setting' although it wasn't that romantic sitting by myself in candlelight alongside canoodling couples. The old guidebook had mentioned that the 'old Kuta hands' who remembered Jenik's restaurant would find Poppies familiar – it had the same owner. I asked the waiter if Jenik was still around. 'Yes, she is here,' the waiter said, motioning towards the bar.

When I explained to Jenik, who couldn't stop smiling, that I was travelling with the old guidebook, she pulled up a chair and told me her story. 'In the late sixties, there was a restaurant called Poppies in California,' Jenik explained. 'But the restaurant closed down and the owners went on a holiday to Bali with their American friends.' Three of those friends met Jenik, who had been running a small *warung* (restaurant), and they decided to stay and open a restaurant with her. So, they enlarged the kitchen of Jenik's Balinese home and added a bar. 'Poppies opened in 1973,' Jenik said proudly. 'Then we added some cottages in 1974 and built a pool in 1987.' The Poppies' empire had grown even more since then, with another 20 luxurious cottages, two more restaurants in Bali and a boutique hotel in Ko Samui, Thailand.

Jenik disappeared for a minute and returned with a menu from 1973. It didn't seem that flash, but I supposed that in 1973, fried eggs on toast and banana pancakes were as 'fine dining' as it got in Bali. Now, you could order everything from chilled gazpacho to seared sesame-crusted tuna steak, to chicken Provençal with baked aubergine, and even Hungarian goulash soup.

And instead of banana pancakes, Poppies now offered pancakes 'flambeé à l'orange'. Since the old guidebook had insisted that fish and seafood were 'as popular in Kuta restaurants as are frog's legs', I ordered the nasi campur. The delicious and suitably flash dish consisted of steamed rice with the 'daily selection of tasty accompaniments'. But no frog's legs.

After my meal, I did what any true-blue Aussie would have done: I went out on the town in Kuta and got trashed. I stumbled from bar to bar (Kuta must have the highest per capita of population who are working members of a band, as every pub had a local Balinese ensemble belting out such traditional Balinese music as 'Sweet Child of Mine') and ended up at Paddy's Club, whose slogan was 'Get wet, get food, get drunk, get fun'. And not necessarily in that order, I imagined. A leggy local girl gave me a flyer for the upstairs 'Snow Party – with Sexy dancers/Drinking Comp/18+ games'. Instead, the second floor was filled with pissed Australians, mostly in white Bintang singlets, drinking buckets of some nasty firewater disguised with fruit juice. And I say 'mostly' wearing singlets because many were actually shirtless and doing the limbo (while still clutching their buckets of rocket fuel).

I headed back downstairs where there weren't quite as many drunken comrades and watched a local cover band with sublimely talented musicians. I started chatting to a couple of the band members and, after a few more beers, ended up on stage with them, belting out a few songs. By two in the morning, I too was a pissed idiot. And like the other pissed idiots, I staggered back through the streets trying to remember where the hell my guesthouse was.

5

Ubud and Beyond

By far the best way of seeing Bali is to hire yourself a
motorcycle for a week.
South east Asia on a shoestring, 1st edition, 1975

Think carefully before renting a motorcycle.
Southeast Asia on a Shoestring, 15th edition, 2010

'The hippies smelt very bad.' Oka Wati winced,
pinching her nose. I was in the foothill town of Ubud,
having lunch with Oka Wati in her restaurant, Oka
Wati's Warung, which overlooked the rice paddies
behind Monkey Forest Road. Back in 1974, Oka Wati's
Warung was an 'Ubud institution directly opposite the
temple'. Oka Wati's had since moved to a location down
a series of narrow lanes and a few hundred metres away
from the temple. The once-simple restaurant was now
accompanied by nine villas that overlooked a small
pool surrounded by perfectly manicured gardens. I
was thrilled to discover my villa was decorated with

traditional Balinese furniture, an impressively large stone carving on the wall and a huge four-poster bed.

Like everyone I'd met in Bali who was years older than me, Oka Wati looked younger than me. 'I'm sixty-two,' she beamed. It was amazing how young Oka Wati looked after hearing the story of her life. While I ate my traditional Balinese pizza, Oka Wati talked. 'I opened a warung selling simple food by the temple in 1974,' she said, nodding serenely. 'I was twenty-four and already married, but my husband was no good. He had no job or house, so I worked very hard to buy a house. I also rented out two rooms in my house.'

'What sort of people stayed in your house when you first opened?' I asked.

'It was the hippies, and they would smoke grass all day,' Oka Wati said, trying to control her giggling. 'But there wasn't much to do. Ubud had no electricity. There were only rice fields and you could walk in the middle of the road because there were no cars at all – only bicycles. And lots of ducks going "quack quack" all day.'

Things got tough for Oka Wati after she divorced her husband. 'It was a big scandal. I was very alone and had three young children. My husband took the house, so we had to go to the market each night to ask for a room. I worked very hard, so I could get another house and send my children to school. They are all very successful now,' Oka Wati said. 'I was very lucky. An American man stayed with me twenty years ago. He stayed for weeks and was stoned every day.' Oka Wati gave me a cheeky smile. 'He loved Oka Wati, so he bought me some land and I built some beautiful villas. A few years later, I worked hard and I bought this land and built more villas.'

Oka Wati's face suddenly wilted. 'But I don't have the other villas anymore. I had remarried and my husband got sick in 2002. I had to look after him and support his six children and my three children. He had not worked for many years and it was very hard work looking after him.' Oka Wati paused as tears welled up in her eyes. 'My husband died in 2007 and my stepchildren wanted everything. Lawyers are too expensive and law not good for woman anyway, so my stepsons took my beautiful villas. They are so greedy. They also got my rice field, gallery and my three-level house.' Oka Wati put her hand gently on my arm. 'I've had a hard life, but a good life,' she said with a smile. 'Lots of people love me. I'm lucky. Very lucky.'

I felt lucky to have met this wonderful woman. Oka Wati seemed at peace, even though she had gone through so much. After lunch, I spotted her heading out with a large basket of flowers, fruit and neat packages of rice perched on her head. She was on her way to the temple with gifts meant to express gratitude to benevolent spirits and placate demons, to prevent them from disturbing the harmony of life. Those cheeky demons had sure done their best to disturb Oka Wati's harmony of life. That was why her offering basket was so huge. She wasn't taking any chances.

The old guidebook had suggested a walk 'through the rice paddies from Canderi's to the small monkey forest and temple'. The road that had once been a dirt track between rice paddies and quacking ducks had now been transformed by queues of cars honking down the two-kilometre strip of Balinese restaurants and shops selling jewellery, Dolce & Gabbana and those God-awful Crocs shoes.

The Monkey Forest was now called the Sacred Monkey Forest Sanctuary. In the early '70s, only a handful of people visited this site every week. Today, there were up to 10,000 visitors a month. As I wandered along the path through the forest that was more of a jungle, I noticed that the tourists in the sanctuary outnumbered the monkeys – even though the population of the long-tailed macaques had also increased from about 50 in 1974 to around 350 today. Most of the visitors were daytrippers bussed in from Kuta. You could tell by all the white Bintang singlets and the glazed eyes from way too many Jäger bombs. The monkeys took full advantage of this, ransacking their bags for food and even packets of cigarettes – which they promptly opened and shredded. (Members of the anti-smoking lobby, perhaps?)

The stifling afternoon humidity wasn't fit for man (or monkey), so I headed back to Oka Wati's for a dip in the pool. (I had to have at least one swim while I was in Bali.) That night, I set out to find Canderi's, a restaurant that the old guidebook had deemed 'Ubud's

other institution' where 'the whole travelling population gathers at night to see Canderi perform miracles
in her tiny kitchen'. I asked a young waitress shoving
menus in the faces of passers-by at the entrance of the
Tropical Restaurant if she knew where Canderi's was.
She hadn't heard of it, but I knew it had to exist because
Oka Wati told me it was still there. I trekked up and
down Monkey Forest Road and finally asked one of
the hundreds of men offering 'transport' if he knew it.
He pointed directly across the road from the Tropical
Restaurant, and the same young waitress.

Canderi's didn't have the candles and mock waterfalls of the Tropical, but I liked it, anyway. It was simple
and unpretentious. And while the Tropical had been
chock-full, Canderi's had only two tables of diners. The
whole travelling population might not have been gath-
ering there at night anymore, but Canderi was still in
her tiny kitchen performing miracles 35 years later. Ibu
Canderi was a diminutive woman who greeted me with
a huge toothy grin as she took my hand and welcomed
me to her restaurant. 'I'm a very young seventy-eight,'
she told me when I told her how surprised I was to find
her still cooking in the kitchen. When I asked Canderi
what Ubud was like in 1974, I got the same answer that
Oka Wati gave me: 'There were no cars, no electricity
and ducks going "quack, quack" all day.' And also like
Oka Wati, she'd had a tough life and had worked hard. 'I
trained as a schoolteacher,' she explained, 'but there was
no work for me after the coup.' In 1965, a communist-led

group had attempted a coup against President Sukarno. Unfortunately, the repercussions spread across all of Indonesia with 80,000 people (or five per cent of Bali's population) killed in the process. 'We had to eat,' she said. 'So I opened a homestay and restaurant.' Canderi opened her *losmen* (guesthouse) in 1970, and the restaurant followed in 1972. Both were set within the family compound of her traditional home, and the surrounding four rooms were made available for rent. 'They were open-sided rooms,' Canderi said. 'And there were no beds or bathrooms.'

I asked her if the restaurant and homestay had changed much since 1974. 'The homestay has new nice rooms with walls,' she grinned. 'But the menu is much the same.' The food was a mixture of Balinese fare and backpacker food, from the ubiquitous nasi goreng to cheese and tomato jaffles. Canderi's favourite traditional dish of 1974 had been the *lawar*. Though the menu showed no description of what it was, I ordered it anyway.

I was handed a plate of mixed beans, spring onion, garlic, chilli, grated coconut, lime juice, and lots of other stuff I didn't recognise. Even with its serious, burn-your-tastebuds-off kick, at least I was eating traditional Balinese food. I later read that the dish was very traditional Balinese but not traditionally eaten by tourists. And those ingredients I couldn't recognise included pig's blood, Balinese shrimp paste, the root of the galangal plant and boiled young jackfruit.

Though the food and ambience at Canderi's and at Oka Wati's was delightfully simple and homely, I was surprised to discover that neither of them had made it into the current *Southeast Asia on a Shoestring*. Pity, really.

When I finished my meal, Canderi's son, Taviv, came over and introduced himself. He had the same warm smile and gentle demeanour as his mum. He was also the same size – shorter than me (which says a lot). 'Is Taviv a Balinese name?' I asked him.

'No, it's a Soviet name.'

Taviv was born in 1965, the same year as the coup. 'It was a bad year. My father was a lawyer and he was murdered.' Taviv pointed to a framed faded black-and-white photo of his father on the wall. 'He was murdered because people said he was the leader of a communist group. They were just jealous because he was successful.'

Giving your baby a Soviet name probably didn't help, I thought.

'Forty-five people were murdered that day,' Taviv said musingly. 'They were all buried in one hole and my father was put on the top.' He had been only a few months old and the youngest of five children at the time that his father was killed.

When Canderi returned from the kitchen, Taviv put his arm around her. 'She is the most beautiful mother in the whole world.' He squeezed her tightly. Following a light discussion about Taviv's family and children, he made a mention of 'Grandma'. 'Is she still alive?' I asked him.

Canderi's mum, Niketutmerti, was not only still alive, but the oldest person in the village. In fact, she had just turned 108. Canderi and Taviv then led me to a tiny room at the back of the house, where I met a thin woman who was propped up in bed, listening to a crackly radio. The room was thick with incense smoke. Niketutmerti's big smile revealed her one remaining tooth.

Back at my table, I ordered another beer then spotted someone I recognised walking past in front of the restaurant. It was Tony Wheeler. I leapt out of my seat and, old guidebook in hand, rushed up to him. 'Excuse me, can you help me?' I asked. 'I'm trying to find a hotel, but my guidebook seems a little out of date.'

'Maybe you should get a new one,' Tony said, laughing.

Meeting Tony would have been an incredible coincidence – if it hadn't actually been planned (although bumping into him in the street that night was a coincidence). I'd timed my visit to Ubud to join him on a motorcycle jaunt around the island, following his suggested route from the old guidebook. Tony happened to be in Bali as a guest of the Ubud Writers and Readers Festival. As he sipped his beer back at Canderi's, I noticed he had brought along photocopied 'Bali' pages from the old guidebook. 'I wanted to see what had changed, too,' he said. Tony wouldn't have been as confused as me, however. He had also brought along the current *Lonely Planet Bali* guidebook.

Tony Wheeler was a busy man. He'd only just flown in from Kazakhstan where he'd watched a tourist get jettisoned off into space. Kazakhstan was the 140th country that this intrepid explorer had visited. 'I've still got a few more countries to see yet,' he grinned. There are 192 countries in the world, according to the UN, and 235 according to Lonely Planet. I believed Lonely Planet. Although Tony was in his early sixties, he still travelled extensively and arguably recklessly at times for most of the year. Only recently, he'd travelled through all the 'Axis of Evil' countries, including Afghanistan, Iraq, Libya and North Korea for his book *Badlands*. Tony had stayed in tents with Bedouins eating boiled camel penis while most other 60-year-olds were holidaying in a villa in Tuscany or driving a campervan around Queensland. Tony also enjoyed staying in nice places, but why not? He'd certainly earned it. And yet he still jumped at the chance to join me in the search for smelly old guesthouses.

I almost squealed with delight when Canderi approached our table. 'Canderi,' I gushed. 'This is *the* man who wrote the old guidebook. He's . . . Lonely Planet.'

'Hello, Mr Lonely Planet,' Canderi said.

'This was my favourite breakfast place in all of Bali,' Tony told her. 'Do you still make those delicious tacos?'

Those 'delicious tacos' were still on the menu. They were so popular, in fact, that in 1984 the Australian band Redgum mentioned Canderi's tacos in their hit song, 'I've been to Bali, Too'.

Tony Wheeler is actually quite shy, which is surprising considering he ran a hugely successful company and is a popular guest speaker all over the world. However, when the talk turned to travel, Tony's eyes lit up and he became a different and more voluble person. I reminded him of a quotation of his that has inspired me in my travels: 'I love travel because you may be uncomfortable, hungry, hot and sweaty, cold and shivering . . . but damn it, you will never be bored.'

'That's true,' Tony said and laughed. 'But it's also about the buzz of arriving somewhere new and the thrill of returning to a favourite place.'

'I feel exactly the same,' I said – then realised I sounded like I agreed only because my all-time travel hero just said it.

'It's good to see places like this haven't changed,' Tony said, glancing around the simple restaurant. 'You know, this place was full every night. You couldn't get a table if you got here later than five. And the entire restaurant was only lit by a couple of oil lamps.'

A few minutes later, the power went off and the room was plunged into darkness. But I could see Tony still smiling, in the gloom. 'It's just like old times,' he said, then took a sip of his beer.

I awoke early to join Tony on a *jalan jalan* (literally 'walk, walk'). As part of the Ubud Writers and Readers Festival, Tony would be leading a morning stroll through the rice fields and along the steep ridges that overlooked the town. The event, which had sold out weeks ago, consisted of a small crowd of, well, 'writers and readers' who traipsed behind Tony, hanging onto his every word. After all, Tony was, as *The New York Times* dubbed him, 'the most influential man in travel' and 'the trailblazing, patron saint of the world's backpackers and adventure travelers' ('The End of the World on 10 Tugriks a Day'). While Tony walked and recounted anecdotes about his travels and the history of Lonely Planet, I too shuffled as closely as I could to him, frantically scribbling into my notebook.

I already knew a few of the stories he shared, but during the two-hour walk I also discovered many other interesting tidbits. For example, the name 'Lonely Planet' had been a 35-year mistake. The name actually came from a misheard line in the song 'Space Captain' by Joe Cocker, on the *Mad Dogs & Englishmen* live album in 1970. The actual words were 'lovely planet', but Tony simply heard 'lonely planet' and liked it. And did you know – stop me if I start boring you – that Lonely Planet's biggest selling guidebook is *Australia*, followed by *Thailand*, *New Zealand* and *India*?

When we arrived for breakfast at the way-too-expensive-for-the-likes-of-me villa, which overlooked the almost-too-perfect-to-be-real rice fields, Tony pulled me aside. 'You're doing a panel with me at the festival this afternoon.' He smiled apologetically. 'I sort of roped you in.' Since author Matthew Condon had pulled out of the festival at the last minute, Tony had been asked to fill in on one of his sessions. 'I told them that we'd do it together,' Tony said. 'The topic is about how Bali has changed.' I'd only been in Bali three days of my life. And besides that, I wasn't quite dressed for public speaking. My one remaining clean T-shirt (well, the one I was wearing) was full of holes.

At the end of the walk, a fleet of cars was waiting for us – after all, writers and readers can only walk so far. On the drive back, I arranged to meet Tony for lunch, so we could figure out what the hell I would talk about. I arrived at Casa Luna Restaurant to find him frantically texting his wife and fellow Lonely Planet founder, Maureen. 'She says that she is here in the restaurant, but she's obviously at the wrong one,' Tony huffed. Maureen had skipped the space launch in Kazakhstan and met up with him in Bali. After about ten minutes of texting, and cursing, the two figured out they were actually at the same restaurant: Tony was upstairs and Maureen was downstairs.

'You'd think after all these years of travelling, we could at least find each other in a restaurant,' Maureen chuckled, as she sat down.

Although Maureen shared the same passion for travel as Tony, she wasn't too keen on 'roughing it' anymore. 'I'm very happy with my nice villa, thank you very much,' Maureen said.

Bali was one of Maureen's favourite places in the world. 'It's still the same here as it was in 1974,' she said. 'It's still the same women taking the same offerings of fruit and rice to the temple. And you only have to walk five minutes out of Ubud to get to the rice paddies, where local men are still chopping grass the same way they have been for centuries.'

'Not exactly the same,' Tony said. He then went on to explain how the Balinese now used modern fertilisers. The grass grew quicker and longer, he continued, but also weaker. While it used to last six or seven years on the roofs of traditional Balinese homes, it now lasted only two or three years.

I asked what types of tourists came to Bali in the '70s. 'When we first came here in 1972,' Maureen began, 'there were two groups of tourists – surfers and overlanders. We were part of the overlanders, but the two groups didn't really mix.'

On the Lonely Planet Thorn Tree Travel Forum website, I found a long thread of old hippies reminiscing about visiting Bali in the '70s. One of the surfers, 'tezza', commented:

> . . . the beach at Kuta was fantastic – good surf which was why we junior tube-shooters were there – lovely sand backed by coconut palms and behind that rural bliss with [rice paddies], water buffalo . . . Oh yeah, and all along the beach were these naked hippie chicks.

The Wheelers had returned to Bali for two months in 1974 to do research for *South east Asia on a shoestring* and returned in '77 and '83 to make updates – for the second and third editions. So I guess Tony must have liked all those naked hippie chicks, too.

By the time we'd finished our lunch, I realised we hadn't discussed a single thing about our panel session. And we were due on stage in ten minutes.

'Good crowd,' I whispered to Tony, as we sat down in the modern and spacious Indus Restaurant – which was a stark contrast to the Ubud from the old guidebook.

'Most are probably expecting Matthew Condon to talk about his new novel,' Tony whispered.

The talk went well, as in Tony regaled listeners with interesting anecdotes about Bali in the '70s while I concurred: 'Oh, yes, Bali has changed *so* much from when I first came.'

After a quick bite at Canderi's (I had to have the famous tacos – which were absolutely nothing like Mexican tacos but tasted delicious, nevertheless), I met up with Beth, an American writer I met on Tony's walk. Well, more like I chased her down the road after the walk because I thought she was cute and bubbly in that excitable American way (as well as that big hair, big blue eyes and perfect teeth American way). We'd struck up an immediate rapport after discovering we were both travel writers, worked in advertising and loved getting lost (although most of my getting lost was often not planned). And little did I know that Beth would become a big part of my trip and ultimately a big part of my life. But that's getting ahead of the story.

We'd organised to meet up at the Jazz Café for what the writers festival had listed as a 'fun cabaret evening of singing and dancing writers'. Except that it wasn't much fun. The pub was packed, uncomfortably hot and sticky. And there wasn't much singing and dancing. As we arrived, a Dutch poet was performing. Not that there is anything wrong with poetry; it's just that Dutch is not the prettiest of languages for poetry. Next up was a fellow doing Arabic poetry, which was even worse: it was like Dutch poetry combined with a serious case of whooping cough.

'Shall we get out of here?' I said to Beth. We'd only been there ten minutes and hadn't even finished our beers. We happened upon a Hindu ceremony not far from the Jazz Café and joined the throng of onlookers sitting on the ground. The locals participating in the ceremony donned white robes and *udengs* (traditional headdress), while others wore huge monster masks – looking very much like baddies in a *Scooby-Doo* cartoon. The procession slowly wound its way up the street and into a packed open-sided temple to the accompaniment of crashing and tinkling gamelan music. We watched, jaws dropped, at the beauty of this event. Like me, Beth had brought her current Lonely Planet, but to her American eyes, this was another planet completely. 'This is exactly how it would have been a hundred years ago.' And just as I said it to Beth, a kid dragged a digital camera out from his very traditional Balinese robe and snapped a photo of his friend who was pulling a funny face.

'Hiring a scooter is by far the best way of seeing Bali,' Tony had recommended in the old book. So, that's what I did, in spite of the fact he'd also warned readers, 'Be careful, Bali is no better than any other place in the world to come home from in a box.' In 1974, a scooter cost 2000 rupiah a day (which was just under five dollars). I hired a scooter for five days for 30,000 rupiah a day (which was just under five dollars). Though I didn't fancy coming home in a box, I felt relatively safe with my scooter. It seemed a newish bike and came with a Be-Seen-Be-Safe fluoro-pink helmet.

With Tony busy all day, I thought I'd tick off a nearby sight recommended in the old guidebook. The Gunang Kawa temple near Ubud had been described as one of the best sights in Bali. The road out of Ubud certainly wasn't, however. It was one big shopping strip (the road from Kuta was much the same) selling huge stone carvings, woodcarvings, mosaics, brightly coloured paintings, ceramics, clothes and every other tourist trinket you could possibly think of – or, in some cases, hadn't thought of. Thankfully, the road to the temple turned off the main drag and swept through fields and rice paddies so luminously green, it looked as if someone had turned up the colour setting on the TV.

I found the temple surprisingly easily (or should I say *amazingly* easily, considering my map), but it looked nothing like the description in the book. The burial towers had been described as 'impressive both for their sheer size and their setting in the rice paddies'. I agreed that the sheer size of the temple was impressive, but I couldn't see a single rice field. The temple now stood in the middle of an overgrown jungle of palm trees and thick vegetation. Then again, 35 years was probably enough time, I supposed, for a jungle to spring up.

When I approached the gate to hire a sarong (everyone must cover their legs to enter a Hindu temple), I asked the employee what had happened to the rice paddies. The young man and I shared a long confusing conversation, until I finally figured out there were two temples with the same name. Well, at least that's what I thought he'd said. Even more confusing was trying to find the other temple. I managed to get myself hopelessly and utterly lost. But I loved it. I rode down narrow, windy lanes through tiny villages (in fact, lots and lots of tiny villages – as I said, hopelessly and utterly lost) without a single mosaic shop in sight. I also saw lots of locals herding cattle, carrying shopping, tending fields and sitting by the side of the road – and spoke to most of them when I stopped every few hundred metres to ask for directions.

I knew that I was getting close to a major tourist attraction when I passed a long row of woodcarving and painting shops on the way to the entrance. I parked my scooter and walked through a throng of relentless sarong sellers, who all offered me a 'special morning price'. Instead, I hired a sarong at the entrance gate for an 'early-morning *very* special price'.

Ah, so there was the impressive size and setting. And the rice paddies. I spent an hour trudging up and down the steep steps admiring the rice paddies then headed out to face the doggedly determined sarong sellers again. It didn't take them long. The second I walked out of the entrance, a man called out, 'Sarong, sarong!'

'No, thank you,' I said, without looking back.

'Hey, you! Mister! SARONG!' he shouted.

'NO!' I bellowed, and kept walking.

Another woman now joined in. 'SARONG! SARONG!'

I was just about to turn around and tell them to shove their sarongs up their . . . when I noticed that the woman wasn't even selling sarongs. She was, however, pointing to the hired sarong that I was still wearing and walking away with.

I got lost on the way back too (surprise, surprise) but ended up in the Monkey Forest Sanctuary, dodging gibbering monkeys and jabbering tourists.

'We were the experts on getting lost,' Maureen told me later, when we met for an afternoon drink at Oka Wati's. We'd been discussing Tony and Maureen's motorcycle trip across South-East Asia in 1974 and the two were reminiscing about their first visit to East Timor. 'The Perola Oriental in Baucau was terrible,' Maureen groaned. 'It was just one room and one very large mattress with twenty people sleeping on it.'

'I thought it was okay,' Tony shrugged. 'Particularly if I was squashed up against two women.'

Maureen flicked through the old guidebook and chuckled to herself. 'This is such a Tony list.' She had just started reading the 'Rated Features of South East Asia' list at the back of the book. The rollcall included Best Food Bargain, the Most Attractive Hotel and the Most Interesting Museum, as well as the Weirdest Colour Scheme, the Most Dirty Postcards Centre, the Funkiest Funghi, the Biggest Geckoes and the Hippest Hookers. Ubud had made the list for the Most Aggressive Pick-pockets: the monkeys in the Monkey Forest. Sadly, I'd missed the Best Food Bargain because Mama's in Kuta was no longer there.

Upon receiving our drinks, I asked the waitress if Oka Wati was around to meet Tony and Maureen, but she had already left for the temple. 'She was so beau-tiful,' Maureen commented. 'All of the backpackers would fall in love with her.'

The talk turned to the motorcycle jaunt Tony and I were about to embark on. 'Now, no riding at night,' Maureen waved her finger at her husband. 'And no riding fast. You're not twenty-five anymore.' Tony rolled his eyes, but Maureen wasn't finished. 'And make sure you take some spare underwear.'

That night I met up with Beth again for a 'literary dinner' at Casa Luna Restaurant. I wasn't that keen on going (there's something about the word 'literary' that just sounds so vaingloriously grandiloquent), but I was keen to see Beth again and this literary dinner came served with lashings of margaritas, Corona beer, Mexican food and mariachi music. The main speaker at the dinner was Mexican novelist Alberto Ruy-Sánchez, whose writing was described as 'overflowing with erotic conviction that allows us to read with all the skin' by the Ubud Writers and Readers Festival program. Although Beth and I missed most of the talk. And no, we weren't overflowing with erotic conviction. We spent most of the evening chatting to each other as if no one else was in the room.

As I was escorting Beth back to her guesthouse at the end of the evening, I suddenly had an idea. 'Would you like to join me for some of the trip?' I asked. And I wasn't surprised at all when Beth said yes. Although we'd only spent two evenings together, we'd really hit it off. And besides, we could be a couple travelling together just like Tony and Maureen, I thought. It turned out Beth wanted to spend more time in Bali, but she agreed to meet up in Malaysia and travel to Thailand together. Well, that's if I didn't get hopelessly lost in Sumatra on the way.

I was late picking up Tony. That was because the Four Seasons Hotel, which looked like a giant, five-star flying saucer hovering over the rice fields, wasn't around in 1974. That meant that it wasn't on my map and I'd driven past it. Three times. We finally met in the hotel's five-star scooter park, where Tony was dressed in a suitably five-star floral shirt, pants and dress shoes. Not quite backpacking attire, but that was because Tony had been to a 'literary lunch' at the Four Seasons. At least he wasn't wearing a beret or a cravat.

As soon as we turned onto the main road, Tony raced off ahead of me, my newish bike and hot-pink helmet. And I mean raced. I didn't have a chance to admire the view, because I was concentrating so hard just to keep up with Tony, who was zipping in and out of the traffic like one of the suicidal locals. When he started overtaking large trucks on blind turns at 80 kilometres an hour, I almost wet my pants. I didn't think Maureen would have been happy (that's about Tony speeding, not me wetting my pants). But Tony was right in his element. This was how he researched the old guidebook – zooming around South-East Asia like a madman.

When we eventually stopped, I nearly fell off the bike because my knees were like jelly. I'd been so focused on keeping up with Tony that I hadn't even noticed we'd climbed a mountain road high over Lake Batur, with a spectacular view over the still-active volcano of Gunung Batur. Within a few seconds of stopping, a woman appeared out of nowhere with an armful of sarongs and T-shirts. When the lady said to Tony, 'For you special price,' I laughed. 'You must have heard that a few times.' In almost four decades of constant travelling, I guessed Tony would have heard that several hundred thousand times.

The road down to Lake Batur was steep and twisting, but that didn't stop Tony from trying to break the land speed record for a Honda scooter. By the time we stopped at a dirt clearing on the lake's edge, I was so happy to get off the bike. I hadn't even driven that fast in a car before.

I mentioned to Tony that he was trying to kill me and he told me that for a few years some people thought that he'd died. 'I kept hearing all these stories that I was dead,' Tony said. 'From a bus or motorcycle accident, or from malaria or eaten by a rhino. One time, I was standing in a bookshop in Singapore and there were two ladies next to me. One of the women picked up a Lonely Planet guidebook and said, "This is much cheaper to buy here than in Stockholm," and the other one said, "Yes, it's such a pity that Tony Wheeler is dead, though."'

Tony looked very much alive as we hiked along the shore past simple fishermen's huts, tiptoeing over fishing nets spread out to dry like huge spider webs. Suddenly, Tony stopped. 'It was around here somewhere,' he said. We were looking for the 'pleasant and small' Wisma Tirta Yatra guesthouse. Tony finally asked one of the fishermen, who pointed directly in front of us. Tony hadn't been here for over 25 years, but he'd stopped in exactly the right place.

The guidebook guru giggled with excitement as we climbed up to the whitewashed – or formerly white-washed and now more greywashed – guesthouse overlooking the lake. Tony's level of enthusiasm abated, however, when we were shown one of the rooms. It still had the same 1974 electric fan in the corner that flapped weakly towards the two 1974 beds with sheets covered in 1974 stains. 'It looks exactly the same,' Tony said. 'Except the sheets were cleaner.' I wasn't surprised when Tony whispered that the guesthouse hadn't been featured in a Lonely Planet guidebook for more than 20 years.

At least it was an almost-1974 price of $4.50 a room. Tony suggested that we could probably afford to get our own room each. He couldn't stop laughing after inspecting my room more closely, only to discover my squat toilet totally covered in a platoon of ants fighting over some rather questionable stains. 'That's all we ever had,' Tony said when he spotted the *mandi* (bucket shower). 'We went for months without seeing a real shower.' Tony must have been one of those smelly hippies at Oka Wati's.

With no restaurants listed in the old guidebook, we opted for a wander into the nearby village of Toya Bungkah to find one. The first restaurant we happened upon, the Volcano Breeze Restaurant, sported a large 'As Recom-mended by Lonely Planet' sign out the front. 'We have to go here,' Tony grinned. Unfortunately, being recom-mended by Lonely Planet wasn't working too well for the Volcano Breeze Restaurant. We were the only diners.

In my travels, I had seen 'As Recommended by Lonely Planet' signs in front of restaurants and guesthouses in just about every corner of the globe. And in some places, it became a little bit out of control. I'd visited the Lonely Planet-recommended Lac Thanh Restaurant in Hue, Vietnam, which was run by a deaf-mute cook. The place had always been full of travellers, so another deaf-mute cook opened a restaurant next door called Lac Thien. Then another deaf-mute cook (yes, I'm serious) opened Lac Thuan across the road. All three were highlighted in Lonely Planet, and all three had put up large 'As Recommended by Lonely Planet' signs out front.

The Wheelers had often heard complaints that they helped to ruin certain destinations because of their guidebooks. 'There's no question; we are a little bit responsible,' Tony admitted. 'But change is inevitable and guidebooks don't inspire travel so much as to channel it. It's better to have educated travellers than clucks on tour buses.'

Lonely Planet also deliberately changed things around, and omitted and added different restaurants when they updated a book. 'Particularly if it's a small place,' Tony said. 'It keeps it fresh, and if we didn't, it would make it tough on everyone otherwise.' What he said was true. All of the three deaf-mute restaurants, which were in the guidebook when I travelled to Vietnam, weren't listed in the current *Southeast Asia on a Shoestring*.

We joined a few of the locals for a beer on the verandah overlooking Lake Batur. One of them was Wayan Balik, the owner of the Wisma Tirta Yatra guesthouse. 'I lived in a different village for forty years,' Wayan told us. 'Then I married a local girl and moved here.' He smiled sheepishly. 'In Bali, usually the wife follows the husband wherever he goes.' Wayan had purchased the four-room guesthouse from the original owner in 1985. 'Not many people stay now,' he said sadly. Luckily I didn't tell the owner that he was sitting with the founder of Lonely Planet, or Tony may have been pushed to put the guest-house back in the guidebook again.

We were in bed by nine (there wasn't much else to do), but it took me a while to get to sleep. As I pulled back the sheets revealing 1974 in all its glory – more like, in all its gory – I noticed stains that made me shudder to imagine where they came from. I spent a lot of the night like a contortionist, trying to avoid lying on them.

I was up at 6 am, but not because I wanted to get up early. The local roosters and dogs, which must have been on some sort of a roster, had taken turns howling and crowing. At least I didn't have to use the question-able toilet and mandi, though. Only a short walk from the guesthouse, a series of hot springs fed into Lake Batur. Since Tony's first visit, where you simply jumped in, a rather flash hot-water springs complex had been built, housing hot pools, spas and showers. It was so flash, in fact, that the entrance fee was more expensive than a room at the Wisma Tirta Yatra.

After a quick breakfast, I bid farewell to Tony, who was heading back to his nice villa in Ubud with unstained sheets. It was such a privilege travelling with Tony, even for a short time. He has a wonderful sense of adventure that undoubtedly started when he traipsed around the world with his parents (his family lived in Pakistan, West Indies and the States) and he has never lost it. I still hope to be gallivanting around the world when I'm in my sixties – hang on a minute, that's not that far off.

Aside from his breakneck speed, my bike trip so far had certainly been a lot easier following Tony. Now I was on my own with only a fairly basic 1974 map of Bali – okay, an incredibly basic map. But at least I could admire the view out of the village. From there, it was downhill all the way to the coast. It was a pleasant (and pleasantly slow) journey with no traffic and spectacular views over a lush green landscape down to the north coast of Bali. By the time I hit the coastal town of Singaraja, I was cruising – at not much more than jogging pace – while looking for the turn-off to the temple of Pura Medrwe Karanga. It had a 'good example of extravagant sandstone carvings', according to the guidebook.

My thoughts were seriously interrupted when an older couple on a scooter tried to overtake me. As they attempted to avoid an oncoming car, they clipped my bike. It all happened in slow motion, as the three of us flew over our handlebars in perfect unison. Thank the Hindu gods for compulsory helmets or I would have been toast. I landed face first then slid for about 20 metres along the road. I pushed myself up, dazed. Boy, is that road hot, I thought, followed by, this is not good. I seemed to be covered in an extraordinary amount of blood. Further up the road, the female pillion passenger was lying on the ground in a heap and moaning. Even though I felt completely out of it, I somehow managed to move my scooter to the side of the road, and by the time I'd sat down in the gutter, quite a crowd had gathered around the scene. The sight of my own blood threw me into a dizzy spell (as it normally does). I'd torn a few layers of skin from my legs and arms and spotted a big nasty gash on my hand. Thankfully there were no broken bones. Well, my bones at least. When I checked on the couple, I discovered the woman had broken her arm. After that, I had to sit down again straightaway, because I thought I was going to faint. My shirt was so soaked with sweat, I may as well have just jumped out of a pool. A local man sat down next to me. 'We need to go to the doctor,' he said.

He looked okay to me.

'I'm all right,' I said.

'The woman needs doctor. You must pay for doctor.'

I watched in horror as blood gushed out from a wound on my knee. My shorts were drenched in blood, which actually bothered me much more than the crater in my knee. This had been my only pair of shorts, as all my other clothes were still back at Oka Wati's in Ubud. Still, seeing the doctor was probably a good idea.

'Quick, before police come,' my newly acquired friend said, grabbing my arm.

I jumped on the back of his bike. But as we turned off the main road and down a dirt track, I started to worry. Where was he taking me? To a brand-new house and doctor's surgery it seemed. I thought there might be a good chance the doctor's surgery was unchanged since 1974, but it was spotlessly clean and the doctor even had his iPod playing on a Bose SoundDock.

The young doctor – who looked about 21 – had some bad news. 'I'm sorry,' he said as he lowered his head. 'I will have to amputate your leg.' Okay, he didn't really say that. Despite all the bloodiness, I didn't even need stitches. Though while he was cleaning up the blood, I almost fainted again (yes, I know, I'm a wuss).

'You must pay money to the doctor,' my friend said. 'You give me the money.'

But when the doctor said that I didn't have to pay, the man looked more distressed than I was (there went his commission).

As the doctor finished bandaging my leg, the two other accident victims arrived with the police. After the doctor gave the woman some painkillers, we were escorted straight to the police station.

The police station was like a sauna, and I had sweat dripping from my chin like a tap as two officers inter-rogated the couple for nearly two hours. And for most of that time, I had no idea what was going on. 'This will cost you a lot of money,' my friend, who'd been acting as my translator, said. As the couple got up to leave, the policeman handed me back my passport. His next words to me sounded very much like 'go away', but my friend interjected with, 'You have to pay police ten million rupiah.'

I stared back at him. 'I don't have that much money on me. I need a bank.'

'It's Sunday. No banks open today.'

'I have to pay tomorrow,' I said. 'I'm staying here in Singaraja.'

'Okay, we meet out the front of the police station at nine o'clock.'

'See you tomorrow,' I waved.

Yeah, right. I was out of there.

I was shaking with fear as I mounted the bike. Thankfully, the only damage consisted of a bent brake grip and a smashed front headlight.

But I wasn't going to stay in Singaraja – even though it was said to be 'packed with reasonably priced losmen and lots of places to eat'. Instead, I headed 11 kilometres down the coast for 'something completely different'. The Tasik Madu beach cottages sounded nice and quiet and, more importantly, the police might not find me if, in the end, they did come looking for their money.

Shortly thereafter, I began to doubt whether I'd find the beach cottages. Several kilometres out of Singaraja, I passed an endless procession of resorts, hotels, bars and restaurants. Those few beautiful cottages on the beach had turned into the full-blown resort town of Lovina, which the current guidebook described as the 'north coast's beach-bum magnet'. Feeling a bit weary, I stopped at an empty bar for a mixed juice.

Fortunately, the fellow behind the bar was able to confirm the Tasik Madu cottages were still around. 'Yes,' he said, pointing across the road. By sheer luck – and I deserved some after my day so far – he'd pointed directly over the road. 'It's a bit old,' he added.

I waddled up to reception in sweat-drenched clothes and caught the young guy at the desk staring at my bloodied shorts – probably wondering whether a travelling mass murderer was about to check in. The guesthouse was meant for longer stays, but with so few guests, the fellow at reception let me stay for one night. The hotel brochure even looked as though it was from 1974. The faded copy read:

Puri Tasik Madu is the oldest of the home stay in Lovina. Some rooms are old building and are much basic, the other ones are worth staying.

'Is the owner still around?' I asked. 'I'm going to kill him next.' Okay, I didn't really say that. But, the guy did look petrified when I asked for the owner, so I told him that I was writing a book about Puri Tasik Madu.

'Yes, but he lives in his village,' he said. 'I come from the same village fifty kilometres away.' He didn't tell me much about the owner or the hotel, but he did tell me all about his grandfather. 'He is famous in our village,' he said. 'He has been married twelve times and his son, who is my dad, has been married six times.' I wasn't surprised when he told me that his grandfather and his father had no money. 'They don't have a big wedding ceremony,' he said. 'Just bananas and coconuts.'

All the time that we were talking, he kept staring at my bloodied shorts, so I told him about the accident. 'Bali is crazy.' His eyes widened. 'Too many motorbikes. A family might have three children, but they will have five motorbikes. At high school, every kid had a motor-bike.' He then went on to say that more than 20 people died every month in motorbike accidents.

Suddenly, I was feeling very fortunate. Then again, I still had to ride over the mountains to get back to Ubud.

My room was 'much basic', but I was just deliriously happy to lie on the bed under the fan. Three hours later, I awoke even weaker. I hadn't eaten any lunch and it was almost 4.30. So I went for a walk, or more like a zombiesque stagger, along the black-sand beach. There were no restaurants listed in the old guidebook but I now had hundreds to choose from. I settled for the Sea Breeze Café because its name said it all, from its beach to its breeze. As a spectacular sunset dropped over the mountains, I instantly became the official nice-roman-tic-shot-of-couple-at-sunset photographer.

Feeling extremely lucky that I had come away from the accident relatively unscathed (just a little shaken up and a couple of extremities torn to shreds), I decided to celebrate my good fortune with a few drinks. The fellow at reception had recommended the Poco Evolution Bar.

'It is the happening place with the best good band in Lovina,' he said.

The Poco Evolution Bar wasn't quite happening, however – with only a Dutch couple sitting at one of the tables and a handful of locals leaning against the bar. I didn't know if the band was the 'best good band' in Lovina, but their cover songs sounded identical to the original versions. When they had a break, I approached the lead guitarist and, as usual, talked my way into singing a song with the band. I suggested 'Sweet Home Alabama' – which I later remembered was actually from 1974. Halfway through the song, a fight broke out between two of the locals at the bar. It began with yelling, then threatening one another with beer bottles. But, that wasn't quite enough action for one of the fellows, so he threw his beer bottle directly at the other guy's head – which luckily missed and smashed into pieces against the wall. The missed target then went so ballistic, his friends had to hold him back. Soon, two security goons dragged out the bottle-thrower, as he howled and swung his arms.

And all this, while I happily belted out the lyrics to 'Sweet Home Alabama'.

When I sat back down next to the Dutch couple, I said: 'I think we have to pay extra for that entertainment.' I'd had enough, though, and it was time for bed. That was just way too much excitement for one day.

*

I spent the entire night repeatedly rolling on to my wounds and waking up squealing in pain. But the early start the next morning was a good thing. The fellow at reception had told me that the mountains became covered in cloud as the day went on, and when it rained, you could only see a few metres in front of you. One accident was enough, thank you very much.

I was rather tentative on the scooter to begin with. Not only because I was still feeling a little shaken up from the accident, but I was also a little worried that I might be on Singaraja's Most Wanted list. What if the fine was legitimate and police were on the lookout for a man in bloodied shorts riding a scooter with a broken mirror? I still had to ride through Singaraja to get back into the mountains. And if I rode too slowly, it would look suspicious, and if I rode too fast, it would look like I was trying to make a speedy getaway. I tried to ride at a non-criminal everything-is-okay-with-the-world pace, but everyone seemed to be eyeing me suspiciously. Okay, maybe I was a little paranoid. But many of them did look like they could be undercover cops. They did, really.

Once I left my paranoia and the traffic of Singaraja behind and headed up the quiet mountain road, I relaxed. And I felt totally calm and peaceful by the time I hit the 'calm and peaceful Lake Bedubal'. Perched on the edge of the lake was what the old guidebook had called the 'pleasant little waterside temple of Ulun Danu' with 'the nicest no entry sign in Bali'. The same sign still stood proudly: 'It is forbidden to enter women during menstruation.' (I'd agree with that.) The Ulun Danu temple today was famous all over Indonesia because it appeared on the 50,000 rupiah note. This made it the most photographed temple in Bali. I parked my scooter in the busy car park and made my way down to the lake's edge where an impressively large and largely impressive ceremony was taking place with a neat line of local folk dressed in white and gold robes sitting under yellow umbrellas. I watched as offerings were being thrown into the lake, including baskets of food and a live duck. When the duck was first thrown in, it swam back to shore. The duck was tossed in again, and again it swam back. 'You have go,' the duck-chucker said to me. He handed me the squirming duck and I threw it, rather pathetically I might add, all of about three metres. The duck was back to the shore in seconds. Now it was getting serious. The brawniest man in the group grabbed the duck, wound it up like a baseball, then launched it 50-odd metres out into the lake. The duck didn't come back this time, but that was probably because the poor thing was in shock.

The old guidebook had devoted a whole section to ceremonies, Balinese dances and gamelan music: 'Temple festivals are splashes of colour,' it read. 'They can be for all sorts of reasons, but the most usual are temple birthdays held every 210 days.' The old guidebook went on to describe the temple decor – flowers, umbrellas, streamers and a feast of food offerings. This type of information would never go out of date – except that you couldn't now get 'cassette tapes of gamelan performances' at the temples. Today, you could purchase CDs, DVDs and maybe even a 'Throw the Duck in the Lake' Wii game.

Three hours after I left the temple and got lost a dozen times or so, I was back in Ubud. When I hobbled up to the door of Beth's villa to meet her for dinner, she asked me what had happened. 'Oh, not much,' I said. 'I almost died in a scooter accident, got into a bar brawl and threw a duck into a lake.' I was feeling very sore and tired but wasn't going to miss out on our last date together before Malaysia. I may have been a bit smitten. Or delirious. Or both.

The old guidebook had listed three restaurants in Ubud (and the only three restaurants in Ubud back in 1974, Tony had told me). All three were still there. Beth and I headed to Ibu Rai's, although it wasn't quite 'on-the-cheap' anymore, with linen napkins and proper wineglasses. Then again, six dollars for a main meal was cheap in the scheme of things. Mind you, those tight-arse hippies would have skipped it for a three-cent bowl of mouldy rice from the side of the road. The old guide-book cited the bean soup and Balinese-style porridge as 'tasty treats not to be missed'. Though neither were on the menu, one could at least order potato and leek soup and Balinese-style spaghetti bolognese.

I asked the waitress if Ibu Rai was around, but she told me with a sweet smile that she was dead. However, the waitress did introduce me to Ibu Rai's son, Dewa

Gede. 'My mother passed away in 2004,' he explained, after he'd joined our table. 'She was seventy-nine years old.' As Dewa briefly told me the story of Ibu Rai's life, I discovered it to be strangely similar to Canderi's. Ibu Rai's husband had died in the late '60s, and she'd been determined to provide her six young children with a good education. Four of the six children ended up graduating from university. 'Grandma started by opening up a small warung,' Dewa continued, 'and it made it into guidebooks because she served up food that was safe for foreigners. In the early '80s, she gave up the warung and sold paintings. Then I opened this restaurant in 1992 and named it after my mum.' Dewa's smile told me just how proud he was of his mum.

'Did your mum ever talk about what Ubud was like before you were born?' I asked.

Dewa thought for a moment. 'Yes. Mum would talk a lot about all the quacking ducks.'

6

Java

The National Museum has a big relief map on which you can pick out all those volcanoes you have climbed.
South east Asia on a shoestring, 1st edition, 1975

The National Museum has a big relief map on which you can pick out all those volcanoes you plan to climb.
Southeast Asia on a Shoestring, 15th edition, 2010

In the old guidebook, Hotel Kota in Yogyakarta was the only hotel actually marked on the map. All of the other hotels had been bundled together under 'Other Cheap Hotels'. And they must have been cheap, because one of them was called the 'Inexpensive Losmen'. But these Other Cheap Hotels receive a bad rap in the book: 'With the exception of Hotel Kota, the majority of Yogya's hotels are remarkably dull and unimaginative for a supposedly artistic city.' Mind you, the Kota hadn't fared much better: 'The Kota is often full and rather noisy.'

But at least the Hotel Kota was still there. As I walked out of the airport, the first taxi driver I approached said, 'Of course I know Hotel Kota. It's a very plain hotel.' The hotel appeared suitably plain from the outside and looked more like the dusty train station directly across the road. The inside of the hotel, however, wouldn't have looked out of place in Marrakech. The foyer and sitting room had exposed, dark-wood beams with hanging iron lamps, bright green and yellow leadlight windows, and chequered tiled floors. The receptionist, who looked about 12, didn't know when the hotel was built. 'I think it might have in the brochure,' she suggested. 'But my English not much good.' Whoever wrote the copy in the brochure didn't have 'much good' English, either:

Hotel Kota is the only hotel in Yogyakarta which still remains the iriginal style of building. Though rooms in Hotel Kota are a little bit smaller than those of common, you can enjoy your stay because all rooms are dealing with the history of years ago. Hotel Kota building which was bulit in 1950 and used by the Ducth for dormitory of its 'vip' men still remains its original style to depict the history. All ceilling were built so high that guest will feel confortable. We also had been renovated in 1995.

I wouldn't have really called the room 'vip', and the renovation looked as if it had been done in 1975, not 1995. But I did feel 'confortable' with the high 'ceilling'. And it had air conditioning and CNN on cable. The room felt a little stuffy, so I opened the window – which opened up into the busy corridor. Then again, I had asked for the cheapest room. Still, at $40 a night for a basic room, the Hotel Kota probably didn't fit the bill for 'on a shoestring' anymore. It wasn't listed in the current guidebook, anyway.

The old guidebook noted that Yogyakarta was 'the most popular city in Indonesia'. It certainly was. In 1974, Yogyakarta had a total of around 35,000 international tourists of whom backpackers comprised the major proportion. In comparison, Kuta had only around 15,000 tourists.

It relieved me to discover that, because Yogyakarta was so popular, the old guidebook had provided a reasonably detailed map. Letting my stomach dictate where I would start my tour, I headed first to Maliboro Street, the main street for eating as well as shopping, according to Tony. I noticed quite a change from Hindu Bali to Muslim Java. The women wore headscarves, the men didn't wear skirts, and not a single person asked me if I wanted a massage.

There were three restaurants listed in the old guidebook, including the 'particularly popular' Happy Restaurant. It was even more popular today, I discovered. And still very much happy – but that's only because they now sold McHappy meals. It was a McDonald's. Then there was the Helen Restaurant, with 'terrific iced juice'. It now had terrific iced donuts. I couldn't believe it – Helen Restaurant was a Dunkin' Donuts. It certainly was a different world from 1974 – or more like it was now part of one big homogenised world. The main street of Yogyakarta hosted a McDonald's, a Dunkin' Donuts, a KFC, a Starbucks and a Pizza Hut. Next door to the Pizza Hut was a Novotel Hotel that looked identical to the other 5000 Novotels around the planet. And often those mega hotel chains had identical room layouts, whether you were in Yogyakarta, York, Yokohama, Yangon or Yazoo.

I feared the Restaurant Cirebon – the remaining restaurant on the list – was now a KFC. I was close. The restaurant was still there, but a KFC was next door. The interior of Restaurant Cirebon looked straight out of 1974, with its high ceilings and groaning ceiling fans that struggled just to do one rotation. Except that it had opened in 1930, according to a sign on the wall. This popular destination for Muslim families housed large 'HALAL' signs throughout, although it wasn't quite kosher halal. Fried pork was listed on the menu and the fridge was filled with large bottles of Bintang.

I asked the waitress for the most famous dish on the menu and she suggested the house specialty: fried frog. So, I ordered the frog (when in Rome . . .) plus a lobster omelette. After the waitress returned with my beer, she showed me an old framed photo of Yogyakarta from the 1930s. It looked pretty much the same – minus all the cars, scooters and fast-food restaurants. My fried frog – as in an entire bullfrog – had been cut up into bits like something from a botched high-school science class, then deep-fried in batter. All things considered, it didn't taste too bad (it was frog, after all). The only problem was that I couldn't tell if I was eating a leg, a head or a brain. Clichéd as it may sound, it tasted like chicken. Or more like a froggy chicken. The lobster omelette didn't resemble lobster flavour, either. Or an omelette, for that matter.

With a stomach full of frog, I hit the streets for Kraton, the huge palace of the Sultan of Yogya, which was actually a city within a city, according to the old guidebook. There, a 'traditionally dressed guide' was to show you around its 'sumptuous pavilions and halls'. I don't think that my guide was wearing traditional dress, however. Unless of course it was a Chelsea football top, Levi's jeans and Nike runners. Though he attempted to show me around, there really wasn't much to see. The Sultan of Yogya still lived there and he obviously didn't like people traipsing around his sumptuous pavilions and halls anymore.

The Taman Sari, or 'Fragrant Garden', had been described as:

. . . a complex of canals, pools and palaces built within the Kraton from 1758 to 1765. Damaged by Diponegoro's Java War and further by an earthquake, today it's a mass of ruins crowded with small houses and batik galleries. Parts are being restored.

Amazingly, that exact same passage was in the current 15th edition of *Southeast Asia on a Shoestring*. Even the bit about 'parts are being restored' (or as it should now read, 'parts are *still* being restored').

According to the old guidebook, the bird market near the water palace was well worth visiting. It's now even more worth visiting because as well as birds of every variety of squawk and titter for sale, there are also bats, frogs, lizards, snakes, squirrels, mongooses, hamsters, lemurs, monkeys, mice, spiders, bees, crickets, ants and some particularly squirmy worms. For a dollar, I could have purchased a whole bag of frogs, and one of the stallholders hassled me for ten minutes to buy a pet bat.

When I got back to the hotel, it was time for dinner. Well, it was actually way too early for dinner, but my frog brain and mystery omelette lunch hadn't quite filled me up. For dinner, the old guidebook recommended the 'good, cheap warungs' all along Jalan Pasar Kembang, known for 'very nice' gado gado at a 'good value'. So, that's exactly where I went and that's exactly what I ate. It excited me whenever I followed advice from the old guidebook and not only the same place, but the same value still existed. That said, I was surprised the restaurants hadn't been swamped with backpackers. The current guidebook described Yogya as 'one of the nation's most enjoyable and cosmopolitan cities', and yet I hadn't seen a single backpacker since I'd arrived.

It was still early, so I went for a wander near the hotel to see if I could find a bar – although being in a Muslim city, I wasn't sure if I'd have much luck. I followed a narrow lane near the hotel that eventually came to a halt at a brightly lit street filled with restaurants, bars and guesthouses. No wonder I hadn't seen any backpackers – the entire backpacker area had moved from the train station area a few blocks away.

I ended up in a bar overflowing with backpackers. They spoke the same schtick of every backpacker the world over: *Where have you been?*, *Where are you going?* and most importantly, *Here's where you should have gone.* I wondered if this same conversation played in backpacker guesthouses in 1974. Apparently not. According to Agnieszka Sobocinska in an article in *The Australian*, 'Hippies Blazed a Trail to Those Far-Out Reaches', about travel in the '70s, travellers spent most of their time boasting about all the tortures they had suffered. The article went on to explain how 'whingeing about inconveniences of every kind was a way of proving that a traveller had experienced the "real" Asia and had a genuine experience'. This contradicted the most common scenario I'd heard so far. Hippie travellers were far too busy getting stoned to complain, and the only thing that probably would have passed their lips was, 'Can you pass me the joint?'

*

I'd planned to catch an early-morning bus to Borobu-dur, which ranked with Pagan and Angkor Wat as one of the great South-East Asian Buddhist monuments, according to the old guidebook. This time, I decided to skip the local bus and do what all the other Lonely Planet-wielding backpackers were doing – join a tour. I almost didn't make the 5 am departure because I'd been traipsing through the dark streets in search of a bunch of other weary-eyed travellers. 'Are you Superman?' the tour guide asked when I finally found them.

'Um, no,' I said.

'I'm Superman,' the Dutch fellow beside me inter-jected.

'What about you?' the tour guide asked, staring straight at me.

'I'm . . . er, Brian.'

'No, what *are* you?'

'Batman?'

'Superman' was actually the name of a guesthouse, I discovered. I'd thought something was fishy since the Dutch guy hadn't been wearing red underpants over his clothes. The guide just wanted to know which guest-house we were staying in. Incidentally, Superman was so popular that they made a sequel: there was now a Superman 2 guesthouse.

The beefy Frenchman next to me, however, wasn't Superman 1 or 2. 'I'm Lucy,' he offered. He was staying at Lucy guesthouse.

The first signs of dawn painted a warm glow over the packed car park, as we pulled in next to a line of vehicles that almost outnumbered the lines of stalls selling tourist trinkets. The old guidebook suggested buying 'good whistling tops for the kids'. And these particular toys were still being sold – except that the stalls all now had credit card machines.

According to the 1974 guidebook, the ancient Buddhist ruins of Borobudur had been about to get an eight-million-US-dollar restoration job that was due to be completed by 1978. Thirty years later, it was still being restored. Even though it was swarming with tourists (at 6.15 am I might add), the ninth-century terraces and stupas lent a mystical feel to the soft morning light and mist that hung over the surrounding countryside. Unfortunately, I didn't have quite enough time to view all of the 1500 panels, 472 Buddha images or even the 57 stalls with 'whistling tops for the kids'.

While I was waiting back at the bus for the remaining passengers (as a former tour guide, I knew there would *always* be passengers who were late back to the bus), I chatted to our guide, Agus (yes, another one). 'Where are you going next?' he asked me.

'I'm catching the train to Jakarta tomorrow.'

Agus stared back in disbelief. 'You won't get a train tomorrow. It's the end of Ramadan and everyone is on that train. I booked a ticket for my brother a month ago and they were sold out the next day.'

'What can I do?' I asked.

Apparently, I could fly to Jakarta or wait a week for the next available train.

'Maybe you can look for shifty people out the front of the station to buy a black-market train ticket,' Agus suggested.

So when we arrived back in Yogyakarta, I headed to the entrance of the jam-packed train station. I approached the first man milling about who looked sufficiently shifty enough, but before I even opened my mouth he said, 'Do you want a train ticket?'

'Yes, to Jakarta for tomorrow.'

'The train is full.'

'Yes, I know.'

He looked around from side to side as though being watched. 'Okay, one minute.'

He shuffled off and spoke with a couple of other shifty-looking characters (there were plenty to choose from) and one minute later he returned with a ticket. 'I'm sorry,' he said. 'You have to pay a bit more than normal ticket.' I had no idea what the price of a normal ticket was, anyway. All I knew was the 1974 price for the 'express train', which was just over two dollars. He handed me the ticket, which was for the overnight train leaving at 6 pm.

'Is it possible to get a ticket for the morning train?' I could play hardball too.

'Okay,' he said with a smile. Two minutes later, he returned with an executive-class ticket for the morning train. The man explained that the ticket was normally

160,000 rupiah ($20), but that I would have to pay 240,000. For an extra ten dollars, I didn't mind. And besides, trains were 'by far the best way to get around Java', according to the old guidebook. When our dodgy deal was done, my shifty friend leant in and whispered, 'Okay, you want a nice Indonesian girl for tonight?'

I politely declined and my shifty friend disappeared among the throng of other shifty-looking characters at the entrance.

The next morning, I arrived at the train station early in preparation for the ensuing madness, but there wasn't any. The platform was virtually empty and most of the train passengers were already aboard and in their seats. 'Choose your trains for comfort, speed and destination,' the old guidebook had suggested. Well, I got two out of three. The train was heading to the destination I wanted (or I hoped it was) and seeing as it was an 'express train', I assumed it would be fast. But it didn't quite live up to the comfort part. My executive-class seat didn't get me air conditioning and when I opened the window, a hot stuffy wind buffeted my face. The rest of my body fell victim to all the thrashing around, as if the train were having an epileptic fit. For most of the day, the train trundled through a flat landscape of vivid green fields tended by folk in conical hats, and past country lanes where the only traffic was that of bicycles. It felt like 1974 – until we flashed through towns with large billboards advertising mobile phones, the latest cars and laptop computers.

Throughout the journey, local people strolled up and down the carriage aisle selling water, tea, coffee, snacks, cigarettes, newspapers and Dora the Explorer dolls. Whenever we stopped at a large station, we were mobbed by hawkers selling watches, wallets, DVDs, belts, plastic toys, books, magazines, soap and deodorant (a few people on the train desperately needed some of that). You even got to try before you bought. A seller would throw something down on your lap then return a little time later and enquire whether you were interested in purchasing. Over the trip, I had a wooden ladle, a plastic gun, a leather cowboy hat and a huge bouquet of pink plastic flowers placed in my lap.

The best way to block out the constant screaming of the hawkers was to listen to that great 21st-century invention, the iPod. Back in 1974, travellers certainly wouldn't have had that luxury (the first Walkman didn't even come out till 1979). They may have been able to pick up the local radio stations, but then again they probably would have been better off without it – particularly if the radio was playing the big hits of 1975. Those hits included the number-one selling song 'Love Will Keep Us Together' by The Captain and Tennille, plus other top-50 songs such as 'Morning Side of The Mountain' by Donny and Marie Osmond, 'Thank God I'm A Country Boy' by John Denver, 'Bad Blood' by Neil Sedaka and 'Mandy' by Barry Manilow. I think I would have preferred the annoying hawkers to Donny and Marie.

While I was listening to Neil Sedaka's Greatest Hits on my iPod, I read *Ghost Train to the Eastern Star* by Paul Theroux. In the travelogue, he retraced the trip he took for his 1975 book *The Great Railway Bazaar: By Train Through Asia*. Sound familiar? Yes, it was somewhat similar to the premise of this book, except he was following the journey he'd taken himself 30 years earlier. I'm a big fan of Theroux's travel books and, yes he can get a bit grumpy and comes across as rather misanthropic at times, but I do admire his prose. It was very interesting comparing his journey to my own. He too had discovered places that were exactly the same and had also met up with some of the same people from 1975. One of my favourite stories involved him travelling to Maymyo in Upper Burma, where the author visited the same guesthouse he'd originally stayed in. The original manager's son (who was now the manager) recognised him straightaway and led him to the same room he had stayed in previously. He even remembered that Theroux had worn a black shirt, smoked a pipe and had a favourite table by the window where he loved to sit and write.

As we approached shantytowns built under modern highway overpasses and the ubiquitous squalor and rubbish piled everywhere, I knew we had entered a huge, third-world capital city. There had also been plenty of squalor around in 1974, according to the guidebook: 'Jakarta is an often squalid and dirty city that many travellers try to give a miss, but actually has quite a lot to offer.'

After almost ten hours (two hours longer than the time listed in the old guidebook), the smell in the carriage had become a nasty mix of urine and body odour, all in the suffocating heat. It took me ten minutes to unstick myself from the seat to stand up and stretch my legs. As I stood near the open carriage door, I chatted to a local 19-year-old university student. When I commented on the heat, he replied, 'The problem is, Indonesians are always hot and confused.'

'Confused about what?' I asked.

'Oh, everything.'

Gambir Station was chaotic with locals returning from the Ramadan holiday. I must have been the only tourist because every taxi driver, tuk tuk driver, motor scooter taxi driver and mule driver jumped on me at once. As I made my way through the train station car park, the price lowered and lowered. The fare started at 50,000 rupiah. But, by the time I reached the exit, the drivers were pleading with me to get into their taxis for 15,000 rupiah. Relief swept over me when the taxi driver knew of my 1974 guesthouse recommendation. The heat had drained my ability to schlep through the streets in the dark looking for old guesthouses that may or may not exist anymore.

Wisma Delima guesthouse was on Jalan Jaksa, a street filled with backpacker guesthouses and bars.

But back in 1974, Wisma Delima had been the most popular 'resting place' in Jakarta, according to the old guidebook. Luckily, it had shrunk in popularity and there was a room available. Even better, a room was only 40,000 rupiah a night. Not many capital cities in the world gave you a room right in the heart of the city for five dollars. Though the guesthouse did have some rather strict rules. A large sign at reception announced 'RULES!!' that included:

Keep room very clean.
NO DRUGS (we will call the police at once).
All payments are made in advance due to negative experiences in the past – besides it saves time and effort.

The old guidebook had been right when it described Wisma Delima as 'a little chaotic at first glance, but is actually quite comfortable and very friendly'. Except that it was still chaotic at second glance. Beyond the reception was an enclosed courtyard, home to the family's living room, kitchen and dining room. It was all so randomly ramshackle, but I loved it. I had to walk through the middle of the living room and up a groaning staircase to get to my tiny room, which had an even tinier lumpy bed with a whopping big dip in the middle. But that was nowhere near as disconcerting as the walls, which were covered in blood splatter. Had there been a murder? No. Just years and years of people squashing mosquitoes.

Still drenched in sweat from the Sauna Express, I headed downstairs to the shared bathroom for a shower. This consisted of frigid water dribbling rather pathetically from a hose, but it was bliss. I decided also to have a shave, which meant standing outside in the courtyard by the bathroom sink while the owner's family sat at the dining table watching me. It wasn't often that you got an audience while you shaved. Sadly, there was no standing ovation when I finished.

I decided to have dinner at the guesthouse because the old guidebook had described the meals at Wisma Delima as 'probably the best value in Jakarta'. So, I had the nasi goreng, a dish recommended by the old Lonely Planet guidebook in just about every city in Indonesia.

Afterwards, on the way out for a drink, I noticed the manager sitting at the front desk. I told him that I was writing a book and showed him the old guidebook. 'Ah, Tony Wheeler,' he said. 'He was last here in 1995.'

'Are you the manager in the book?' I asked. In the old guidebook, the manager had received a nice rap: 'The manager speaks perfectly fluent English and knows everything there is to know about things to see, places to go and how to get to wherever you are going.'

'No, my name is Jahja Lawalata and I am his son,' he replied in perfectly fluent English, just like his father. 'My dad died last year. He was ninety-five.' Jahja suddenly looked sad.

I'm never quite sure what to say when people tell me that someone close to them has died. To me, saying sorry just doesn't make sense (it's usually not your fault) and I couldn't really give him a hug. Instead I smiled. 'So, when did your father set up the hostel?' I asked.

'The hostel was opened in 1968 by my father when he was the secretary-general of the Association of Indonesian Youth Hostels,' Jahja said. I later read in an article I found on the history of Jalan Jaksa that it was Jakarta's first youth hostel and was managed by the National Police. However, it didn't stay in business long, because the hostel was already run-down before it was even a hostel. 'When the hostel closed down,' Jahja continued, 'they moved it into our house because we were closer to the city. We then added more rooms for tourists.'

'When did backpackers first start coming to stay?' I asked him.

'The hostel was listed in the youth hostel guidebook in Australia and our first guests were forty Australian tourists. Our rooms were not finished, but they said that they would sleep on the floor in their sleeping bags. After that, we would hang around the airport and bring back guests in a becak.' (A becak was a cycle rickshaw that was considered an icon of Jakarta but banned in the late 1970s, due to concerns of public order.)

'What was Jalan Jaksa like then?'

'Oh, the street was totally dark,' Jahja told me. 'Guests were too scared to leave the hostel at night. The locals in the street would say to my father, "Why you open a cheap hotel? You will not make any money." They said that my father was completely mad crazy.'

It was at this point that Lonely Planet could truly lay claim for the shaping of a city – or the backpackers' part of the city, at least. After appearing in *South east Asia on a shoestring* (and it still did today after 15 editions), so many tourists began turning up that Jahja's family had to rent out one, then two, then three other houses in the street for extra rooms. Jahja motioned towards the street. 'Now everyone is happy and everyone loves our family.' There were now 26 hotels and guesthouses along the road, with just as many bars and restaurants.

I headed out to one of the many backpacker bars for a beer. It reminded me of numerous backpacker streets the world over, with the accompanying flotsam and jetsam that hang around tourist strips asking if you want transport, drugs, souvenirs, a tour or 'something special for you' – wink, wink. One fellow decided to cover all bases and asked me, 'What do you want?'

'Nothing,' I said.

'You want nothing? I can get it for you.'

What I should have asked for was a new mattress. Not only did my bed have a Grand Canyonesque dip in the middle, but I also spent a long time trying to find a spot with the least amount of rock-hard lumps. Plus I had trouble getting to sleep, because the room was so hot that I had to point the fan right at my face and it was like sleeping in the cockpit of a 1974 twin-propped Vickers Viscount.

*

I think Tony might have been a little bit excited about the sailing ships in Jakarta. Not only had he written that Jakarta had the 'most impressive reminder of the age of sailing ships to be seen anywhere in the world', but he also claimed that the old Dutch port of Sunda Kelapa was the 'best sight in Jakarta' and that you could see 'more sailing ships and magnificent Makasar schooners, than you would ever think existed'. Sunda Kelapa was my first port of call, so to speak, but like many occasions during this trip, I got lost trying to follow the 1974 hand-drawn map. Admittedly I'd probably be just as lost with a detailed map. I somehow ended up on a side street where the footpaths were clogged with fetid and rotting rubbish and the gutters were filled with stagnant brown water covered by a film of hideous black oil. I could see the harbour ahead but couldn't get to it. Well, actually I could get to it, but that meant one of three options: walk in the middle of the road while trying to dodge the nonstop maniacal traffic; walk on the side of the road through the noxious water; or, walk over the piles of rancid rubbish on the footpath. In the end, I decided to run over the rubbish – while blocking my nose and keeping my mouth tightly shut. But after only a couple of steps, a wall of flies rose from the garbage and moved towards me. I screamed, letting a few flies (and probably a good dose of hepatitis and diphtheria) into my mouth. Halfway across the Great Wall of Filth, my thong flew off. When I finally reached the other side, I looked back to see my thong sticking out of some nasty-looking brown sludge surrounded by flies. Hmm . . . no, I decided. I was better off walking around in one thong than picking up another half-a-dozen diseases.

The harbour, decorated by majestic Buginese wooden fishing boats with huge billowing sails, was almost worth the months I was going to have to spend in the infectious diseases hospital once I arrived home. I spent a pleasant hour strolling up and down the dock watching deckhands clean and paint the hulls while the captain called out, 'Ahoy there, me hearties!', a lot. (He was speaking in Indonesian, but I'm sure that was what he was saying.) When I asked an old man with two remaining teeth for directions to the town square in Old Jakarta, he grunted then pointed to his long, narrow boat (actually more like a log with a hole in it) squeezed in between the hulking hulls of two fishing boats. He jumped aboard then motioned for me to follow suit. I very tentatively hopped aboard, not wanting to fall into the oily, black water and possibly the bubonic plague. After a short tour across the harbour and even more rubbish, I was unceremoniously dumped onto a rickety wooden walkway on the edge of an even more rickety shantytown. Built mostly on stilts over the water, the village was linked by a series of precariously narrow planks that I had to share with a scrawny army of cats. I passed homes and stalls selling fish (hence all the cats), and soon asked a large, shirtless man for the way out of this maze. He smiled, lifted his bottom and farted. 'Thank you,' I said, and gave him a round of applause. It was the best foghorn I'd ever heard.

I managed to find my own way to the Old Town square without having to backtrack down Diseased Fly Road. Okay, strictly I didn't find the way back by myself; I jumped in a taxi. According to the old guidebook, the Old Town was 'gradually being restored'. At the rate of one cracked cobblestone a week, by the look of it. The only buildings that didn't look as though they were going to fall over any minute were in Fatahillah Square (formerly Stadthuize Plain, when Jakarta was called Batavia). The refurbished Dutch colonial government buildings now housed a history museum, puppet museum, fine arts museum and the Cafe Batavia. I skipped the museums and instead had a beer at the Cafe Batavia because it had air conditioning. Although the building dated back to 1805 – it had been a popular coffee shop until the 1930s – the Cafe Batavia had also served as a warehouse and office in 1974. It had only opened as a restaurant in 1993. The Cafe Batavia hosted a grandiose array of Baroque mirrors, teak floors, capacious comfy couches and a bar made from cowhide. The menu offered 'modern Australian cuisine' at modern Australian prices. The cost of the Australian rib eye steak was the equivalent to a week's accommodation at Wisma Delima.

By the time I returned to the hostel for a dribbling shower, it was close to dinnertime. Only a short walk away in Jalan Haji Agus Salim was the popular Natrabu Restaurant where 'the food can be good', according to the old guidebook. It must have been, on this particular night: I couldn't get in. There was a private function going on. I did get to speak to one of the waiters, however, who told me that the restaurant had opened in 1967 and was now so popular that there were eight Natrabu eateries in Indonesia, plus another two in Malaysia. 'There were only four tables back then,' he said. 'Now we have room for five hundred persons. We also have won many, many awards.' According to the restaurant's website, they had won many, many awards, including first place for 'Table Service', 'received during The Seminar on The Prospect of Restaurant in Facing The Global Era of The 21st Century', back in 1995, and the 'Awarded Certificate of Hygenic', in 1996.

The old guidebook had also suggested the food stalls in the streets around the Natrabu Restaurant for 'reasonably priced nasi goreng'. The vendors were still there, but at this rate, I was turning into a nasi goreng.

The monuments in Jakarta were described in the old guidebook as 'inspired tastelessness'. Being quite a fan of tastelessness myself, particularly the inspired kind, I headed out in the morning to check out what the 1975 guidebook had described as 'Sukarno's last erection'. The giant column in Merdeka Square did look conspicuously like a monolithic erect penis (a 'cockument', if you like), but the locals must have liked erect penises because there was a huge queue to get into the enclosed garden that surrounded the monument. This was probably not in the hippie spirit, but I climbed over the surrounding wall and into an ornamental garden in order to bypass the queue. But hippie karma got me in the end. Because I didn't have a ticket, I couldn't go to the top.

The next sight on my list was the very un-penis-shaped Sarinah Department Store, which had one floor devoted to 'a very good collection of local handicrafts' and 'reasonably priced T-shirts', said the guidebook. This had been the first department store to open in Jakarta in 1967 – and was still the only one in 1974. There were now hundreds of department stores in Jakarta – all full of reasonably priced T-shirts. The Sarinah Department Store was still located on the 'main drag' and still had a floor devoted to handicrafts, but it all looked a little run-down and tired – although the no-fuss simplicity had a certain charm about it. As a comparison, I went to Senayan City in the business district, the newest shopping centre that had only recently opened. The seven-storey glass tower, chock-full of cashed-up and dressed-up locals, was ritzier than anything I'd ever seen in Australia. And you can't get much fancier than a 'designer' pet wear store. In fact, there were three designer pet wear stores all selling cute sequined jackets for poodles. There was even a long, neon-lit plastic tube slide in the middle of the mall, so shoppers could hurl themselves down from the seventh floor to the ground floor in about 12 seconds (for the price of two nights at Wisma Delima).

There were plenty of suitably salubrious restaurants in the shopping centre, but instead I headed to the Hotel Indonesia, where hopefully there would still be a hotel with Sunday *rijsttafel* night. The hotel, I discovered, was still there, but had only been open for a couple of months after a five-year refurbishment, plus the addition of a colossal – and colossally expensive, I imagined – 289-room glass tower behind the original building. The Hotel Indonesia Kempinski (as it is now called) had been the first five-star hotel in Indonesia when it opened in 1962, but its prestige had declined over the years. The refurbishment had revived its status as the most exclusive hotel in Jakarta (read: expensive) and the Signatures Restaurant still had rijsttafel on Sundays – of sorts. It was now a 'lavish themed brunch that will dazzle you with a Western, Indonesian and Japanese buffet presentation'. Luckily for my wallet, the outrageously exorbitant buffet was only served at brunch. So instead, I returned to Wisma Delima and had nasi goreng number 21.

7

Sumatra

Indonesia's new frontier.
South east Asia on a shoestring, 1st edition, 1975

Indonesia's new frontier.
Southeast Asia on a Shoestring, 15th edition, 2010

The old guidebook claimed that Padang has nothing to offer except wonderful and fiery food. Tony did forget to mention, however, the wonderful and fiery sunsets. As my taxi drove me into town from the airport along the coast road, the fiery sun was dropping into the sea in front of a Sumatran-tiger-striped sky. 'So, you do know where the Tiga Tiga Hotel is?' I asked the taxi driver. He didn't seem exactly sure when I asked him at the airport.

'Yes!' he said, with a big smile.

The Tiga Tiga Hotel was 'very popular with the travelling community', although it did have its 'fair share of skeeters so burn your mosquito coils', the old guidebook warned.

Not long after we entered the outskirts of Padang, the taxi stopped. 'Hotel Tiga Tiga,' my driver announced, with that same big smile. Yes, it was the Hotel Tiga Tiga, but it was dark and empty – as in abandoned – and every single window was smashed.

'Do you know the Olo Hotel?' I asked.

'Yes, Olo Hotel,' he said, giving me the thumbs up.

'Does it have windows?'

'Yes, Olo Hotel.'

A few minutes later we pulled up in front of a hotel with all of its windows intact. 'Olo!' the taxi driver said.

'Are you sure this is the Olo Hotel?' I asked, pointing to the large sign for the Hotel Djakarta Makmur.

'Yes, Olo,' he said.

Had the hotel changed its name? No, it hadn't. After a long conversation, I figured out that the hotel was in Jalan Belakang Olo – Olo Street – so my driver thought that was close enough. Actually, it was close enough for me, too. It was too dark and I was too tired and hungry to track down the original hotel. Even the receptionist at the Hotel Djakarta Makmur couldn't help me. He knew the Olo Hotel, but he said, 'I don't know where it is anymore.'

My room was a bit strange. To begin with, two mattresses on the floor took up the entire space, while one wall was covered in huge mirrors and thick red-velvet curtains concealed the opposite wall. I pulled back the curtains, but there wasn't a window, just a brick wall with a set of chains mounted to it. Okay, I made the chains bit up, but it did look like the sort of hotel room that caters for guests with lascivious nocturnal activities in mind. I checked the sheets (a habit now from all the dodgy hotels I'd been staying in) which had neat cigarette burn holes all over them. My suspicions were right: I'd checked into the Bondage Room.

According to the old guidebook, you couldn't come to Padang without eating Padang food, and the best place to eat Padang food was Simpang Restaurant. The restaurant, which was a ten-minute walk from the S & M Hotel, had a '70s theme going on – they had '70s-style Formica tables and chairs and most of the waiting staff were in their seventies. Twelve seconds after I was seated, 14 different plates of food were thrust in front of me, plus a large glass mug of tea and a bowl of water. Every table was also laden with plates, so I figured that it must be a set menu of some kind. (I tried asking the waiting staff, but no one spoke any English.) I knew the bowl of water was to wash your hands: everyone in the restaurant was eating with their hands – or right hand to be precise, because we know what the left hand is used for. Most of the food in front of me was swimming in thick chilli paste or baked in a crust of chilli. There was fried chicken, boiled eggs, some sort of meat, vegetables, tomatoes and . . . that was about all I recognised, actually. I tried the fried chicken first, because it looked the most like food. I took a mouthful, but it was so hot – as in chilli hot – that I had to eat four large handfuls of rice and down half of my mug of tea so the insides of my mouth didn't burst into flames. The meat wasn't as hot, but I had no idea what animal it came from. The tomato dish, which looked deceptively mild on the chilli front, almost blew my head off. After three mouthfuls of food, my nose was dripping like a tap and I was sweating like a marathon runner. Even my fingers were stinging as if they were on fire.

Rather impressively I ended up trying 11 of the 14 dishes. I skipped the eggs, which were fire-engine red with chilli, the dried meat that looked like shoe leather and the bowl of brown sludge that looked like something you produced after you'd eaten all this chilli. (Incidentally, a bit later on I decided that Johnny Cash must have been to Padang and got inspiration when he wrote the lyrics, 'Burns, burns, burns, the ring of fire'.) The biggest mistake I made, however, was rubbing my eye when I finished my meal. When my retina began peeling off from the searing heat, I screamed in pain and the entire restaurant glared at me. Then, as they were all staring at me, I bent over the bowl of water and began to frantically scoop up the water and splash it into my eye. I may have looked totally ridiculous, but at least it did eventually put a stop to my howling.

When I went to pay, I discovered that you only pay for the plates of food that you've eaten. All the other tables had untouched plates of food (the ones you don't eat get recycled to another table, I'm guessing).

On the way back to the hotel, a fat guy on a moped slowed down and said to me, 'I like pens.' Well, I thought that's what he said: it was a bit hard to hear over the traffic noise.

'That's nice,' I replied.

'I'm Gary.'

'Hello, Gary.'

The traffic noise stopped for a second. 'No, I'm gay.'

'Oh, that's nice.'

Then it clicked. He wasn't saying that he liked pens. He liked penises.

He then asked if he could come back to my room. He probably knew that I was staying in the Bondage Room.

I skipped a shower in the morning, because the shower room reeked of urine, and headed straight to the bus station. I'd booked a bus at the hotel reception to the 'cool, easy going mountain town' of Bukittinggi, but I was a little apprehensive. In the old guidebook, Sumatran buses were described as uncomfortable as hell. They also had a tendency to 'pelt through towns, stopping only for meals (the drivers seem to have enormous appetites)'.

I didn't have to worry about an uncomfortable Sumatran bus, however. It was a new 4WD. I also got the front seat, although that's probably because I paid three times the price that the locals squished into the back were paying.

The passing landscape was a stark contrast to Java. We drove in the shadows of imposing mountains that seemed to be covered in green plush carpet and through groves of palm trees and banana trees while troops of monkeys sat nonchalantly by the side of the road. As we wound our way up into the hills, the air became cooler even though we were right near the equator.

According to the old guidebook, there were no stand-outs, but plenty of accommodation options in Bukittinggi. Only three were listed: the 'very pleasant' Jogja Hotel, the 'quite good' Grand Hotel and the Zakiah Hotel, where 'the man at reception is a positive encyclopedia on Sumatran cheap travel'. I asked a local at the chaotic bus station if he knew the whereabouts of the Jogja Hotel and he stared at me blankly. When I asked about the Grand Hotel and the Zakiah Hotel, I got more blank stares. I had more luck with a bemo driver. He only gave me two blank looks, before I mentioned the Zakiah Hotel and he pointed down the street. After walking the full length of the street, I asked someone else and again they pointed in a vague direction down the street. I trudged up and down the street three times, and then stopped and said aloud, 'Okay, I give up.'

There were a few hotels to choose from in the street, but I chose the Hotel Singalong because I liked the name (it was actually called the Hotel Singgalang). They only had 'basic VIP rooms' for 300,000 rupiah a night (about $40), but the manager did tell me that the room was very inviting. The room was basic, but inviting enough. The manager was sure proud of it: 'You have western toilet and hot water and a fridge and . . . [pause for effect] . . . a TV.' He smiled and pointed to a tiny ancient TV in the corner.

'It will do,' I shrugged.

As he was handing me a registration form back at reception, I asked, 'Have you heard of the Zakiah Hotel?'

'Yes,' he said. 'But it is now called the Murni Hotel.'

'Oh, do you know where it is?'

'Right across there.'

Directly across the road was the former Zakiah, now Murni, Hotel. I decided to go check it out.

It may have once been the Zakiah Hotel, but I was pretty sure that the man at reception was no longer a positive encyclopedia on Sumatran cheap travel. That's because the man at reception was a monkey. As in there was a real live monkey manning the front desk – or more like just sitting there scratching himself. The monkey ignored me (desk clerks in hotels can be so rude some- times) when I asked if I could check out a room. After a few minutes, a human came out. His name was Emil (the man, that is – I didn't catch the monkey's name). Emil was the son of Zakiah, who had passed away in 2002. 'Why did you change the name of the hotel?' I asked Emil.

'It was time to update the hotel.'

Update in name only, it seemed. The rooms hadn't been updated since 1974. My room was quite a bit more basic than the basic VIP room at the Singalong. There was no western toilet, no hot water, no fridge and no TV. In fact, it had a bed and that was it. There wasn't even a bedside table. The squat toilet and shared mandi were outside. But I liked it – because it was five dollars a night compared to $40 at the Singalong.

After I dumped my bag and handed my room key to the monkey, I headed out to explore what the old guidebook described as the 'most pleasant town in Sumatra'. I hit the market first because the old guide-book promised that market day would be fun. With all that chilli in Padang food, I wasn't surprised to see piles and piles of chillies and chilli paste, powder and sauce on show at the market. I was surprised, however, when I accidentally stumbled into the meat section. On sale were cows' blackened lungs and hoofs, pigs' intestines, goats' tongues and large white gelatinous things that looked like the internal organs from the Blob. The smell alone was enough to turn me into a vegetarian – well, until dinnertime, at least.

After all the dead animals, it was time to see some live ones at the zoo with the world's longest name: the Taman Marga Satwa dan Budaya Kinantan Zoo. I cursed Tony Wheeler a few times as I climbed up and down steep steps and then climbed up and down the same steep steps trying to follow the old map. Eventually, I came to the zoo entrance at the top of the hill, which had terrific views over the town below. The zoo was still the same as it was in 1974 – and I mean, sadly, exactly the same as it was in 1974. Most zoos around the world had moved on from tiny concrete pens without any greenery, but not this zoo. It was one of the most pitiful sights that I'd ever seen. The elephants were chained up with no room to move. The crocodiles were lying on piles of rubbish – and I mean massive piles of plastic bottles and chip packets. The bears looked as if they had given up on life. The monkeys were acting as if they had gone mad – one was rocking uncontrollably while another was staring at its hand while hitting the side of its head with the other hand. The one enclosed deer almost made me cry. The poor thing was caked in wet mud and, although the day was warm, it was shivering. To me, probably the saddest of all, however, were the giant turtles. Yes, they had a tiny pool in a concrete enclosure just like the rest of the animals, but the tragic thing was that turtles live for a long time and they could very well have to put up with a hundred years of this. I didn't stay long. This was one time that I wished things had changed dramatically since 1974.

All the restaurants listed in the old book served Padang food, but my bottom needed a bit of a rest from chilli for a day, so I opted for a backpackers' restaurant/bar/internet cafe and did what all modern globetrekking backpackers do – I had a burger. I sat at a table with A. J., a young English fellow who was following the Banana Pancake Trail through South-East Asia (with the help of the prerequisite *Southeast Asia on a Shoestring*, of course). As I scoffed down my burger, so I could get to Panorama

Park, which according to the old guidebook was 'worth a look at sunset', A. J. told me that there was no need to rush because the sun didn't set until 6.29. 'How do you know that?' I asked him.

A. J. held up his iPhone with the 'Sunset Times Around the World' app – or something similar.

The entrance to Panorama Park was lined with stores selling tourist crap, but crap wasn't the only thing on sale. I was followed through the park by gangs of teenage boys trying to sell me magic mushrooms or offering to take me down to their magic mushroom farm at the bottom of the canyon. All along the edge of the deep canyon were playful troops of monkeys, including one very large monkey sitting on the railing eating a packet of popcorn. As I was watching the 6.29 sunset, a young woman, who looked straight out of 1974 with her tie-dye dress and long blonde unkempt hair, marched past with a small pet monkey perched on her shoulder. The monkey, who had a very nice gold chain around his neck, was called Oki (she kept repeating his name). The popcorn-eating monkey jumped off the rail for a closer inspection, so the girl went all *Gorillas in the Mist* by going down on all fours and swaying from side to side. In a split second, the larger monkey scampered past and grabbed Oki then disappeared over the rail into the vegetation. The girl screamed hysterically and jumped the rail – except that beyond the rail was a narrow ledge then a sheer drop of several hundred metres to the canyon below. There were only a few tufts of grass stopping her from tumbling over the edge. Her two Indonesian friends dragged her out and were trying to calm her down when Oki turned up – minus his gold chain. Mr Popcorn was just a common monkey mugger. The girl kissed Oki all over then suddenly ran away squeezing the poor monkey to death. I didn't think she'd be back in a hurry. As soon as the excitement had died down, the locals returned to trying to sell me magic mushrooms.

Back at the Murni Hotel, I had a freezing-cold bucket shower in the dark because there were no lights in the bathroom. Also my room was like an oven and my bed was like sleeping on a kitchen table. What's that saying again? 'If you pay peanuts, you get monkeys.'

The next day I risked life, limb and lungs by hiring a scooter to ride to Harau Valley – which was not in the old guidebook but recommended in the new one. I didn't need a map, however. I was joined on my expedition by A. J. who had what a hippie backpacker in 1974 certainly didn't have: a GPS. It was the same chaotic maniacal and suicidal traffic that I'd encountered on the drive to Bukittinggi, except I was the one now driving in it. And to make my driving task even more difficult, just about every bus, car and scooter was clapped out and belching vile black smoke. The traffic cleared when we got out of town (and so did the black smog, thankfully) and soon we were turning off the road into a narrow country lane flanked by a neat line of trees and surrounded by sheer limestone walls topped with waterfalls.

We had to pay to enter the park (although it did look as if a local had just set up a ticket office – or shack – in the middle of a field), but it was an almost-1974 price of 12 cents. We stopped for lunch at a small restaurant – which was recommended in the current guidebook, of course – and the manager insisted on showing us one of the eight huts that overlooked the river. 'You bring back girlfriend next time,' the manager said, giving us a wink. 'You have, you know, disco in the room.'

We rode further up the valley along the base of the steep limestone walls that sheltered a lush valley filled with rice paddies, palm trees and Sumatran tigers. I thought we might actually see some tigers when A. J. announced that we were only 12 kilometres away from the equator. Soon after, the tar road ran out and we rode deep into the jungle down a narrow gravel track, which turned to dirt, then to mud, then to a combination of gravel, dirt, mud, small boulders and the odd chicken. When we came to an incredibly rickety wooden bridge, A. J. announced that we were only 30 metres away from the equator. We tiptoed across the bridge and then A. J. walked around in circles with his GPS for a few minutes. 'This is exactly the equator,' he exclaimed. 'We should ride to the Northern Hemisphere.' That meant riding across the bridge that seemed to be more holes than bridge. We made it across, stopped, remarked how cool it was in the Northern Hemisphere, and then turned around and rode back to the warmer climes of the Southern Hemisphere.

When we got back to Bukittinggi, I was ready for another dose of stinging lips. Simpang Raya was described as 'very good' in both the old and current guidebooks. I dragged A. J. along as well, which meant that at least there was no aimless ambling around town: we just followed the up-to-date, and up-to-scratch, map in the current guidebook. Simpang Raya was in a large two-storey building in the main square above town and was filled with locals and tourists (although the waiters almost outnumbered the patrons). We were ushered upstairs and seated at a heated marble table (to keep the food warm, we figured). I asked our waiter when the restaurant opened and he said, 'A long time ago,' before running off. It took 23 seconds this time for our 12 plates of food to arrive, and it was the same fiery-red chilli eggs, chicken and fish – with the added bonus of things that looked like the scary animal parts that I saw in the market.

A. J. took a mouthful of food then ran to the toilet to be sick (although telling him about the black cow lungs and hoofs probably didn't help). I only had three plates of food this time (and lots of rice), including a delicious fish dish in chilli coconut sauce. The bill came to around three dollars. I paid for it because A. J. had eaten only a mouthful of food.

I skipped the cold bucket wash in the dark room, even though I was still covered in dust and soot from the scooter ride, and went straight to bed. (I figured that if I went to bed clean I'd just end up covered in dust and soot from the sheets anyway.)

I spent the morning in an internet cafe. I know it's not very 1974, but travelling sure is easier nowadays. I booked a flight to Malaysia (my next country), paid a couple of bills online, transferred some money, skyped my folks, updated my blog and, more importantly, updated my status on Facebook: 'I'm sitting in an internet cafe in Bukittinggi.'

After a very traditional Indonesian ham and cheese toastie for lunch, I joined up with A. J. and we jumped into a mini-van with a Canadian, an American, a Belgian and Michael Schumacher. Or that is what we soon dubbed our driver on the 17-hour bus journey to Lake Toba. Even though most of the Trans-Sumatran Highway was perilously narrow, Michael would race around impossible bends and barrel through villages at a hundred kilometres an hour scattering startled children playing on the side of the road in the process. He would also overtake, well . . . everything and anything at any time.

The way backpackers travel overland has also changed since the 1970s. Noticeboards at backpacker hostels are now full of ads for transport services. These privately run minibuses are jammed with backpackers, who are shuttled from one must-see town to the next. The minibuses are a lot quicker (and often smell a lot better) than public buses, but travellers miss out on interaction with locals (and the odd chicken or goat). I must admit that even though our direct minibus was a lot quicker (and I mean out-of-control quicker), I do prefer sitting with chickens (and the odd local) on a bus. We did stop for something to eat and, when a local bus pulled up, and scores of locals piled out, I felt a tinge of regret. I felt as if I wasn't seeing the real Sumatra in our air-conditioned van full of backpackers.

Lake Toba was described in the old guidebook as a relaxed and easy-living place – which is exactly what we would need after 17 hours on the Trans-Sumatran Racetrack. We were all heading to the Singapore-sized island of Samosir in the middle of Lake Toba, which Tony declared was a 'delightful island with no electricity'. There was a lot of space in the old guidebook devoted to Samosir Island, so I guessed it must have been one of the groovy places to hang out in 1974. Bill Dalton described the island in the *Indonesia Handbook* as: 'Mellow – if Bali is no 1, then Samosir is no 2.' Although there was something helping all that mellowness along. Dalton advised to stay at tribal houses where smoke was 'laid on for you'. 'There is so much weed,' he added, 'people use kilos of it for a pillow at night.'

I was looking forward to mellowing out for a few days – that's if we ever made it there alive, I thought. The bus ride got even scarier when night fell. It was like being tossed around in a clothes dryer as Michael raced down winding roads through a very dark jungle.

At some point, I managed to get some sleep – or I was knocked unconscious, I wasn't quite sure – and when I awoke in the middle of the night our driver's head was slumped back and his eyes were closed. My heart almost jumped out of my chest, until I realised in my dazed state that he was in the passenger seat and some random local fellow, who he'd picked up – and who must have gone to the same Daredevil Driving School – was behind the wheel. When I woke again at six, the sun was coming up and Michael was back in the saddle again. His eyes were drooping and he'd slowed right down, but then he chain-smoked three cigarettes and went back to driving like a loon.

We were dropped off, all rather bleary-eyed, at the lakeside town of Prapat where we boarded a small ferry to the wonderfully named village of Tuk Tuk (named not after the auto rickshaw, but apparently after the Dutch linguist Herman Neubronner van der Tuuk!). The hour-long trip across the tranquil pale blue water of Lake Samosir would have been delightful if it wasn't for the gaggle of accommodation touts who followed us onto the ferry. 'Where you stay?' they asked, then recommended a place that was 'much better for you'.

'I have somewhere to stay,' I said, rather hopefully, to one of the touts.

'Where you stay?'

'Losmen Carolina.'

'There is no Losmen Carolina.'

Oh, bother. I was hoping Losmen Carolina would still be around. It got one of the best write-ups in the entire book and in Tony's list at the back he rated Losmen Carolina as the Most Attractive Hotel in South-East Asia. And, even more impressively, for having the Best Fruit Salad in South-East Asia. He also described the rooms at the 'up market' Losmen Carolina as 'the nicest cheap accommodation I've seen anywhere in Asia, with fantastic views across the lake'.

I showed another tout the Losmen Carolina listing in the book and he said, 'It is now called the Hotel Carolina.'

'So, it's still there?'

'Yes, but I have better place for you. Much cheaper.'

'But the Carolina *is* cheap,' I said, as I flipped open the old guidebook again. 'See, it's only 600 rupiah a night.' (That's around seven cents at the current exchange rate.) The expression on his face went from confusion to 'you've got to be kidding'.

'I'll give you my chicken shed for that price,' he huffed.

My fellow bus passengers were heading to various guesthouses listed in the current guidebook or recommended by the touts, but when I showed them the write-up in the old book they decided to join me staying at Hotel Carolina. The touts weren't very happy. 'Don't listen to him,' my chicken-shed tout scoffed. 'It is not that cheap.'

The touts got off at the main ferry port then we were all dropped off at the Carolina's own private pier. The hotel, which was one of many resorts along the water-front, was made up of a series of traditional Batak cottages with tall and striking dark-timbered roofs. On the way to reception, we walked past perfectly manicured lawns and a male staff member raking the perfectly manicured private beach. On the lake's edge were sun beds and a couple of diving boards. 'This place is magic,' the American girl said.

The smiling staff at reception were all wearing crisp clean uniforms. The old guidebook did say that it was 'up market' – which probably meant expensive. The others almost collectively wet their cargo shorts when they saw the price. A basic room was 20,000 rupiah (just under three dollars). And that was with an ensuite and a view of the lake. I decided to lash out and paid $11 and got a huge room with a wide verandah right on the lake, with a hot-water shower and a minibar.

Before I met the others down at the beach for a swim, I went for a quick wander around the resort. Our super-cheap resort also had an internet cafe (with high-speed broadband), scooter hire (with just about brand-spanking-new scooters) and a large open-sided restaurant with spectacular views over the lake. In Australia, with views like this and rooms like this, you would expect to pay at least $400 a night. On the way back past reception, I asked if the owner was still around. The owner was Carolina, or Oma as the receptionist called her (Dutch for Grandma), and she was still very much around. 'How old is Oma now?' I asked.

'Maybe ninety-something.'

'Can I meet her?'

'Yes, but later. She is having a lie-down.'

When I met up with the others, they kept telling me how wonderful Hotel Carolina was and I felt quite chuffed that the old guidebook had brought us all there.

The water in the lake was crystal clear and surprisingly warm and after our swim we sat in the sun while our waiter brought out cocktails and cold beers. I then had my first hot shower in eight days. I thought I had very tanned feet, but they were just really dirty.

For lunch, I had to try the best fruit salad in all of South-East Asia. And 35 years later, I'd have to agree that the concoction of papayas, bananas and pineapples, sitting on a thin layer of condensed milk, mixed with lime juice, then topped off with shaved coconut and sprinkles of Milo was still a worthy winner.

Tony described Tuk Tuk as 'what Kuta and Kathmandu were like until they became international freak centres'. Tony mentions 'freaks' a number of times in the old guidebook. The freaks were the hippies – they did not call themselves hippies, preferring the term freaks – while other travellers – those who were not freaks – referred to themselves as overlanders. Tony and Maureen called themselves overlanders, but I'd seen a few of their photos and Tony's flared pants and flowery shirts looked suspiciously hippie enough to me.

I went for a wander into town, but there were no tourists around – or freaks, for that matter. The place was totally empty. Every pleasure a backpacker could wish for was here – cheap guesthouses, cheap restaurants, cheap cafes and cheap bars – but they all sat forlornly empty. I walked past a stretch of deserted shops selling wood-carvings and the usual tourist crap and none of them had a single customer. Kids were playing games on the floor of the shops because there was no need to get out of the way for anyone. The shop owners waved and smiled, but bless them, there was no Bali-style hassling.

Before dinner, I went back to reception and met Carolina's grandson Sonny. 'Oma is Dutch,' he told me. 'She married an Indonesian man and moved here sometime in the sixties.' I asked again if I could meet her. 'Oma is having a lie-down,' he told me. 'You can meet her tomorrow.'

The old guidebook promised 'amazing food' at Samosir and recommended starting with dinner at the Carolina for its 'tremendous fruit salads and nightly smorgasbords'. There were no smorgasbords anymore, but I did have a delicious chicken satay as the sun dropped over the mountains, turning the lake the colour of molten gold.

After dinner, we all headed into the village to see a traditional folk music and Batak dancing show. (I'd seen a sign advertising the show on my walk earlier.) On the way there, a local on a scooter stopped and asked us if we wanted to buy some magic mushrooms.

'No, thank you,' I said.

'How about marijuana?'

'No, but do you have any LSD?' I said with a cheeky grin.

'Yes, I get it for you.'

The Bagus Bay Band and Batak dancing show started at 8.15. We arrived at 8.25 and the place was empty and bereft of any music or dancers. 'Sorry,' the barman said. 'There was no one here, so the dancing girls went home.' The band, which was made up of two guitarists, a bongo player and another two vocalists, were still there, however, and they started playing a beautiful harmonic folk song – which was even more impressive because they were all a bit trashed on palm wine. After taking huge mouthfuls of the wine in between every song, they managed to hold it all together for almost an hour – although one fellow was having trouble staying upright.

When the band eventually got too drunk to play, they put a DVD on of themselves performing sober. The band members skolled a couple more palm wines then left, leaving all their instruments behind. I got up first. I wanted to play the bongos – like any good hippie would. The Canadian and Belgian, who could both play guitar, joined me in a rather boisterous 20-minute version of 'The Lion Sleeps Tonight'. Yes, and we'd had a few palm wines by then, too.

*

I hired a scooter and, accompanied by A. J. and his GPS, we set out to ride the 60 kilometres around the island, even though the old guidebook warned that the road around the island was rather bad. The road was great, but that didn't stop me from having an accident. We were riding up a spectacular mountain road when I rounded a tight bend and was confronted by a truck taking up the entire road. There was nowhere to go, so I slammed smack into the side of the truck. Actually, it wasn't as dramatic as it sounds. Luckily I was going quite slowly (and so was the truck) and I managed to hit my brakes, so all I did was basically bump into the truck and then gently tumble over. A. J. fell off his bike, too – but that was from laughing too much.

Each bend, which I took rather tentatively, afforded more dramatic vistas over to the steep cliffs in the distance that tumbled down into the blue-green waters of the crater lake. Incidentally, the lake was formed by a stupendous prehistoric volcanic explosion and is the largest in South-East Asia and one of the deepest and the highest in the world. (It was handy having a current guidebook to peek at.)

We spent the morning riding through the quiet coun-tryside and past small villages of intricately carved Batak houses with tiny front doors. And when we weren't riding through villages, I was falling off my scooter. My first accident (or second if you want to get technical) involved a couple of goats. The goats were fighting on the side of the road, so I slowed down and as I got nearer they jumped out right in front of me and I bowled them both over. All three of us were all right – although one of the goats did take down my registration number. My next crash was on a wooden bridge that was constructed out of ridiculously uneven planks. A. J. rode easily across one narrow plank, but I got two metres in then fell off. That made it three crashes before lunch (which was rather impressive, I must say). It was fortunate that Tony Wheeler could actually ride because I calculated that if he'd had my crash record average, he would have had 297 accidents during his jaunt around South-East Asia.

When we did eventually stop for lunch near the 'relaxing hot springs town of Pangururan' (which were more like a hot trickle), I decided to have a break from nasi goreng and ordered a mushroom pizza. Except that I should have had nasi goreng number. 28 because the mushroom pizza tasted so horrible, I only had two slices.

When I got back on the bike, I started feeling strange. Not sick, but strange – like a buzzing head sort of strange. Or even a happy type of strange. Then it clicked. My pizza was listed on the menu as a 'mushroom' pizza. The quotation marks should have given it away: I'd eaten a magic mushroom pizza. I was high (how so 1974 of me). Luckily I'd only had two slices or I would have been tripping the light fantastic – and probably tripling my accident count on the way back. I didn't feel the sudden urge to say 'man' or 'groovy', but my head was swimming. Some of those groovy hippies back in the

'70s would have felt like this for most of their trip (so to speak). No wonder they were so chilled, man.

Although the journey back was somewhat surreal, it did at least help my riding: I didn't hit a single truck or goat on the way.

I was still buzzing when we pulled up in front of the Hotel Carolina two hours later (it's amazing how fast you can ride when you have no fear). I bumped into Sonny on the way to my room. 'Would you like to see Carolina now?' he asked.

'No, sorry,' I said. 'I need a lie-down.'

'Bloody hippies,' he said as I walked away. Okay, he didn't really say that, but I was a little paranoid he was staring at my glazed eyes.

I spent the rest of the afternoon lying on a sun bed by the lake. Now I could really say that Samosir was a 'magical place'.

The whole gang joined me for dinner again – plus two more Aussie backpackers who had just arrived at Hotel Carolina. I was feeling better and my urge to listen to Neil Young had gone away. We were heading to Bernard's where 'dinner time is like a big happy stoned school dinner, with Pepe, the power in the kitchen running the show'. That's just what I needed. More happy high hippies. But there was no big happy stoned dinner, because there wasn't a single diner in the place. When we wandered in, the lady behind the bar did say hello, but it was more of an 'are-you-lost?' hello.

We ordered a few beers and the American girl ordered a banana milkshake. The waitress had to run across the road to get bananas. And milk. 'Is Bernard still here?' I asked when she returned.

'Yes, I will find him somewhere.'

Bernard, who was a small man with a very big smile, looked way too young to have even been around in 1974. 'I opened the restaurant in 1972 when I was twenty-three,' he said proudly. 'We have been open for almost forty years.'

'Wow, that's a long time,' I said. Particularly as there didn't seem to be any tourists around to eat at his restaurant.

I had to ask, 'What happened to all the tourists?'

'We used to have lots of tourists. When the hippies left in the seventies, we had many Dutch and German people because there were five or six Garuda flights a week to Medan from Amsterdam and Frankfurt. The streets were full of people and the guesthouses and restaurants were full. Then Suharto changed the direct flights from Europe to Bali in 1990 because his children had bought many hotels and land in Bali. So they stopped coming here.'

'Have there been no tourists since then?'

'No, in the late nineties tourists came again because Tuk Tuk was the place for full-moon parties, but then everyone went to Thailand.'

That wasn't the only problem for Samosir. There was also the secessionist war in Aceh, the Bali bombing and the 2004 tsunami to scare tourists off.

Bernard shrugged. 'What can I do?'

'So, is Pepe still around?'

'No, Pepe is dead,' Bernard said musingly. 'He took too many magic mushrooms.'

Bernard suggested the chicken curry, so we all ordered the chicken curry. He then sent the staff out to get the ingredients for our meal: he hadn't had a single customer in more than a week.

I got up early for a swim and paddled out to the floating platform and lay in the warm sun for an hour. I wasn't ready to leave Samosir, but I had to catch a morning ferry back to Parapat. Over breakfast I told A. J., who was staying on the island for a few more days, that I would come back one day. And I meant it.

From Parapat I jumped on a brightly painted local bus to the city of Medan. Sumatran buses made the list at the back of the old guidebook for having the Most Aesthetic Transport in South-East Asia. The bus wasn't very aesthetic inside, however. It was dirty and messy and smoky – and that was just the passengers. The old fellow sitting next to me was the smokiest person I'd ever seen. He chain-smoked one cigarette after another, but thankfully after two hours (and nine cigarettes – I was counting) he collapsed dead. At least there was no more smoking. Actually, as you probably guessed, he wasn't dead: he'd fallen asleep slumped on my shoulder. When he woke up an hour later, he smoked furiously to catch up for lost smoking time.

For most of the five-hour drive, we drove through a cool and pristine landscape of alpine meadows and pine forests then we dropped down into Medan, which was stinking hot and just, well, stinking. The old guidebook claimed that Medan had nothing much to offer and that it was 'a noisy dirty town with a miserable choice of cheap hotels'. If the bus station (or bus slum, more like it) on the outskirts of town was any indication, then Medan now excelled in noisiness and dirtiness. But I had to come to Medan because the city was Sumatra's biggest transport hub and I had a flight out the next morning to Kuala Lumpur.

I jumped into a beaten-up taxi – although every single taxi looked beaten up – and we drove through peak-hour traffic (although I got the sense it was always like this) on a road that had more holes than Blackburn, Lancashire. The city was a mess: there was rubbish everywhere, pollution hung around like a bad smell, there were countless buildings in a state of disrepair (and quite a few in a state of disrepute) and the streets were full of surly-looking and bedraggled locals. After 30 minutes in Medan, I decided that the city was well up there in the Shithole Cities of the World that I'd visited (Cotonou, Benin is currently number one).

The first hotel listed in the book was the Sigura-Gura Hotel, but my taxi driver said that it had closed a few years ago and was now a travel agency. He hadn't heard of the Hotel Irama, but he knew the Hotel Danatoba International which was, according to the old guidebook, 'within spitting distance' of the Hotel Irama. We drove around the area for a while and stopped here and asked there before pulling up again in front of the Hotel Danatoba International. I looked at my watch. It was now almost eight o'clock and I was incredibly dirty and sweaty. 'This will do,' I said.

The foyer of the hotel was all wall-to-wall marble and chandeliers and there was a large sign announcing: 'Comfort is our concern'. It was a five-star hotel, complete with swimming pool, bars, restaurants, gym and room service. Although the hotel was definitely not 'on a shoestring', it was technically in the book, so I took a room – after haggling the price for a basic room down to $52.

When I got to my room, I did the usual things that I do in nice hotel rooms: flicked through *all* the channels on cable, checked the minibar and huffed and puffed about the prices, bounced on the bed, put the shampoo and sewing kit into my bag and, for something new, stole all the spare rolls of toilet paper (those five-dollar guesthouses with a hole in the ground for a toilet never have toilet paper).

I went out to get something to eat and found a good cheap Indian restaurant nearby then finished off with a nightcap in the hotel bar. My beer cost 48,000 rupiah, which was more expensive than most of the rooms I'd stayed in across Indonesia.

Malaysia

Image: YTL Hotels

8

Kuala Lumpur

$M3.10 = $AU1.00
South east Asia on a shoestring, 1st edition, 1975

$M3.10 = $AU1.00
Southeast Asia on a Shoestring, 15th edition, 2010

I flew from Medan to Kuala Lumpur with Air Asia. The airline is a big success story for Malaysia, although I'm not sure how they actually make any money. My flight from Medan to KL cost $21. That same flight in 1974 (with Merpati which no longer flies this route) had been $30. That made the 1974 flight more expensive, although that doesn't even take into consideration inflation and the fact that $30 had been a much higher percentage of the average income at the time. (Incidentally, in 1974, the average Australian yearly wage was $10,491, while in 2009 it was $64,594.) I found even bigger discrepancies by picking out other random flight prices in the old guidebook and comparing them with prices today. For example, a flight from Jakarta to Singapore with Sempati Airlines had been $100. I did a search online and found the same flight with Tiger Airways for $24. It is a great indication of how cheap air travel has become. And boy is it now cheap – I just did a quick search for current flights with Air Asia and there was a flight from KL to Singapore for ten dollars and one from Penang to Langkawi for three dollars (you can't even get a luggage trolley at Melbourne Airport for that price).

It's also a lot easier to get into Malaysia today than it was in 1974. Back then, Malaysian immigration officials were described as 'nasty' and that 'they can brand you a "suspected hippie" and only give you a transit pass that cannot be converted into a visa permit'. Besides having long hair, I'm not sure how they tested for suspected hippies. Did the immigration officials measure the flare width of their bell-bottoms or listen out for anyone saying the word 'groovy' or 'far out'?

As the immigration official stamped my passport, I said, 'Thanks, man,' but he didn't even bat an eyelid.

I changed money at the airport and amazingly, and quite coincidentally, the exchange rate was exactly the same as 1974 at 3.1 ringitt to the dollar. (By comparison, Indonesia went from 500 rupiah to 8000 rupiah to the dollar.) Tony was certainly right when he wrote that the Malaysian ringitt was as 'stable and steady a currency as anything'.

It was less than an hour by bus into the city along a sparkling clean freeway past immaculately manicured hedges and perfectly art-directed coconut groves. Then suddenly we hit the suburbs of the 'hustling capital' and thundered past rows of modern high-rise apartments. Kuala Lumpur is the epitome of a modern and dynamic Asian city, but even back in 1974 (which was only seven years after Kuala Lumpur became the capital of the recently independent Malaysia), the city was noted as 'the most progressive, noisy, trafficy, skyscrapered, cloverleafed town in South East Asia'. The city was still very much 'trafficy' and a hell of a lot more 'skyscrapered' – particularly with the addition of the Petronas Towers (which were the world's tallest buildings from 1998 to 2004) and the towering KL Tower.

At the bus station, I jumped into a taxi to Jalan Tuanku Abdul Rahman. Although there were 12 places to stay listed in the old guidebook, the map only had an area marked for Cheap Hotels and another for Not Quite So Cheap Hotels. According to the old guidebook, a good place to start had been the Coliseum.

The taxi stopped in front of the Coliseum Theatre.

'Is this the Coliseum?' I asked with a here-we-go-again sigh.

'Yes,' the taxi driver nodded enthusiastically.

'Can you sleep there?'

'No,' he said, pointing next door to the Coliseum Café & Hotel.

The hotel reception desk was located in the bar, or actually at the bar, where a posse of old-timers in crumpled suits looked as though they'd been sitting there since 1974. The bar itself looked straight out of the 1930s with its high ceilings, low tables, huge Deco-style comfy chairs and old clunky ceiling fans that just pushed the heat around. A tiny and ancient Chinese man, who was perched on a high stool in front of an even more ancient till, introduced himself as Mr Wong. When I asked about a room, he pointed to a large sign above his head, which read 'Cash Terms Only'. A basic double room was '33 dollars'. Tony had noted that 'Malaysia can be quite expensive', but $33 was a bit steep for on the cheap. Mr Wong handed me a room key and motioned upstairs. 'You go!' he grunted. 'Pay later!' My room was generously proportioned and it did have quite sturdy furniture, including a large double bed with a nice dip in the middle, but the bathroom was a somewhat smelly shared bathroom at the end of the hall.

I headed back downstairs for a drink before dinner and tried to strike up a conversation with the old guys sitting at the bar who were a mix of Chinese, Malay and Indian descent. They were all speaking English, but I couldn't understand them as most of them couldn't speak coherently because they were so plastered.

The cheapest drink on the bar menu was a small draught beer for seven dollars. That was even more expensive than Switzerland. 'How much is that in ringitt?' I asked the barman.

'Um, seven ringitt.'

'But on the menu it says seven dollars.'

'That's right.'

After a few minutes of me asking the same question over and over again and scratching my head a lot, I finally figured it out. It was quite simple, really: Malaysians also call ringitts dollars. So that meant my room was 33 ringitt, which was a more palatable ten dollars, while, more importantly, my small draught beer was only $2.40.

Mounted on the walls around the bar were framed restaurant and bar reviews for the Coliseum. On a page from *The Malay Mail* from 4 January 1922 was an ad for the Coliseum: 'Doctors are agreed that the COLISEUM is the best nerve tonic'. Next to the ad was a story with the headline: 'What to Do When Your Servant Has Malaria.' The Coliseum Café & Hotel opened a year before that story in 1921 where, according to another article, famous English author W. Somerset Maugham was a regular at the bar and it was 'the *in* place where the old crowd of British planters, tin miners and Government service types used to gather for afternoon gin & tonic'.

Some of the restaurant reviews weren't so glowing. 'The waiters are an unsmiling, brusque lot but very efficient,' one reviewer said, while another noted that the food was 'no nouvelle cuisine, but just as good'. I adjourned to the adjoining dining room, which was full of folk, and full of smoke, even though there was a large NO SMOKING sign on the wall. But I discovered it wasn't cigarette smoke – the smoke came from sizzling plates of steak. I was escorted to my table by a small, thin and very old Chinese waiter, who greeted me in perfectly proper Queen's English. And to carry on the very English theme, there was a bottle of Lea & Perrins Worcestershire sauce on the table and mulliga- tawny soup and Welsh rarebit on the menu.

'What is the house specialty?' I asked my waiter.

'You must have the crab,' he replied in his clipped accent.

I asked him why he had an English accent.

'Many British people used to come here.'

And he should know. My waiter's name was Captain Ho Singong and he'd been working at the Coliseum for 49 years (the title of captain is given to the longest serving waiter). 'This was my first job when I arrived from China,' he said. The captain was now 88 years old, but he still worked long hours. 'I work for four hours in the morning and another four hours in the evening and I have one day off a week.' No wonder the waiters are 'an unsmiling, brusque lot'; I would be, too, after serving up crabs and steak for 49 years. The captain had outlived or outlasted three separate owners. 'They never change anything,' he said, sweeping his arm around the room. Or paint anything, I was tempted to add. The walls were stained with decades of grime and smoke. 'They still have the same menu as when I started in 1961,' the captain said. 'Oh, except we have one new addition. The sizzling steak was added in 1982.'

I asked the captain if he remembered when young travellers started turning up in the '70s. 'They were very scruffy,' he said, shaking his head. 'People who came here wore nice suits.' He told me that backpackers still stayed at the hotel, although I hadn't seen any since I'd arrived – or anyone in a nice suit, for that matter.

The captain had other tables to attend to, so he left me to eat my meal, which was a crab shell filled with crab meat and onions and 'accompanied with a pink sauce'. Oh, and a salad, if you could call it a salad: it was two slices of tomato and half a lettuce leaf.

After dinner, I went for a stroll in the rain, which was belting down and coursing in torrents through the gutters. (Incidentally, this was my first rain in over five weeks of travel.) My mission was to check out the other hotels listed in the book, but I didn't have much luck. The Rex Hotel was now a Bata shoe store and the Tivoli Hotel was now . . . take a guess. No, not McDonald's, but a KFC. In the KL restaurant section of the old guidebook, they suggested that 'if you feel like copping out there's two Kentucky Fried Chicken havens'. I walked a kilometre up the street and passed four KFCs (as they are now called because the 'fried' part didn't sound very healthy, even though they still serve exactly the same unhealthy fried chicken as in 1974).

I quite liked this part of town. It was less bustling and on a smaller scale to the rest of KL, although there was one very modern addition. Looming above the street at the main intersection was the city's monorail. And as a sign of the times in this overtly modern and overly commercial world, the monorail stations were sponsored. Bukitt

Bintang station was now called 'Handycam' (formerly Coca-Cola) and Chow Kit station was now called, and I'm not making this up, 'Julie's Bakes Better Biscuits'.

By 9.30 I was snuggled up in bed – or more like stuck in the dip in the middle of the bed. I could hear laughing and shouting from the bar below, but I hadn't seen any other guests upstairs – though there were telltale signs that some of the intoxicated patrons sitting at the bar were staying. The floor of the shared toilet was covered with badly aimed wee.

In the morning, I headed to the train station. Not because I was catching a train anywhere, but because the old guidebook noted that the railway station 'must be the world's most bizarre'. I caught the monorail there, but I couldn't pronounce the name of the station (Mahara-jalela), so just asked for a ticket to 'Prudential' station.

When I got out at 'Prudential' – which is an important part of a sound financial plan, apparently – I tried to follow the old map and ended up on a bridge without footpaths. That was because the road shown on the old map was now a major overpass for the freeway and I was toddling along the side of the road while cars zoomed past only centimetres away. I had to wait 15 minutes to cross and even then I hightailed it across the highway screaming in panic.

The old train station looked like a fanciful castle of Islamic arches and spires. A marble plaque at the entrance read: 'The old Kuala Lumpur railway station was built in 1892 and it was one of the nicest buildings in the city.' Okay, ticked that one off. Next. The Masjid Negara National Mosque was near to the railway station, which the old guidebook proclaimed looked 'more like a "real" mosque than this space age building'. It still looked very space-age, in a *Jetsons* sort of way, and it certainly had plenty of space. The mosque was stark and empty. You couldn't go inside the actual mosque, however, unless you were Muslim. Which was a pity – it had air conditioning. Mind you, I was given the option to become a Muslim. I was handed a brochure, or more like an invitation, that read: 'Becoming a Muslim is a lot easier compared to getting a visa or a passport.' The brochure also suggested that it was 'better for you to have a Muslim name', and according to tradition, 'the best names in the sight of Allah are Abdullah (Slave of Allah) and Abdur Rahman (Slave of the Merciful)'. I'll stick with Brian, thanks (Slave of the Ancient Guidebook).

I stopped for lunch, replacing the Indonesian staple of nasi goreng with the Malaysian staple of nasi lemak, then devoted the rest of the afternoon to wandering aimlessly around the city trying to follow the guidebook's hand-drawn maps. And I figured there would have been lots of aimless wanderings in Asian cities in the late '70s with those hand-drawn maps.

On the way back to the hotel, I stopped at the Medan Pasar car park for dinner. Back in 1974, the car park was home to 'some of KL's best eating at the tables that set up at dusk'. I arrived just before dusk and there were only a couple of tables set up with one woman selling socks and another selling underwear. Mind you, there were plenty of diners – they just all happened to be in the huge Burger King that overlooked the car park.

I had dinner back at the Coliseum (I had to try the sizzling steak) and a new waiter served me. Well, he wasn't that new. Mr Lai was 75 and he'd only been working at the Coliseum for a mere 33 years, compared with the captain's 49 years of service. 'I used to come here with my parents for dinner when I was a child during the war,' Mr Lai said as he put my plastic bib on. 'It was full of Japanese soldiers and their rifles were hanging from the hatstands.' When Mr Lai started working here in 1966, the area was mostly Chinese. 'All the shops and restaurants were Chinese; now they are Indian,' he said. 'Indians are very rich. You want to buy something, you buy from an Indian. You want to rent, you rent from an Indian.'

The sizzling-steak chef came out with a trolley and while we were talking, he cooked the steak in front of me. It really is a small culinary world: the steak was from New Zealand, the wine was from Australia, the sauce was from England and just about everything else in the restaurant was made in China. Including all the waiting staff.

After dinner, I told Mr Lai that I'd spoken to Captain Ho and mentioned that the captain had started 16 years before him and he huffed, 'I'm waiting for him to die, then I will be the oldest and I will be the captain.'

In the morning, I headed to the airport. Not because I was catching a plane anywhere, but because I was picking up Beth. I was really excited about seeing her again. My marriage had fallen apart and it felt wonderful to have a connection with someone again. And Beth was up for an adventure, even though I had warned her that we would be traipsing around cities trying to find hotels and restaurants that may or may not exist anymore. She seemed okay with that – although I hadn't mentioned the possibility of stained sheets or toilets covered in ants.

Beth was easy to spot in the throng walking out of the departure gate with her long blonde hair, big blue eyes and a backpack that was bigger than her. We were both quite nervous as we hugged and made our way to the taxi rank. Not only was this the beginning of a travel adventure together, but we both were already sensing that this was the beginning of something a lot bigger.

I took Beth to a new hotel (or an old hotel, you could say). I chose the Tai Ichi Hotel, in the Not Quite So Cheap Hotels street of Jalan Bukit Bintang, which had air conditioning and a private bathroom, hopefully without wee all over the floor. Mr Wong at the Coliseum told me that the Tai Ichi Hotel was still there, but when our taxi driver dropped Beth and me off at the address, all we could see was a large, brightly lit Subway® sign. I was about to storm off when I saw Tai Ichi Hotel in small black type near the restaurant entrance. Subway® now took up the ground floor of the hotel. 'I'll have a double room and a Chicken and Bacon Ranch Sub,' I said to the girl in the tiny reception area that was tucked away behind the dining section.

Our room was small, but nice enough – although it did smell like a Meatball Sub. What a romantic way to start our time together. 'At least for room service we can get a Seafood Sensation Sub,' I said to Beth as we unpacked our bags.

We headed out in the rain to check out Petronas Towers, the pinnacle of 'skyscrapered' Kuala Lumpur and the formerly highest building in the world. It wasn't the perfect introduction to Malaysia for Beth: we had to queue for ages to get tickets for the Skywalk that linked the two towers and when we finally got up there, it was raining so hard we couldn't see much, anyway. Then we wandered around the massive shopping mall underneath, which could have been the Mall of America, and most of that wandering was because I was looking for a toilet. All the toilets we found had a two-dollar entrance fee, and there was no way I was paying that – not when you could get an airline ticket for that price. So, in the spirit of being a tight-arse backpacker on a shoestring, I searched five levels of shops – and almost wet my pants in the process – because someone told me that there were free toilets in the mall somewhere (hiding in a back corner near the broom closets). Beth was probably wondering what the hell she had got herself into. And even more so, when we squeezed under an umbrella in the pouring rain and went on the hunt for one of my old restaurants. Although there was nothing old on Jalan Ampang – it was all ultra-modern glass skyscrapers, embassies and banks. I was searching for number 33, but the problem was that many of the buildings didn't have numbers, just names. (Were the buildings too big and important to have numbers?)

After trudging in the monsoonal rain for an hour, we came to a row of decrepit old buildings. 'Go to Bilal Restaurant for something a bit flash,' the 1975 guidebook suggested. Bilal Restaurant was as run-down as the rest of the buildings, but at least it was freshly painted – even though it looked as if it had been painted in a hell of a hurry.

The man sitting on a stool at the entrance began shaking his head when we walked in. 'No beer,' he said.

'That's okay,' I said.

'No beer.'

'We just want food.'

'No beer here.'

'Yes, I understand, no beer,' I said, grabbing Beth's hand and waltzing in.

It wasn't quite flash inside. It was like a morgue. Literally. Not only was it dead, as in we were the only customers, but the floors and walls were covered in blood-splatter-proof white tiles. And, to make dissecting body parts easier, the whole place was lit up with banks of bright fluorescent lights.

'We have no beer,' the waiter told us as we sat down. 'And the special today is mutton.'

The food turned out to be quite nice. Not quite flash either, but nice. We had the mutton buhara, chicken korma, basmati rice, roti and mango juice. The food came from a bain-marie (which hopefully had not been sitting there since 1974) and was served on plates that had once been white and were now a dirty sort of pink colour.

While it felt as if we were eating in a morgue and the freshness of the food was perhaps questionable, I loved the restaurant. Although that was mostly because it was so nice having a dining companion for a change (and one who I just happened to be incredibly attracted to as well). In my travels I had spent so many meals dining solo that it felt good to have a conversation instead of reading a book or studying the menu for an hour.

It was also wonderful to have someone to cuddle up with in bed, although Beth did liken our bed to a ping-pong table, so I had strange dreams that night about playing table tennis with a Subway meatball.

The Batu Caves had been described in the old guidebook as one KL sight not to miss. They were now just hard to find. There was a detailed description of the caves in the old guidebook but no directions on how to get there, only that they were '12 kilometres to the north'. I asked at the NEC monorail station and they suggested catching a local bus, although they weren't sure what number bus to catch.

When we spotted a scruffy-looking backpacker hopping onto a bus clutching a Lonely Planet guidebook, we jumped aboard. I asked the guy how long the bus trip was to the caves and he checked his Yellow Bible. 'Twenty minutes,' he said. 'It's thirteen kilometres to the north.' So the caves had moved a kilometre north since 1974.

The suburbs of KL sprawled all the way to the caves. One minute there were high-rise apartments and industrial estates, the next we pulled up in front of a vast open square and the steep steps leading up to the caves. Towering over the steps was a monumentally new addition since 1974: a 42-metre-high gold statue of the Indian deity Lord Murugan, which was unveiled in 2006.

To get up to the caves, the old guidebook offered you the option of climbing the 272 steps or taking a 50-cent funicular ride. But we discovered they'd taken the funicular away – which meant a slow, sticky ascent to the top past cheeky macaques that were very keen on getting their grubby mitts into my daypack.

The main cave was called the Cathedral Cave – Tony wondered, insightfully, if it got its name because it was 'big enough to put a cathedral in'. There were actually two large caves and they were both filled with elaborately painted sculptures of various Hindu gods – plus some monkeys, pigeons, a couple of cats and three chickens. The book also recommended visiting the Dark Cave, which was 'a long winding cave filled with thousands of squeaky bats. Spooky.' What was spooky was that they now charged 35 ringitt to get in (you could get two nights at the Coliseum for that).

On the bus on the way back, Beth asked, 'Where do we get off?'

'Easy, just follow the guy with the Lonely Planet.'

'What if he doesn't know?'

'We'll all get lost together,' I said.

We didn't get lost. But we did when we headed out to dinner later on. We walked around in circles for half an hour until we found Petaling Street, which was, and still is, KL's Chinatown. The old guidebook promised that at night the market comes alive with street vendors and that it was a 'really good place to wander' with 'lots of nice things to nibble on'. That's if you like nibbling on Nike runners and YSL handbags. The street vendors were mostly selling big-brand copies and pirated DVDs.

'I have a T-shirt,' one vendor said to me.

'You have a few, actually,' I said in return.

We attempted to find a restaurant that didn't have plastic menus with full-colour pictures of every item on the menu, but they were all the same. We ended up picking the busiest restaurant, which was yellow – as in all yellow. The building was yellow, the chairs and tables were yellow, the menus were yellow and the staff all wore matching canary-yellow polo shirts. And to go with the yellow theme, we both ordered the 'lemon glass chicken' from the ridiculously extensive menu. The meal was a bit disappointing, however. It didn't taste like lemongrass at all – or even lemon glass, for that matter.

9

Malacca

Malaysian long distance taxis are a great travel bargain.
South east Asia on a shoestring, 1st edition, 1975

Malaysian long distance taxis are an expensive way
to travel.
Southeast Asia on a Shoestring, 15th edition, 2010

'Are you sure you want to stay at the Cathay Hotel?' the taxi driver asked.

I nodded hopefully. 'Yes, the Cathay Hotel.'

'It is not very famous.'

We'd jumped in a taxi at the bus station after a two-hour bus trip (in 1974 it took three hours) from KL to Malacca in a newfangled state-of-the-art bus that looked as if it had just driven straight off the assembly line.

'Maybe I think you like this better,' our taxi driver said as we pulled up in front of the Marriott Renaissance Melaka Hotel. What was wrong with the Cathay Hotel? In 1974, it was the first hotel listed and was described in the old guidebook as 'super-clean and quite comfortable'.

The Cathay Hotel wasn't quite in a Marriott Renaissance-style part of town, but it had been updated. 'Look, it's now the *New* Cathay Hotel!' I beamed. That probably meant that it was now even more super-clean and comfortable. The hotel, which was above a row of ancient-looking shops that sold sweets, plastic buckets and mobile phones, didn't look so new inside, however. The rickety wooden stairs leading up to the first-floor reception area weren't particularly sturdy, and perhaps even more disconcerting was the locked cage around the grimy reception desk. I called out and a grimy man popped his head up from underneath the desk. (I tried not to think about what he might have been doing under there.) 'Um, do you have a room?' I asked.

He stared at us for a while before answering. 'Yes.'

'Can we . . . have a look at one, please?'

He unlocked the cage door and said, 'Walk this way.' He walked with a limp. I was tempted.

We couldn't really see what the hotel was like because the corridor was so dark. And he had to jiggle the room key in the lock for about five minutes before the door would open. When we eventually got into the room, Beth's face was priceless. She was standing there with her mouth agape staring at the bedsheets. Admittedly they weren't the best and had stains that seemed to belong on the set of a slash horror movie that involved soy sauce, sex and mutilated bodies. 'What do you think?' I asked Beth.

Beth leant in and whispered, 'It's full of bacteria!'

'You have to pay extra for that.'

We checked out the bathroom. 'This is nice,' I said. I was getting used to stained sheets and walls with peeling paint. 'It's got a shower and there are no ants around the toilet.'

Beth was still in shock.

'Wow, it's even got air conditioning,' I said. 'This is luxury.'

We took the room after I told Beth that if we just put our T-shirts over the sheets, we'd be fine. Beth said that she would go to bed with all her clothes on because she didn't want to get any of the bacteria on her, so I guessed that a bit of romance was out of the question.

When I suggested that we go for a wander to check out the sights, Beth couldn't get out of the room fast enough. On the way out, we passed a troop (or whatever the collective noun is) of monks in orange robes who were also staying at the hotel. I said to Beth that this must be their final test before they become fully ordained monks: if they could handle staying here, then they could handle anything.

The old guidebook noted that Malacca was Malaysia's oldest and most historic city with a long and compli-cated history and there was plenty to see. Malacca's history *is* long and complicated – in short, it was Malay, then Chinese, then Portuguese, then Dutch, then

British, then Malay again. And there was still plenty to see, including the Porta de Santiago (an old gate made of old bricks), St Paul's Church (an old church made of old bricks) and Stadthuys (an old town hall made of old pink bricks). All the buildings in the main square, including the Dutch Christ Church, were painted an exuberant pink colour. But they were nowhere near as exuberant as the trishaws that were used to ferry tourists around. They were all trying to outdo each other with over-the-top decorations including coloured lights, bouquets of bright plastic flowers, Barbie dolls and massive sound systems that blasted out Bollywood music mixed with a bit of hip-hop.

Stadthuys was the oldest Dutch building in the east and back in '74 it was used as government offices. It now housed the Historical, Ethnographic and Literature Museum, which showcased traditional costumes and artefacts from the history of Malacca. We went in for a look, but there was nothing from 1974 – although the pants worn by locals in the 1880s had a great 1970s-style bell-bottom.

There were no restaurants listed in the old guidebook, so I asked cage man at reception for a recommendation. He suggested Capitol Satay, which was 'very old and very famous'. It was very famous: there was a queue to get in even though it was only five o'clock. When we eventually got in, we were shown to a round metal table with a big hole in the middle. As soon as we were seated, the waiter lit a gas burner underneath the table and placed a pot of bubbling brown goop in the hole – which actually wasn't goop but satay celup, where sticks of raw food are cooked by dipping them into a boiling pot of aromatically rich and spicy peanut sauce. There was a huge variety of raw foods available, including vegetables, prawns, pork, chicken, beef, fish balls, quail's eggs, cockles, squid, pig's liver and braised pig's ears. Oh, and camel. Well, that's what I told Beth the beef was at least.

We grabbed a plate full of things on sticks and when we sat down, the waitress pointed to each stick, instructing us, 'Cook that for one minute; this one, five minutes; this one, three minutes . . .'

'Did you catch all that?' Beth asked when she left.

'Um . . . that one is for three minutes, no, five, no, maybe one . . .'

The food was delicious and it even got the seal of approval from the popular Australian TV soap *Neighbours*: above us on the wall was a framed and signed picture of the cast.

When we got back to the Bacteria Hotel, I laid out a pile of T-shirts on top of the sheet. 'See, it's fine now,' I said to Beth. I didn't tell her that I'd tried this once before on a similarly execrable bed in Dahab, Egypt and ended up rolling over onto the sheets in the middle of the night and woke up swimming in a sea of bacteria.

When Beth woke up screaming, I decided that it was probably a good idea to move hotels.

I thought we'd try the Majestic Hotel – although it was listed as an 'oldeworlde place with oldeworlde rooms' and probably now had even more oldeworlde rooms with matching oldeworlde sheets. I'd asked cage man at reception if the Majestic was still around and he said, 'Yes, it is very nice.' Then again, he also told us that our room at the Cathay was 'very nice'.

Although the Majestic Hotel was in a run-down-looking area, the grand and very much olde-worlde colonial building did look suitably seemly and there wasn't a bit of peeling paint in sight. When we shuffled into the elegantly immaculate and bacteria-free hotel lobby, a doorman in a dapper suit handed us a cool, scented face cloth. This was much too grand a place for the likes of *South east Asia on a shoestring*. I casually waltzed up to reception trying to look stylish in my cargo shorts, scruffy T-shirt and backpack and picked up a brochure. The Majestic was now part of the Small Luxury Hotels of the World brand. This place would not be cheap. I enquired the price of a single room for one night which was the equivalent price to 24 nights at the New Cathay Hotel.

'I love this place,' Beth enthused. It wasn't hard to love the place: it looked like a palace after the New Cathay Hotel.

'Well, I suppose it is in the guidebook,' I whispered to Beth. 'And we have to stay where the book says to stay.'

Beth looked as if she'd just won the lottery.

We got a room on the seventh floor of the 'new wing' and it was my turn to look like I'd just won the lottery when the desk clerk said, 'Your stay includes lunch and dinner.' I asked the dashing young chap at reception if he knew anything about the history of the hotel and he giggled and handed me a fact sheet. According to the sheet, the hotel started life in 1929 as a private mansion owned by Leong Long Man, a Chinese merchant who had made a fortune from rubber plantations. When Leong succumbed to tuberculosis in 1931, his number-one son then lost the entire family fortune on an extravagant lifestyle, that included 'numerous mistresses', and he was forced to sell the grand residence in 1955. It was then converted into the Majestic Hotel and its 24 rooms were often filled with guests that included the 'political elite of the day, local and foreign dignitaries and a smattering of artists and movie stars'. By the '70s the Majestic had faded and became the 'favourite haunt of hippies', but by the '90s the Majestic ran into financial difficulties. In 2000 the land was bought by the state of Malacca and the hotel was closed and its surrounding land used as a car park for the adjacent hospital. The old mansion looked destined to end her days as landfill when YTL Hotels bought it in 2006, restoring the original hotel and constructing a 15-storey block behind it, plus a swimming pool, gym and a 'wellness centre'.

Our room was . . . hang on, I'll let the brochure describe it:

Bespoke furnishings call to mind the glory days of old Malacca, while floor to ceiling windows framed by silk drapes bathe the room with soft light. Standing on warm timber floors is an inviting king-size four-poster bed finished in rich teak and dressed in cool cottons with an ornate silk runner. A matching silk-upholstered chaise lounge provides a cosy spot to gaze out over the river and let your imagination take you back in time.

We were most excited about the four-poster bed because the Egyptian cotton sheets didn't have a single stain on them. Beth couldn't wait to get into the shower. 'This is the best shower I've ever had,' she called out while I bounced happily on the bed. We then spent the next couple of hours in the room just enjoying all the cleanliness.

After our delectably inclusive four-course lunch, which included an incredibly spicy chicken dish and huge prawns cooked in lemongrass and chilli, we dragged ourselves away from the hotel to check out the Museum of Enduring Beauty and Kites. Beth was particularly interested in the enduring beauty part while I was more intrigued in what beauty and kites had in common – I mean how good-looking can a kite be?

For a start they got the name wrong: it should have been called the Mutilation Museum. It was, according to the sign at the entrance, dedicated to 'the suffering that people go through in the quest to look good'. The sign also warned that: 'The different levels of pain one has to endure during the beautification process are shown in full.' Those levels of pain included foot binding, neck stretching, teeth filing, scarification, corsetry, skin tattooing, stretching lips by the insertion of round discs and, my favourite, moulding heads into oval shapes. Each torturous concept of beauty was accompanied by photos and paintings showing all the gory details of body parts being unnaturally stretched, squeezed, pierced and rammed into jars. It was all rather gross – but the Kites Museum on the top floor did have lots of pretty kites.

When we got back to the hotel, I dressed up for dinner – I cleaned the mud off my hiking boots and even ironed my cargo shorts. The Mansion Dining Room was in a big room upstairs. We were shown to our table while a pianist played a ragtime version of 'Imagine' on a grand piano, then the waiter pulled back our chairs and put linen napkins on our laps. This was very flash, indeed. We only had one glass of wine, though. A glass of Australian sauvignon blanc was 50 ringitt. I could have got three nights at the New Cathay Hotel for that.

10

Penang

Cheaper rooms have no bathrooms.
South east Asia on a shoestring, 1st edition, 1975

Cheaper rooms have shared bathrooms.
Southeast Asia on a Shoestring, 15th edition, 2010

'I've never heard of it.'

'I've not taken people there before.'

'I take people to the Travelodge or the Holiday Inn. Would you like to stay there?'

We got all that and more as our taxi driver did her very best to persuade us not to go to the New China Hotel. We were in Georgetown on the island of Penang and admittedly, after nine hours in a bus from Malacca, the Travelodge did sound nice. Mind you, we would have arrived another three hours later if it had been 1974. Back then, you had to catch a ferry across to Penang. There is now a bridge, built in 1985, and at 13.5 kilometres long it is one of the longest bridges in the world.

The bus dropped us off in Georgetown, which the old book described as one of the most likeable cities in South-East Asia with 'easy going kampongs, sandy beaches, warm water, good food and supply of things to see'. The New China Hotel was noted as the most popular place in town with 'big airy rooms and super clean toilets – although the manager is very surly'. The old guidebook listed the name of the street that the hotel was in, but no street number, so we drove up and down Leith Street searching for it. I eventually jumped out and asked a man if he knew where the hotel was. He burst into laughter. 'There it is,' he said, pointing across the road. That's why we couldn't find the hotel: it was now The Chocolate Boutique. 'The hotel closed a few years ago,' he said, still chuckling.

'Your book is too old,' our taxi driver pointed out when I got back in. 'You need a new one.'

Next was the Tye Ann Hotel, which made the list at the back of the book for the Best Porridge in South-East Asia. We pulled up out the front of a row of shops, but I couldn't see a hotel sign anywhere. I hopped out for a closer inspection and spotted a tiny hand-painted sign next to a doorway for the Tye Ann Hotel. I gave Beth the thumbs up then bolted up the stairs to see if they had a room. There were no rooms and they didn't serve porridge anymore – although I bet they serve a very good writ. The Tye Ann Hotel was now Peter Siew & Tan Advocates and Solicitors.

When we pulled up in front of hotel number three, the Hotel Noble, our taxi driver said, 'You like cheap places very much.'

'You won't believe this,' I said to Beth. 'It's full. They have no rooms.'

I was on a mission now – even if I was spending my entire trip budget on one taxi ride. Next on the list was the Wan Hai Hotel, which back in '74 'only cost $M4 but their toilets are a bit primitive'. There was a blackboard out the front that had 'Dorm room $M7' scrawled on it. At two dollars a room, it had only gone up a dollar since 1974. Although the reception area was dark, the door was unlocked, so I crept in and was immediately hit by an incredibly strong smell of oil. That was because four scooters were parked in the middle of the tiny ground-floor foyer. I could hardly make out the reception desk through all the boxes of junk piled up everywhere, so I called out a hearty hello, but there was no answer. Which was probably a good thing – it all looked a bit decrepit and creepy, anyway. And besides, at that price, which was a third of the price of the New Cathay Hotel, I can't imagine that they would have updated the primitive toilets.

Just down the road from the Wan Hai Hotel was the Pin Seng Hotel, which was our last chance to snare a hotel from the old guidebook, even though Tony didn't give it a very good rap: 'I didn't like this hotel at all. A very unpleasant manager (even for a Chinese Hotel) and the drains smell.' The new manager seemed pleasant enough, although watching him wander around in his baggy underwear was very unpleasant. A little old lady showed us to a room where the bed had clean sheets, but was, as Beth described it, like a picnic table. We looked at another room, but the bed sagged in the middle – from lots of action that I'd rather not know about. Just like the story of 'Goldilocks and the Three Bears', the bed in the third room was just right. The only slightly disconcerting thing was that there was a plastic sheet underneath the sheets. Did guests at the Pin Seng Hotel wet the bed? Perhaps they just couldn't face the trip to the toilet which was downstairs, out the back door and down a dark and dingy lane.

Oh, and I had a good sniff of the drain from the sink in our room and it smelt just fine.

'We'll take it,' I said.

Tony sure gave the Indian food in Georgetown a good serving: 'I found myself gravitating to the super delectable Indian restaurants, a hundred times better than the Indian food you find in India.' It was hard to gravitate towards any of them, however, because it was 10.30 pm and most of the restaurants were closed. Eventually we stumbled upon Kallammans, which was the only Indian restaurant that still had its lights on. There were no diners, but there was a small contingent of waiters who looked a bit surprised when we wandered in. We ordered some chicken butter cream, dahl, naan bread and a mango lassi, and as soon as our food was served, the staff began cleaning up, putting chairs on tables – as in all the chairs – and sweeping the floors. When they finished, they all stood around watching us, waiting for us to finish.

In the morning, I asked the Wan Hai Hotel manager, who was still in his underwear, where the best porridge in Georgetown was. He sent us around the corner to the Café Little Angel, which had a large sign out the front advertising the house specialty, frog porridge. It's not quite a bowl of Quaker Oats with brown sugar sprinkled on top; this was Asian porridge, which is like Chinese congee made with rice and fish sauce and, in this case, frogs. 'Frog porridge' sounds like something you'd say to someone with a terrible hangover who you are trying to make throw up.

Thankfully, there were other options besides frog: there was also chicken, fish, pork and porridge with anchovies (although the last one is up there with frog porridge and a fish milkshake for the spew factor). It was the best porridge I've ever had. It was also the only porridge and probably the last porridge I'll ever have. I'll eat anything (as my loyal readers would know), but fish sauce and chilli is a bit much for breakfast. Beth on the other hand loved it and finished her entire bowl. Then again she probably likes fish milkshakes for an afternoon snack.

After breakfast, we went to check out The Choco-late Boutique (formerly the New China Hotel). The old bedrooms had been turned into different 'chocolate rooms' including tiramisu, fruits, health, sweetheart, coffee, panned chocolate and Malaysian treats. They also had chocolate frogs, but I was happy to see that they weren't real frogs.

The manager was at the cashier's desk (I bought a couple of blocks of chocolate which later turned into a gooey inedible mess in my backpack from the heat), so I asked him about the hotel. 'The hotel closed nine years ago,' he said.

'What happened?'

'It's a long story, but it was a very bad place and in the end they went bankrupt.'

I looked up the hotel on the Net when I got home and found a blog post from two years before it closed. It sounded bad, all right: 'An Australian mother and her son were arrested at The New China Hotel for possession of heroin. They were both sentenced to death, but given that they were staying at the New China, I don't think a death sentence would have fazed them.'

'We have only been open for a year,' the manager said as he dragged out some photos to show me. One of them was of the hotel in its final years and it looked more run-down than the abandoned and windowless Tiga Tiga Hotel in Padang.

First on our list of sights to visit from the old guidebook was the Khoo Kongsi Chinese Clan House, which was described in the old guidebook as the finest in Penang with 'a rainbow of dragons, statues, paintings, lamps and carvings'. Quite surprisingly, I managed to follow the old map and found the Khoo Kongsi easily. 'On the day it was completed in 1898 the roof caught fire,' I read to Beth from the book. 'Clan elders took this as a message from above that they were overdoing things and repaired it in a marginally less grandiose style.' We both agreed that the roof looked suitably and marginally less grandiose.

As we were heading to the next sight in the book, we saw a sign for the Khoo Kongsi. What had we just spent 20 minutes looking at, then? I had no idea. After we checked out the real Khoo Kongsi, it was time for lunch, which I was looking forward to. And not just because I was hungry, but because the old guidebook noted that Penang was a 'fantastic food trip'. We made our way to Chinatown where the 'excellent Hainan Chicken rice really is excellent'. We adhered to the old adage that if it's full of locals, then it must be good and stopped at Wen Chang, which was full to bursting.

We were lucky to get a table and our waiter sat us right next to the open kitchen. As in so close to the kitchen that if the guy chopping off boiled chicken heads swung his large knife a few centimetres more to the left, I would have lost an ear. We noticed one staff member was sitting down eating his lunch, but he'd brought his own – which wasn't a great sign. Then we found out why. Beth asked for a menu and the waiter gave us a puzzled look. There was no menu because the restaurant served Hainan chicken rice and that was it.

Nothing else. I looked around and every single person in the restaurant was eating the identical dish. No wonder the old guy brought his lunch. Twenty years of Hainan chicken rice for lunch every day could get a bit dull.

Our meal started with soup (so there was something else), which was like drinking dishwater, but the Hainan chicken rice was superb. I felt like something sweet after my meal and the old guidebook recommended going to the Cold Storage Supermarket on Penang Road for the 'best soft ice cream in town'. The Cold Storage Supermarket was now a Happy Mart and they sold Drumsticks and Magnums.

We had more temples and mosques to tick off after lunch, including one temple that had been updated. In 1974, the Goddess of Mercy Temple, which had been the oldest and most popular temple in Penang, had two large burners outside where you could 'burn a few million monopoly money, to ensure wealth for the afterlife'. They'd really gone to town on the renovations and they now had three burners. The courtyard, shrouded in thick smoke, was full of folk burning money – although the afterlife might come sooner from breathing in all that black toxic smoke every day.

The old guidebook suggested looking out for medication stalls promising cures for everything from headache, stomach-ache and kidney trouble to malaria, cholera, and even 'fartulence'. We found the street of medication stalls, which had lots of herbal remedies but no cure for fartulence. And I may have needed some

fartlulence tablets because our next stop was Dawood
Restaurant, which was famous for its Penang Special
Kurry Kapitan. The 'Kurry' got its name when a Dutch
sea captain asked the mess boy at Dawood what was
being served and the answer 'Curry, captain' has been
on the menu ever since. And it is now also on menus all
over Malaysia.

Dawood was in a crumbling double-storey shop-
house in the old part of town. A large sign out the front
promised: 'For that lingerin' taste of Muslim food.' Inside
were simple tables and chairs and the popular morgue-
like white tiles on the floors and walls. The restaurant
was busy and the buzzing waiting staff were serving up
plate after plate of house specialties like chicken briyani,
Kurry Kapitan, mutton kurma, duck sammah and fish
head curry. We ordered the Kurry Kapitan (I passed on
the fish head curry).

When I'd finished wiping my plate clean with the
naan bread, I waddled over to the old cashier sitting
at a desk near the entrance. He introduced himself as
the manager: Syed Aliar, the eldest son of the founder
Shaik Dawood. 'My father came here from Keelakarai
in Southern India and opened the restaurant in 1947,' he
told me. Syed started working at the restaurant in 1961
and had never taken a holiday. 'I work every day,' he
said. 'But I take one day off every two weeks.' You could
tell that this was his home here at the restaurant with his
friends and family. He got excited when I told him about
my book and showed him the entry for Dawood in the

old guidebook. 'We are not in the guidebook anymore,' he said sadly. And it was sad that Dawood hadn't been in the guidebook for years: the food was still 'super delectable' and authentically Georgetown.

'Has it changed much?' I asked.

'It is much the same,' he shrugged. Even the menu was pretty much the same as it was in 1947, Syed told me. 'We have mostly regular customers,' he said, waving his arm around the room. He then stood up and grabbed my hand. 'You two must come back tomorrow,' he said with a beaming smile. 'I want to give you the best banquet. You will try everything. It will be on me.' Unfortunately we couldn't, because we only had two more days left in Penang and we wanted to check out the beach. After all, I couldn't leave Penang without going to the 'most popular freak beach centre in Malaysia' where 'the cops have frequent dope and nudity raids'.

The old guidebook's only suggestion for the beachside town of Batu Ferringhi had been a room in a villager's home. There wasn't much chance of that. As we entered Batu Ferringhi, we passed the Holiday Inn, the Shangri-La and a steady stream of monolithic holiday apartments and resort hotel chains. I didn't think that we'd need to eat in a villager's home, either. We also passed rows of restaurants, including one serving Arabic and Italian cuisine. So is that pizza with hummus topping or lasagne kebabs?

I'd asked the taxi driver to take us to where the back-packers congregated, and I knew we were in the right place when we passed a row of internet cafes, restaurants serving banana pancakes and bars with large 'Happy Hour' signs out the front. I even spotted a couple of old hippie backpackers with long hair wearing tie-dye shirts and Thai fisherman pants (which never look good on anyone, in my opinion – hippies or otherwise). Those hippies would have been in trouble if they'd been around in 1974. Batu Ferringhi had been the scene of the 'infamous suspected Hippie clear outs of 1974', according to Tony. 'Armed cops turned up in the early hours,' he continued. 'And every westerner there was given 24 hours to get out of the country.'

I asked our driver to take us to Batu Ferringhi's oldest guesthouse. He did well – Ali's Guesthouse was the first guesthouse to open in Batu Ferringhi only a few months after Tony and Maureen came through in 1974. The lady at reception told us that the guesthouse had been built in 1953 as a family home and began renting out rooms to travellers. Although the current price of 100 ringitt for a room was a bit more than the one ringitt it cost in 1974.

We had lunch across the road from the guesthouse in a restaurant on the beach (as in a table right on the sand), and then spent a pleasant afternoon swimming in the clear, warm water. This was my first swim in the ocean since Baucau in East Timor. Our end of the beach was relatively quiet, but further up towards the large hotels there was a torrent of tourists on jetskis, four-wheel buggies, parasails, horse rides, tube rides and big sausage rides. When we went for a stroll up the beach, the 'beach activity' touts jumped on us. One guy in particular was insistently persistent, but we ignored him. He kept pointing to the water and calling out, 'Look. Look!' We didn't look, so he began shouting, 'Look! Run!' Why was he saying, 'Run!'? I thought. Then I looked up. He'd been trying to warn us that a parasailer was bearing down on us. We dived to the sand just in time as a pair of feet sailed directly over our heads.

When I asked at the guesthouse if there was anywhere old to eat, the girl at the front desk got a little confused. 'You want something old to eat?'

'No, some*where* old . . . but not with old food,' I said, making her even more confused.

'The hawkers' market might be old,' she suggested.

The hawkers' market was located on the main road past an endless array of stalls selling watches, football tops and shoddily made fake Calvin Klein underpants. The small hawkers' market was chock-full of locals and they had my favourite Malaysian dish, nasi lemak, at almost-1974 prices.

When we returned to our room, we discovered a snake hissing at us from under a chair in the corner. When I got down to check it out, it hissed and sprayed me and I almost jumped out of my skin. Except that it wasn't a snake. It was an Ambi Pur diffuser that was plugged into a power point on the wall. Every ten minutes, it would hiss and let out a dose of air freshener. I unplugged it and put it in the corner next to the bed, but a few minutes later it started hissing again. Beth then broke into a hysterical laughing fit (this is a girl who had an uncontrollable laughing fit at her grandma's funeral after the altar boy fell into the Christmas tree). I couldn't take it – the hissing or the laughing – so I threw it into the corridor (that's the air freshener, not Beth).

Beth was very brave: she jumped on the back of a scooter with me to explore the island. The last time she saw me after a scooter ride in Ubud I was covered in wounds with tales of my incompetent riding skills. At least this time the roads were decent and I felt somewhat safe. Well, until we took a wrong turn and ended up on a freeway. Why were the cars beeping at us? I thought. That was because scooters weren't allowed on the freeway. 'I don't like this,' Beth said. And I could tell that she was a bit worried – she kept trying to squeeze me to death.

Our first stop was the Snake Temple, which according to the old guidebook had 'live snakes draped around everything'. Except we drove straight past it because we couldn't get off the freeway and had to drive another five kilometres before we could turn around. There weren't many snakes in the Snake Temple, either. Or so we thought. 'Where are the snakes?' I asked one of the custodians. He pointed to a large framed photo on the wall with a picture of the Snake Temple from 1978. Yes, that's what it used to look like, but . . . ah, there they were. Hissing, slithering snakes were draped over picture frames, hidden under chairs and wrapped around a 'Don't touch the snakes, they are poisonous' sign. And they sounded exactly like the air-freshener diffuser in our room.

We had a quick bite to eat at the temple (there was no snake on the menu), because we had to get back to town in time for our late-afternoon flight to Phuket. When we arrived back in Batu Ferringhi, Beth even complimented me on my riding skills. I didn't tell her that when we were on the freeway I was so scared that I almost pooped my pants.

Thailand

Image: Malaysia Hotel

11

Phuket and Krabi

Ko Samui is a beautiful and so far totally untouched
island. There are a couple of fisherman's huts to stay
in on this pleasantly un-touristed island.
South east Asia on a shoestring, 1st edition, 1975

Ko Samui is beach paradise central with countless
bungalows and resorts and a plethora of restaurants
and nightclubs catering for more than a million
tourists a year.
Southeast Asia on a Shoestring, 15th edition, 2010

I cheated. I asked a Swedish girl on the plane for a
quick look at her copy of *Southeast Asia on a Shoestring*
to find a hotel in Patong. The plane had been delayed
for three hours and I didn't fancy wandering the
streets in the dark asking if we could kip on a restaurant floor. I didn't need to look at any book to know
that Patong Beach on the island of Phuket had grown
somewhat since 1974. Phuket is one of Asia's most

popular tourist destinations and the name Patong is synonymous with package holiday resorts and girlie bars filled with fat, middle-aged westerners consorting with young, skinny Thai girls. Back in 1974, there was only one place to stay in Patong Beach. The Patong Beach Restaurant offered a patch on the floor for three baht (approximately 11 cents) a night – and a mat to put on it for another two baht. Just a few short years later, however, Patong Beach was already on its way to a full-blown resort town. Tony had an inkling of what was to come when he wrote in the updated 1979 *South-east Asia on a shoestring*:

> Patong has all the makings of an instant tourist slum. Phuket's main drawback is a lot of the development seems to be carried out with total disregard for aesthetics or planning. In Patong, there are more than a dozen hotels and guesthouses and innumerable restaurants.

There are now 35,000 hotel beds on Phuket and the island gets more than four million visitors a year.

If only I'd sneaked a peek in the current book at the price for a taxi from Phuket Airport, then we might not have got ripped off. I purchased a taxi voucher from inside the airport for 600 baht, and then discovered that taxis outside were only 300 baht. Our taxi turned out to be something called the 'Airport Limo Service' and we stopped at their office en route, so they could try to get a nice hotel commission from us. 'Do you have a hotel?' the woman in the office asked me.

'Yes, we already have a booking at the C&N Hotel,' I lied.

'I have never heard of it,' she said. Ah, that old chestnut. She then told us that the hotel was full, closed down and had been taken over by government insurgents. When that didn't work, she asked if we wanted a transfer, a tour, a restaurant, a show or anything else so they could rip us off blind.

'This is so luxurious,' I said to Beth as we walked around our room at the C&N Hotel – although my idea of luxurious was stain-free sheets and a shower with hot water. After dropping our bags, we went for a stroll to the appropriately named Bangla Road. Phuket was described in the old guidebook as a 'mini freak centre'. It was now a major freak centre. The most freakish thing were the sleazy men who watched Thai girls perform tricks with intimate parts of their anatomy. The second we stepped into the neon of sleaze that is Bangla Road, we were accosted by go-go bar touts thrusting laminated cards in front of us that listed all the 'tricks' being performed in their particular show. That included, but was not limited to, feats involving catfish, turtles, bottle opening, ping-pong balls, smoking, writing, frogs, knitting, mice and swamp eels. I didn't ask, and really didn't want to know, what they did with all of the above. But I realised there must be a lot of people interested in swamp eels because when I posted a blog about visiting Patong, I noticed on my blog stats page there was a whole bunch of people who had googled 'swamp eel inside pussy' and ended up on my blog.

'Oh. My. God!' Beth exclaimed every time a new card was shoved under our noses. 'Why us?' she squealed. 'Do we look like the sort of people who go to these shows?' Beth was just as amazed at all the old, fat, red-faced westerners with their young Thai girlfriends. 'How old are those girls?' Beth hissed. 'Thirteen?' A lot of the men were sitting in bars drinking beer, while their girlfriends sat staring into space looking bored out of their minds. When I told Beth that men pay to have a 'girlfriend' for the duration of their holiday, she couldn't believe it – there's not much of that going on in Minnesota. 'They are not ashamed, either,' Beth said. 'They're walking around holding hands as if they are their real girlfriends.'

We wandered down a side street past a row of neon-lit go-go bars and an overly made-up schoolgirl wearing a very much under regulation-length school skirt accosted us in front of School Girl a Go Go Bar. 'Come in,' she said, giving me a wink. 'It's very nice for you.'

'Do you want to go in?' I asked Beth. 'We'll just have a quick look.'

I was blasé about the whole thing because I'd been to plenty of sex shows. And no, I am not a sex tourist – I worked as a tour leader in Europe and on every trip we took the passengers to a sex show in Amsterdam. Just as we were walking into the School Girl a Go Go Bar a couple marched out and the girl was shaking her head saying, 'No, no, no!' We took two steps inside the bar and caught a glimpse of girls dancing onstage who were no longer in their school uniforms – but thankfully, there were no catfish or swamp eels in sight. Beth lasted all of eight seconds. 'I can't,' she cried, before scurrying back out into the street. It was a pity. I was interested to see a woman knitting.

'Tony Wheeler was right,' Beth said as she sipped her coffee at the hotel buffet breakfast. In the old book, Tony wrote: 'Thais make terrible tea and coffee – it tastes like the two have been mixed together and left to stew for a month.' After breakfast, we walked through bright sunshine down to the beach, which was totally deserted with rows and rows of empty sun beds. The tourists were obviously still in bed (and half of them probably with their Thai 'girlfriends'). We had a quick splash in the water then followed the advice in the old guidebook, which suggested that if you had the cash you could 'splash out and spend a night with the richies at Rawau beach'. The richies were spread out all over Phuket now, and the island had some of the most exclusive (read: expensive) resorts in the world. I'd booked us one night with the richies at Indigo Pearl, which was described on their website as 'a luxury resort unhindered by imagination with raw sensuality and industrial chic'.

Even backpackers on shoestrings like a bit of luxury sometimes – even though it is better if you don't pay for it. My favourite freeloading trick is sneaking into a five-star hotel to lounge by their pool. It's easy: just waltz through reception as if you're a guest and drop a, 'Darling, we must have a facial rub at the spa later,' then plop yourself down on a sun bed by the pool. I actually got away with it for two days in a flash hotel in Marrakech, until the poolside waiter got suspicious when I tried to charge a pina colada to room 201.

It would have been difficult to sneak into Indigo Pearl. We had to drive through *Jurassic Park*-esque metal gates and the security guards even put mirrors under the taxi to search for bombs (or backpackers, I guessed). While we filled in our registration card in the reception area that was bigger than most of the hotels I'd been staying in, we were given a chilled drink of frangipani juice with exotic herb extract, or something similar. We were driven to our room – sorry, make that 'Private Pool Pavilion' – in a golf buggy. The bellhop tried to take my dusty backpack into the villa, but I grabbed it and said, 'No, it's okay.' I couldn't afford the tip anyway. We both gasped when we walked through the large metal door into our villa. It was unlike any place that I'd stayed in before (not that I stay in flash places often, mind you). It was no bland Hilton and the decor was 'a spectac-ular interplay of rich wood and stone', with 'spot-lit wonders of imagination' (their words, not mine). A CD of soothing music that had been mixed by the 'resident DJ' was playing. 'The CD is for you to take home,' the bellhop said.

'Really?' I said, although I was planning on stealing it anyway.

Instead of your standard fruit bowl (well, standard for five-star at least), there was a delicate fruit flan accompanied by linen napkins and designer cutlery that I was tempted to steal as well. The bedroom-cum-lounge area had wide glass doors that opened out to our own private garden with a swimming pool, large outdoor bath and a day bed covered with bright red cushions. The bathroom had the biggest shower I'd ever seen. 'You could get an entire football team in there,' I whispered to Beth.

When the bellhop left, I went through every drawer and cupboard and read everything, including the laundry menu. On the itemised list, among the socks and dress pants, was a safari suit (how very 1974), which cost 200 baht to have laundered. That's the same price as a night at the New China Hotel.

In the 'Guest Services' book – and it was a book – was an extensive directory of hotel services, including a 'Special Bath Menu', a service where someone comes to your room and fills up your bath with rose petals, milk and scented candles for 1000 baht. (That's five nights at the New Cathay Hotel.)

After opening all the shampoo bottles and sewing

kits, we met up with Panchan Noimeecharoen, Indigo Pearl's PR manager, at the Tin Mine Restaurant. While I was eating the best red curry chicken that I'd ever had, I asked Panchan where the clientele mostly came from. 'We have lots of Europeans,' she said. Very fussy Europeans too, by the sound of it. 'Indigo Pearl has its own beach and beach club,' she continued. 'But the locals also have their fishing boats in the water. Some of our guests complained, so we asked the fishermen if they would move their boats.'

'What did they say?'

'They laughed at us.'

'What else do guests complain about?' I asked.

'The most common complaint is the weather,' Panchan sighed. 'Guests expect that we can change it for them.'

After lunch, Panchan took us on a guided tour of the resort in a golf buggy. 'This is swimming pool number five,' she said. 'And this is swimming pool number six.' We stopped at the poolroom bar. 'You have to see the toilets,' Panchan gushed. The toilets were so grand that I took photos. In fact, the toilets were nicer than a lot of the hotel rooms I'd stayed in so far on the trip.

We finished our tour at the beach club, which had perfectly raked sand and those annoying fishing boats about 50 metres out in the water. Although it was stifling hot, the waiters were rushing around in starched white long-sleeved shirts and pants serving pina coladas to tanned European tourists (the men in dick-dacks and the women topless).

We devoted the rest of the afternoon to lounging about in our room – sorry, pavilion. We swam in our pool, napped in the sun, lay on the day bed and even had a bath (minus the budget-busting rose-petal-scented milk), then finished off our indulgently opulent afternoon with a cocktail down at the beach club (for the price of a night at Yadi Asa in Denpasar). We were treated to a perfectly choreographed sunset, which Beth said must have been ordered by one of the demanding hotel guests.

After showering in our room-sized shower, we had dinner with all the cashed-up Europeans. These same Euro-cash jetsetters were probably unwashed and un-cashed-up hippie backpackers in the '70s. The hotel had a selection of restaurants, but we opted for the Thai restaurant, Black Ginger, because it had 'Unique Thai delicacies in a riot of flavours served in a modern masterpiece floating on the lagoon'. Back in 1974, Tony noted that most Thai restaurants were actually Chinese restaurants that served a few Thai dishes among the Chinese dishes. Our food was very much Thai and we were treated to an incredible banquet that included crispy fried shrimp and battered cha-plu leaves drizzled with sweet chilli sauce and pak tai yellow curry fish. All for the price of eight nights in a standard room at the Hotel Carolina on Samosir Island.

When we returned to the room, our bed had been turned down, scented candles were burning, our slippers were tucked under the bed, the soothing Indigo Pearl music mix was playing and there were chocolates and a present (a stuffed silk toy elephant) on the pillow. 'It's just like the New Cathay Hotel,' I said to Beth.

We were taken to the dusty and busy bus stop in a shiny, dent-free hotel car driven by a man in a suit. We were catching a bus to Krabi, which was described in the old guidebook as a 'small fishing village with untouched beaches'. I had contemplated going to the untouched beaches of Phi Phi Island, but I didn't need to go there to know that it is now far from untouched. When Tony and Maureen went to Phi Phi in 1974, the locals followed them around because they hadn't seen foreigners before. Well, not any in bell-bottom pants, at least.

By the time we got into Krabi, it was already late afternoon, but the mini-van driver very kindly dropped us off in front of the Vieng Thong Hotel, which had 'very pleasant rooms for 35 baht or noisier ones for 30 baht', according to the old guidebook. We took a noisy room overlooking the street. After our indulgence at Indigo Pearl, we had to cut back a bit.

'Has anyone here been working at the hotel a long time?' I asked the young fellow at reception.

'Oh, yes,' he replied proudly. 'I have been here twenty-four hours!'

'No, sorry, I mean were any staff members working here thirty years ago?'

He gave me a look as though I was crazy. 'No!' he gasped.

He had to ask a couple of people, but he found out that the hotel opened in 1974. The Vieng Thong Hotel would have been brand spanking new when the Wheelers passed through.

Our not-quite-brand-spanking-new room had a bed with the usual big dip in the middle, wires hanging out of the lamp and light switches, and no shower curtain (only curtain rings where it had been torn off just like the shower scene from *Psycho*). Next to the bed was a greasy-looking Bakelite phone. 'Don't touch that,' Beth exclaimed. 'It's covered in bacteria.'

'And hepatitis and cholera,' I added.

Ah, welcome to the real world of backpacking again.

The old guidebook recommended the 'very good' hotel restaurant, which served 'Thai food and, great and rare joy, has an English menu'. It may have once been very good, but we were the only diners in the sprawling restaurant. And the menu would have actually been more of a great and rare joy if it wasn't in English. Listed on the menu were such culinary delights as pig entrails fried with pickled lettuce, imitated crab, fried pig's liver, fried hog's man and frog spare rib fried with chilli paste (that last one would either be an incredibly small dish or a hell of a lot of frogs' ribs). Our food (we skipped the fried hog's man, whatever that was, and ordered the pad thai) and beers came to 200 baht – the same price as getting your safari suit laundered at Indigo Pearl.

We could hear a band playing somewhere outside, so we stepped out the back entrance right into the middle of the weekend night market in the town square. A hip Thai band was getting all jiggy with it, while fanned out around the edges of the square were food stalls with the delicious smell of satays and grilled fish. Two ladies were making elaborate cocktails at one of the stalls. We grabbed a mai tai, which was made with much flourish, and wandered around in the warm evening air with our ice-cold cocktails in hand. It felt good to be out and about among the locals. Yes, I loved Indigo Pearl (who wouldn't?), but I felt like I was really travelling again. I was even happy when we got into bed and the mattress sank so much in the middle that I knew I would have to clamber up a steep slope in the morning to get out.

We had a late-afternoon flight to Bangkok, so we got up early to make the most of the day – although we would have saved time and probably a case of dysentery if we'd skipped breakfast. We had an omelette that came with grey ham. And not only was it grey, but I couldn't pierce it with a fork. Mind you, I thought it didn't taste that bad – even though it was a bit like eating rubber. 'This tastes nothing like an omelette,' Beth said, screwing up her face. 'Or eggs,' I added. Beth was too scared to try the grey rubber ham.

We decided to hire a scooter, even though the old guidebook didn't come with a map of the area. All the old guidebook mentioned was that the road between Phang Nga and Krabi was 'particularly impressive'. The man at the scooter hire shop recommended the best beach to go to – although he had to repeat it five times, because the name (Ao Nang Beach) made him sound like he was talking with a mouth full of pad thai.

The coastal road was 'particularly impressive' with dramatic rock formations soaring from rice paddies on one side of the road and shimmering emerald waters on the other. An hour after leaving Krabi, we arrived at Ao Nang, which had a few guesthouses and one hotel by the beach. We parked in front of a row of cheap restaurant shacks that overlooked the not-so-picturesque car park and picked up a Thai beef salad and some sort of spicy minced chicken salad and had a picnic on the beach. The tide was out, so the locals were walking out through shallow water to a cluster of fantastical limestone outcrops a few hundred metres offshore. After our delicious and spicy repast, we waddled along the brown sand and waded out into the water. But it was like walking through chocolate cake mix. The brown sand also made it virtually impossible to see the tiny crabs (I told Beth that was why it was called Krabi) that were scurrying around. Beth screamed when she stood on one and I said, 'Don't be such a wuss. They are only tiny.' Then, as I was wading in the ankle-deep water, I stood on a tiny little crab and screamed like a little girl.

12

Bangkok

The Bangkok bus service is frequent and frantic.
South east Asia on a shoestring, 1st edition, 1975

The Bangkok bus service is frequent and frantic.
Southeast Asia on a Shoestring, 15th edition, 2010

The Malaysia Hotel was the most popular backpackers' hotel back in 1974, even though you had to 'fight to get toilet paper or towels and your sink may fall off the wall'. In fact, Tony gave it quite a write-up in the old guidebook:

In two years the Malaysia Hotel has completely taken over the No. 1 Bangkok Travellers Hotel title. Or more accurately, the freaks have totally taken over the Malaysia. There can hardly be a more incongruous place on the whole world's cheap travel routes. It is big, air-conditioned, with a swimming pool, bar, restaurant all gradually going to seed. At 78 to

98 baht a night, it is more expensive than any other Bangkok cheapies but people just seem to make the adjustment and it is usually 100% full.

Fortunately for us, the Malaysia was still there and, even better, it wasn't 100 per cent full. A livered doorman greeted us at the entrance and lugged our bags into the clean and bright – and not going to seed at all – reception area. Above the reception desk was a large sign that promised: 'Maximum comfort at minimum cost.' The hotel lobby and the adjoining bar were buzzing with people, but something seemed out of place. 'Do you notice anything odd?' I asked Beth.

'No,' Beth said, looking around.

'Besides the receptionist, you are the only female.'

The place was full of well-dressed men with nice tans. When we stepped into the lift, two men came out holding hands. One had a very bushy moustache and a deep brown tan, while the other was wearing tight little white shorts. 'I think this may be a gay hotel,' I whispered to Beth as the lift door opened again and an old fellow with his young Thai 'boyfriend' joined us. Back in '74, the Malaysia Hotel made the rated features list at the back of the book for having the Hippest Hookers in South-East Asia. That was still the case, but the hookers were now hip-looking young men.

Our room was quite nice: we didn't have to fight anyone for towels or toilet paper (there were two rolls actually) and the sink was firmly attached to the wall. I looked out the window where a large group of men with moustaches and wearing very tiny bathers were sunbathing by the pool. Yes, this was definitely a gay hotel. And a sign above the bed confirmed my suspicions: 'Dear guests, you will be charged at 1,400 baht for any damage of the sheets.'

It was getting late and we didn't fancy traipsing the streets in search of a restaurant, so we decided to lash out and eat at the Malaysia. In the old guidebook, the hotel restaurant was recommended for its 'excellent steak', but only 'if you could afford it'. The restaurant was full of men in tight singlets and white shorts. 'Hi, sweetie,' the waiter said when we sat down. Not to Beth; to me. The steak was still excellent, but I scoffed it down in a hurry because a silver-haired gentleman, old enough to be my father, kept winking at me.

On the way back to our room, I stopped at reception and asked a young staff member if anyone in the hotel had been working here in 1974. 'She has been here a long time,' the very camp fellow said, pointing to a lady on the phone.

Wilai was the phone operator, but she hadn't quite been there long enough for my purposes. 'I started here in 1982,' she said. 'But Somkuan, our doorman, has been here even longer.' It was the same doorman who had helped us with our bags.

Somkuan started working at the Malaysia in 1974, the same year that Tony and Maureen came through.

He probably helped them unload their bags from their motorbike. 'The hotel was renovated twenty years ago,' he told us. 'Then we had another *big* renovation – we put TVs in the rooms.' When I asked him what the hotel was like in 1974, he said, 'It was very popular with hippie people.'

'It's still popular by the look of it,' I said.

'Yes, popular with, um . . . different people, now.'

Somkuan wasn't the only old staff member. The cook in the restaurant had been there since 1978. 'He makes excellent steak,' Somkuan said.

We decided to try one of the other hotels listed in the old guidebook, so while Beth packed I went downstairs to take some last-minute photos. It took Beth about an hour to repack her bag every morning. Mind you, to Beth's credit, we were moving just about every day and she never complained – she just stood around scratching her head, wondering how everything would fit back into her bag (which seemed to contain 'products' for every part of the body). I went out to the pool and, although it was already unbearably hot, men were sunbaking – or more like just baking. They all had dark chocolate-coloured skin. Without Beth by my side, I got winked at twice and caught another guy checking out my bottom.

The hotel reception booked us a taxi and rather appropriately we got picked up in a hot-pink taxi with pink leather seats. Back in '74, Bangkok offered 'hot sticky weather and horrendous traffic', according to the old guidebook. Bangkok was the first place on the trip that I'd visited before and when I'd been here 15 years earlier, the traffic was just as horrendous. But with the addition of the city monorail and new freeways, the traffic was actually moving and was not quite as sticky.

It was while we were barrelling down one of those new freeways that our taxi driver turned around and said, 'Show me map of hotel.' I showed him the map in the old guidebook and he screwed up his face. 'No, no, no,' he squealed, and then dropped us off on the side of the freeway.

What was the problem? Did the hotel still exist? Was it dodgy? Or was it just that the Lonely Planet map was dodgy? We were heading to, or hoping to head to, the Atlanta Hotel, which the old guidebook noted as 'at one time the most popular place going'. The hotel did have a seedier side, however. It was also home to a notorious series of drug raids in the early '70s, which Tony wrote about in the old guidebook:

> Some wide awake (and public spirited) individual saw the fuzz arrive and rushed down the corridors banging on doors yelling 'raid, raid' or whatever one yells at such times of stress. Behind him could be heard a succession of flushing toilets. A less cool individual opened his window and showered the surprised cops below with grass.

We jumped into another taxi (a bright canary-yellow, this time) and when our taxi driver looked at the map, he thought about it for a few seconds, and then said, 'No.' I was going to try one more taxi and if we had no luck then we were heading back to the Malaysia Hotel and guys winking and checking out my bottom.

The next taxi driver said, 'Yes, okay,' even though he looked totally and utterly confused when I showed him the map. He was still sitting there scratching his head when a young local fellow walked past and asked us very politely if we were lost.

'I know the Atlanta Hotel,' he said, when I showed him the map. 'It's not in a nice area.'

That was possibly why none of the drivers wanted to take us because the hotel was in Bangkok's most notorious sex tourism district. This could be really dodgy, I thought as we turned off the main road down a nondescript side street that was mostly filled with old, crumbling apartments. We pulled up in front of a drab concrete hotel, with a large sign above the door that warned: 'SEX TOURISTS NOT WELCOME – The Atlanta hotel does not tolerate sex tourists, prostitutes, drug users, riff-raff or pop music.'

We decided that we weren't any of the above (although Beth does like a bit of pop music now and again) and stepped through the glass doors into another era. The hotel lobby evoked a sleek modern grace, the '50s with hints of the Deco '30s with a polished terrazzo floor, and a wide, winding staircase that seemed to float in space.

The ornately grand furnishings included red leather-ette couches, chandeliers, faux gold-leafed mirrors and, facing the entrance on either side of the lobby, were two pedestalled bronze dachshunds.

There was another large sign above the reception desk, which read: 'Bangkok's Bastion of Wholesome Tourism – Zero tolerance and sleaze free zone. No sex tourists, junkies, louts and other degenerates. Those who object to this policy, and those who wish to spend their time in Thailand whoring, indulging in alcohol abuse, drugs or other illegal activities should stay elsewhere.' And underneath: 'Complaints not permitted (not at the prices we charge).'

They had a room available, and as we were filling in the registration forms, we were given an ice-cold mango drink garnished with a purple orchid. We needed the cold drink because there was no lift and it was a long, hot climb up four flights (as in four incredi-bly sweaty flights) of stairs to our room. The room was notably bereft of anything resembling luxury, but it was comfortably spartan with a fetching pink linoleum floor, a double bed, a desk, a bedside light and an air conditioner. The air-conditioner remote control was bolted to the wall. 'Why would anyone want to steal an air-conditioner remote control?' I asked Beth as I tried to pull it off the wall.

I went downstairs to take some photos while Beth unpacked all her products. At one side of the lobby was the Western Union Travel Section, consisting of a couple of desks and a high table stacked with laminated travel maps. Tucked away on the other side was a small sitting area with an overstuffed sofa and armchair and a writing desk stocked with hotel stationery. On the wall were two glass cabinets filled with signed books from authors who had included the Atlanta in their books or who had stayed there. The first one that caught my eye was a signed note by Elizabeth Gilbert of *Eat, Pray, Make Shitloads of Money* fame. 'For everyone at the Atlanta, thanks for the oasis,' she wrote. Other thankful guests included the gang from the Institute of Nuclear Physics in Krakow, Poland, who were in Bangkok for a conference on 'The effect of Gastrin and CCK-8 on post-radiation recovery of small intestine epithelium'.

On the wall next to the cabinet was a framed painting of the Atlanta's founder, Dr Max Henn, who died in 2002. Underneath was a small plaque that read: 'Dr. Max Henn was a chemist from Berlin who came to Thailand in 1948 to set up a company selling dehydrated cobra venom to the US. Five years later, with business flagging [funny that!], he turned his 2-storey lab and office into the Atlanta Hotel. The outdoor pit, where he kept his cobras, became Thailand's first hotel swimming pool.'

I wandered back to reception and asked, 'Is the owner here?'

'Yes, he is just over there,' the desk clerk said, pointing to a neat, slight figure in khaki pants and a polo shirt.

Max's son Charles was now running the Atlanta.

Or running it when he was in town, at least. Charles, who had a perfectly clipped jolly-what English accent, spent most of his time in England teaching International Law at Cambridge. He told me that he was too busy for a long chat, but in only a few short minutes he still managed to give me a great insight into the hotel's fascinating history.

According to Charles, the Atlanta was once the place to be seen. In the 1950s, the hotel was full of dignitaries, movie stars, diplomats and even royalty – the Queen of Thailand would pop over every Wednesday night for dinner. However, a decade later, partying American GIs on R & R from the Vietnam War took over the hotel and when they left, the hippies – or the 'flower-power people', as Charles called them – moved in. By the time the Wheelers first rolled in to the Atlanta in 1974, the hotel was pretty much a hippie drug den (hence all the raids).

Max Henn had by then given up on the hotel and when Charles returned to Thailand in the '80s after studying at Cambridge, those peace-loving, dope-smoking hippies had made way for porn-loving, heroin-snorting junkies. 'They were the dregs of humanity,' Charles told me.

The Atlanta Hotel was on the verge of total ruin – although Charles didn't want to let the hotel go, nor did he want to run it, either. But Charles had a plan to turn the Atlanta around without having to give up his life in England. He presided over major renovations and instated strict rules against drugs, prostitutes, riff-raff and that nasty pop music.

The Atlanta is now full and buzzing again and, after being blacklisted for many years, is even back in Lonely Planet – the current guide describes it as 'a Bangkok institution, a conceptual art project and a chic refuge from the fast-paced postmodern world outside'.

At last Beth had finished unpacking her products, so we headed out to lunch. Even though there were lots of accommodation options in the old guidebook, there were only two restaurants listed: the restaurant at the Malaysia Hotel and the restaurant at the Thai Song Greet Hotel, which was 'very popular' back in 1974. It was still very popular. It was just now very popular with dead people. The restaurant, which was on the main street near the railway station, was now a coffin shop.

Instead, we decided to go to a restaurant called Cabbages and Condoms. As part of the research for this book, I googled the phrase 'Thailand 1974' and happened upon a restaurant that was set up by an organisation called the PDA (Population and Community Development Association). The PDA, which was founded in 1974, promotes family planning in urban and rural areas of Thailand and today has 12,000 volunteers, plus several mobile health units distributing contraceptives to over 10,000 villages. The restaurant was conceptualised to promote better understanding and acceptance of family planning. We were relieved to find the restaurant's motto was 'Our food is guaranteed not to cause pregnancy'.

We walked into the restaurant's courtyard and were greeted by a strong smell of latex. Standing next to the entrance was a life-sized sculpture of Santa made entirely from condoms. There were red ones for the suit, black ones for the belt and boots, and yellow ones for the beard. Standing next to him was Captain Condom in his blue condom suit and a big, bright yellow C on his chest.

The walls inside the restaurant were covered with framed condoms from around the world, including Rooster Extra Strong from South Africa, Black Jerk from Sweden and something called a 'Tungdom', which was 'Developed by Dr. Lick for the American Institute of Tungology'. There was also a Vasectomy Bar, where you could have a free drink (a stiff one, perhaps?) if you'd had your vasectomy done at the Cabbages and Condoms-run medical centre located next door. We were shown to our table, which had a multitude of multicoloured condoms placed neatly underneath a glass top.

Our lunch was delicious (and totally STD- and pregnancy-free) and after our meal we were each given a small side plate with an after-dinner mint on it. Except that they weren't after-dinner mints: they were condoms.

The old guidebook suggested that Jim Thompson's house was worth a visit, so after lunch we did just that. Jim Thompson was a US architect who fell in love with Thailand when he was stationed there during World War II and is widely credited with reviving the country's long-neglected silk industry. When he decided to live in Bangkok, he built a house by combining six 200-year-old teak houses and lived in it from 1959 until he disappeared in 1967 while holidaying in Malaysia's Cameron Highlands. His home was interesting – if you like traipsing around in muggy rooms looking at a whole bunch of old stuff.

On the way back to the Atlanta, we drove along the banks of the Chao Phraya River past the Oriental Hotel (Jim Thompson was a one-time owner of the hotel along with a group of business partners). The Oriental is a perennial inclusion on top hotels of the world lists and has the room rates to match. Even so, it still makes it into Lonely Planet. Not into *Southeast Asia on a Shoestring*, of course, but it is in the Lonely Planet *Thailand* guidebook.

The content of Lonely Planet guidebooks has changed dramatically since the early years and the Shoestring titles now only make up three per cent of sales. One of the main reasons for the phenomenal growth of Lonely Planet was that the books changed with their readers. The hippies who were the cornerstone of Lonely Planet's rise in the 1970s travelled very differently in the 1990s. Not only did they have less time to travel, they now had kids and money to spend. They didn't want to stay in cheap dives anymore. They wanted a bit of luxury. So that's why Lonely Planet now recommends hotels in Bangkok such as the Grand Hyatt, the Marriott and the Sheraton. In the 'Our Pick' section of the current *Thailand* guide they nominated the Oriental Hotel, which had rooms at up to $3000 a night. That's about three months' travel for a backpacker on a shoestring. In the dining section for Bangkok, the book recommended Le Normandie at the Mandarin Oriental, where the dress code included a dinner jacket. I haven't met many travellers who carry a dinner jacket around in their backpacks. The degustation menu at Le Normandie was 8000 baht. That's $270, or the equivalent of 20 serves of nasi goreng at the hawkers' market in Denpasar. And, if you want to bring your own wine, corkage is 2000 baht. That's $67, or six nights in a deluxe room at Hotel Carolina.

The Lonely Planet *Thailand* guide also recommended Vertigo restaurant on the 61st floor of the Banyan Tree Hotel and the adjoining Moon Bar for a drink. Although it's not quite on the cheap, I figured it was in Lonely Planet, so I booked a table at Vertigo for dinner as a treat for Beth for putting up with moving hotels every day and all the stained sheets.

Thankfully, there were no sweaty staircases to climb at the Banyan Tree Hotel as an express elevator jettisoned us up to the top floor. It was then just a hop up a short flight of stairs to the rooftop and the restaurant, which was (let me just look up my thesaurus because I can't think of words to describe it) spectacular, staggering, startling, stunning, stupefying. The view was more like the sort you get from an aeroplane and the whole city was spread out below us like a sparkling sea. We were escorted to a corner table that was literally hanging over the edge of the building with only a low glass wall between us and potentially a very sudden end to your dinner date. It was so dark that our suit-clad waiter gave us a torch, so we could read the menu. That worked out well because then the waiter also couldn't see the expression on my face when I read the prices. Among the pricier items on the menu were an entree of lobster spring roll (five nights at Wisma Delima in Jakarta) and a main course of broiled Maine lobster with chardonnay cream sauce and truffle potato ravioli (17 nights at the Wisma Tirta Yatra in Bali).

I had the roasted wild Tasmanian salmon with truffle-infused cauliflower puree, but the lofty price tag was well worth it for the lofty views. 'I don't want to go down to the chaos,' Beth said. 'Life is so nice up here.'

'Where would you like to go?' the hotel doorman asked us when we got to the ground floor. I'd asked him to book us a taxi, but I was too embarrassed to tell him that we were going to check out Patpong Road, which even in the old guidebook was described as 'Bangkok's sin centre'. Patpong Road's penchant for sin began in the early '70s when the street was filled with GIs who were on leave from the Vietnam War.

'Um, we're going to Patpong Road to, um . . .'

'Oh, are you going to the Super Pussy Club?' the doorman asked.

Okay, he didn't really say that, but the first bar that we came to on Patpong Road was called the Super Pussy Club – which was next door to Pussy Collection Club.

Not only is the name Patpong similar in name to Patong on Phuket, but it also had the same neon-lit go-go clubs and bars filled with guys from the '70s with their Thai girlfriends born in the '90s. All along the street, women in miniskirts – that were so minuscule that you could see what they had for breakfast – were enticing punters into the go-go clubs. One girl held up a large sign that read: 'Fifty gorgeous girls and a few ugly ones.' There was also the army of sleazy men showing us their laminated cards advertising what was 'on show'. They had a few different tricks to the Patong shows, including a Pussy Chopstick Show, a Pussy Magic Flower Show and, the potentially messy, Pussy Magic Razorblade Show. However, there was one major change to Patpong Road since 1974: running down the middle of the road was now a bustling nightly tourist market with smiling stallholders selling Nike shirts, watches and Thai handicrafts to happy families and the blue-rinse set on package tours.

We had breakfast the next morning in the long, narrow Atlanta dining room with its red leatherette banquettes and Formica tables. On the sound system, they were playing classical music – the hotel played classical in the morning then at noon every day there was an hour of gently swinging jazz by Thailand's clarinet-playing king, followed by jazz standards in the afternoon. The extensive Thai menu included detailed descriptions of the food and even how to eat it. The 'acclaimed' breakfast menu was full of diverse and interesting things to eat.

We had banana pancakes.

I asked Anont, our grey-haired waitress, when she started working at the Atlanta. 'I started in 1973 as a maid,' she said. 'You know, make beds.' I asked her what the hotel was like when it was bad, but she didn't want to talk about it. 'It's nice again now,' Anont said. 'And you know the hotel never closed. It didn't matter. The hotel would get flooded and reception would be filled with knee-deep water for weeks, but we never closed.'

We had quite a few sights to tick off before we caught an overnight train to Chiang Mai, so we set out early and jumped in a taxi to Bangkok's most famous sight: Wat Phra Keo (or the Temple of the Emerald Buddha, which is actually made from Jade) and the Grand Palace. Maybe I should have brought a dinner jacket with me, after all. The old guidebook noted that entrance to the palace required 'coats and ties for men – but dress regulations may soon be more relaxed'. The dress regulations had been relaxed, but there was a large sign at the entrance with illustrations of 'PROHIBITED OUTFITS'. They included miniskirts and tight pants – and definitely no fat knees, either, if the illustrations were anything to go by.

The grounds of the Wat Phra Keo and the Grand Palace were packed with visitors from around the world, including two large groups of tourists that wouldn't have been here in 1974: Russians and Chinese.

'Shall we buy a guidebook and map?' Beth asked. There wasn't much information about Wat Phra Keo and the Grand Palace in the old book (besides that Wat Phra Keo had a 'variety of buildings and frescoes').

'Nah, we don't need it,' I said.

'What's that?' Beth asked when we stopped in front of an architectural wonder of gleaming gilded stupas with polished orange and green roof tiles, mosaic-encrusted pillars and rich marble pediments.

'It's mostly made of gold and it's quite old.'

'What about that one?' Beth said, pointing to another suitably spectacular edifice.

'. . . and so is that.'

As it turned out, we probably did need a map. We, or more specifically, I, got lost trying to find the exit and we ended up waltzing through the staff quarters and going out through the staff car park.

I contemplated going to the 'famous' floating market, but even in the old guidebook it was described as 'a tourist trap'. Instead we went to the 'interesting Thieves Market'. Although I don't think many thieves would be interested in hanging around anymore – unless the thieves were after plastic junk and hairclips.

We returned to the Atlanta for a shower before heading to the train station and it was lucky that we were leaving, because I totally flooded the bathroom – just like the good ol' days.

13

Chiang Mai

Chiang Mai has become a brash tourist trap, full of
noisy motorbikes and souvenir shops.
South east Asia on a shoestring, 1st edition, 1975

Chiang Mai is a quiet world of charming guesthouses,
leafy gardens and friendly smiles.
Southeast Asia on a Shoestring, 15th edition, 2010

'Trains in Thailand are punctual, comfortable, cheap
and serve reasonable food,' the old guidebook claimed.
Our train wasn't punctual. It left three minutes late.
Mind you, that was entirely our fault. We'd got caught
in the 'horrendous' traffic and were dropped off at
the station with only one minute till the scheduled
six o'clock departure. We sprinted through the sprawling Hua Lamphong Railway Station lugging – or more
like dragging – our backpacks, because we didn't have
time to put them on. The train was just about to pull
out when we reached the platform, but the Skinny

Controller waved us down with a big smile and said, 'It's okay; you can go slow.' He waited until we were safely and securely aboard before he blew his whistle.

Our carriage was fabulously comfortable, but it wasn't cheap. Although that's perhaps because we upgraded to our very own first-class sleeper compartment. Train travel in 1974 was certainly cheap – a third-class ticket from Bangkok to Chiang Mai was 68 baht ($2.50). And it still was cheap: the same ticket was now 271 baht (nine dollars). Plus you got the bonus of a 13-hour trip instead of the 17 hours that it took in 1974. Our first-class ticket was 1450 baht ($48), but even that was cheap considering that we got free ice-cold bottled water and a man in a dapper suit who came and made up our bed with fresh stain-free white cotton sheets.

And they did still serve reasonable food. Oh, except Beth almost died after eating the pineapple dessert. Not long after we'd left Bangkok, a woman came around offering a four-course set menu for 150 baht, which included tom yum soup, chicken with lemongrass and cashews, duck red curry and fresh pineapple. After finishing our 'fresh' pineapple dessert, Beth's face turned a scary pineapple-yellow colour. 'My heart is beating really fast,' Beth whimpered. 'And my head feels like it's going to explode.' When Beth started having trouble breathing, she freaked out, which in turn made me freak out. I rushed out to find the carriage attendant, who had one look at her then ran off. I'm not very good in these situations. What could I do? Press the emergency stop? It was dark outside and we were in the middle of nowhere. 'Just try to breathe,' was all I could come up with. Well, in between shouts of, 'I don't know what to do!' The man came back with a handful of tablets. 'Take these,' he said.

'Are they okay?' Beth asked, looking at me with sad, trusting puppy-dog eyes.

'Sure,' I said.

I had no idea what they were, but anything would help, I figured.

Thirty minutes later, Beth was fine, although I lay awake next to her for a while just in case her head exploded in the night.

The rattling train and prattling passengers in the corridor woke us at six to a view of golden clouds, a pinky blue sky, and a lush, deep green jungle interspersed with rice fields. After I found the food lady, we were served a hearty breakfast of fried eggs, ham, toast and pineapple. We both passed on the pineapple.

Chiang Mai Railway Station was frantic and so were the touts out the front.

'You want taxi?'

'You want tuk tuk?'

'You want guesthouse?'

'You want elephant ride?'

'You want trekking?'

'You want silk factory tour?'

'You want bungee jumping?'

This was all in the first minute of stepping out of the station. We took up the offer of a tuk tuk, but before we hopped in I asked, 'Do you know the Je T'Aime Guesthouse?'

'Don't stay there. It's not very nice for you,' the driver said. 'I have much nicer place for you.'

'It's much nice for us,' I said excitedly, although Beth didn't seem too excited about the driver's warning. I still got quite a buzz when something from the old guidebook was still around. Back in '74, the Je T'Aime Guesthouse was the most popular place to stay and was described in the old guidebook as 'very friendly and quiet'.

'Okay then, we go to Je T'Aime Guesthouse,' our driver said with a sigh. (There went his commission.) Then his face lit up again. 'So, do you want go trekking, an elephant ride, a temple tour, bungee jumping . . . ?'

The Je T'Aime Guesthouse didn't seem very friendly. Or quiet. The heavy steel front gate was locked and a pack of rabid dogs was pacing menacingly around the front garden barking and snarling at us. You'd think dogs that lived in a guesthouse would be used to people. Maybe it was because they hadn't seen any other guests for a long time. A lady came out from the main building and said, 'They are okay. They won't hurt you.'

'They don't like me,' I said to Beth as I cowered behind her.

Our cottage was clean, but just a bit dusty. It looked like it hadn't been used for a while. 'It hasn't been used for a while,' the lady said as she showed us around the room. 'And you may have a little trouble flushing the toilet.'

I tried out the bed while Beth jumped in the shower. 'It's firm,' I called out. 'And it sort of has clean sheets. What's the shower like?'

'It sort of has hot water,' Beth called back.

After we'd freshened up, we decided to head into town. On the way out we walked past another guest who was sitting out the front of his cottage. Lorenzo was a middle-aged Italian man from Rome who came to Chiang Mai for six months every year – and had been doing so for the past ten years – to escape the Italian winter. 'I always stay at Je T'Aime because it's only four euros a night,' he said. 'That's cheaper than a coffee in Rome.'

We crossed the moat into the old city where back in '74 you could find a 'couple of tour agencies that run two and three day jungle trips'. We passed about 20 tour agencies in the first ten minutes. And there were more than just jungle trips on offer. You could now hand over fistfuls of cash to partake in everything from bungee jumping, paintball wars, zorbing (rolling down a steep hill inside a massive plastic ball), rafting and go-karting to motocross tours, white-water kayaking, rock climbing, abseiling, off-road buggy driving and something called Flight of the Gibbon. Many of the tour agencies had names like Extreme Sports Centre, X Centre and Max It to the Xtreme Centre (okay, I made that last one up).

All the tour agencies were also selling jungle treks, but they were now mostly catering to planeloads of tourists wanting the Authentic Thai Jungle Experience without getting their loafers dirty. The tour companies would bus them to sanitised villages for elephant rides, handicraft markets and traditional chicken and chips for lunch. We weren't doing a trek because Chiang Mai was one of the places that I had visited before and I'd already been on a three-day jungle trek that included an elephant ride, a bamboo raft trip down a river and a stay in a traditional village (with a single shop selling Coke and Pringles chips). Those same villages probably now have internet cafes, paintball and go-karting.

After spending the morning shambling happily around the tranquil streets, we were ready for lunch. I was keen on finding the Thai-German Dairy Food Stall, which made the Rated Features list at the back of the book for the Best Bacon and Eggs in South-East Asia. But what intrigued me the most was that the same restaurant also made the list for the Worst Hamburgers in South-East Asia.

We found the right address, but it was now El Toro Mexican Restaurant. 'That's close enough,' I said to Beth with a shrug. Back in '74, there was only a choice of Thai or 'Thai with the odd hamburger' in Chiang Mai, but like so many other tourist towns in the world today, there was a plethora of cuisines on offer. I did an online search for restaurants in Chiang Mai and there were the usual suspects of Italian, French, Indian, Mexican,

Japanese, Chinese, Vietnamese and even English (The Red Lion English pub, which has roast dinners), but there was also Spanish, Belgian, German (three restaurants in town including a Hofbrauhaus), American (Duke's American Style Steakhouse), Pakistani, Korean and Israeli (Jerusalem Felafel). There was even a Pink Floyd-themed restaurant (how very 1974) called The Wall, although I'm not sure what kind of cuisine they served – perhaps their dishes are inspired by the band's song titles: 'Candy and Currant Buns', 'Apples and Oranges' and 'Pigs on the Wing'.

The Mexican food was nice (we had the enchiladas) and the restaurant had groovy laminated menus, groovy staff in cool matching polo shirts and a groovy cocktail bar that could have been in Sydney, Santiago or Stockholm.

The majority of the sights recommended in the old book were wats. After our third wat, I began calling each one an AFW – Another Fucking Wat. (When I worked as a tour leader in Europe, after a while every church became an AFC – Another Fucking Church.) At Wat Phra Singh, we did at least time our visit well. It was 'Chat to a Monk Day'. Young monks in orange robes were sitting at tables in the grounds and you could, well, chat to them. When I told a lanky teenage monk from Laos that I was heading there in two days' time, he told me the 'really good bars to get drunk in'.

The old guidebook suggested getting a traditional massage. I'd had a traditional Thai massage in Chiang

Mai before, so I knew that there was quite a bit of pulling and poking involved, but it was all a bit too much for Beth. 'I got the shit beat out of me,' she said when her massage finished. 'They were crawling all over me and pummelling my butt.'

When we headed back to the guesthouse, the entire street was full of rabid dogs. The two psychopathic mutts at the guesthouse must have spread the word around that I was in town. They were all snarling and drooling with anticipation of getting their fangs into my limbs. 'They won't hurt you,' Beth said.

'No, they don't want to hurt me,' I said. 'They want to kill me.'

'Don't look at them.'

'But if I don't look at them, then they can sneak up and attack me,' I whimpered, as I clutched Beth's arm tightly.

We made it back to the safety of our room, but after watching Beth unpack then re-pack then unpack her bags for an hour, I said, 'I want to get some photos outside the guesthouse; will you come with me?'

'You'll be fine,' Beth said as she emptied her backpack again and scratched her head.

'I'm not going out there alone,' I said. 'They will tear me into shreds.'

'They won't,' Beth insisted.

'Okay, but you can ring my parents and tell them that you sent me out to my death.'

I skipped the photos and waited until my blonde bodyguard was ready to join me for dinner. Not far from the guesthouse was, or hopefully still was, Aroon Rai Restaurant, which was noted as one of the best known and reasonably priced Thai restaurants outside of the moat. As usual, we got lost trying to follow the damn map. I stopped in front of a shop and asked a lady sitting on the step if she'd heard of Aroon Rai Restaurant.

'You want massage?' she said.

'Um, no. Do you know where Aroon Rai is?'

'No,' she said, shaking her head. 'You want massage? I give you nice massage.'

'There it is,' Beth said.

It was next door. And even though the restaurant only had a small sign, it was lit up inside with banks of bright fluorescent lights (which seemed to be a feature at most of the restaurants from the old guidebook). The sign read: 'Aroon Rai – Unique authentic Chiang Mai and Thai food since 1957. No branch either in Thailand or in foreign countries. ONLY ONE HERE IN THE WORLD.' The restaurant had the same decor and furnishings from 1957. The rather bedraggled Formica tables were so faded that the once-bright floral pattern was now almost completely white. We grabbed a table in the ground-floor dining area that opened out onto the street.

Our waitress, who started working at the restaurant in 1984, told us that the restaurant was very popular with backpackers. 'We are in the new Lonely Planet,' she said proudly.

The menu had an entire section devoted to frogs. There was fried frog with garlic and pepper, fried frog with tomato sauce, fried frog with spicy chilli sauce, fried frog with curry sauce and, Beth's favourite, fried frog with pineapple. We decided to skip the frog and ordered the house specialty, Thai chicken curry. We finished off our delightful – and delightfully cheap – meal (the whole thing, including two large Chang beers, came to 200 baht) with a heavenly homemade mango ice-cream.

We went for an after-dinner stroll into the old town and stumbled upon the night bazaar, which had taken over the narrow streets. But it was the same, same stalls with the same, same stallholder spiels to sell the same, same novelty T-shirts, including one that had 'Same, Same' on the front. And they had the same lame jokes on T-shirts that you'd find at markets in Kuta, Kuala Lumpur or Ko Samui: 'I'm shy, but I've got a big dick' and 'iPood' with a drawing of someone pooing in a toilet.

In the 'What to Buy' section, the old guidebook recommended 'all sorts of shirts, plain and embroidered at very cheap prices'. There were still all sorts of shirts, but they were now novelty T-shirts, football shirts, beer shirts and, the backpacker's favourite, Che Guevara T-shirts. Although I did see one T-shirt that made me laugh: it had a picture of Che Guevara on it wearing a Che Guevara T-shirt.

On the way back to the guesthouse, we walked past a karaoke bar, so of course we had to pop in for a look. And it would have been rude of me not to at least sing one song. However, inside the bar there were only six customers and the place smelt like a toilet. The decor was also a bit dingy, but they did have nice Christmas decorations up (early or late, I'm not sure). The bar staff were very excited to see us and the manager escorted us to a table and plopped a bulky karaoke songbook in front of me. I flicked through the entire book before I found the somewhat limited repertoire of 40 English songs at the back of the book.

I put my name down for a song and I was immediately called up to sing 'Play That Funky Music'. The song started in a wild disco beat, five times faster than the usual tempo. It was so fast that I couldn't keep up. I looked over at Beth who had just about fallen off her chair with laughter. The six other patrons gave me a polite applause when I finished. I had to try to redeem myself, so I got up to sing 'You're Just Too Good to Be True', but that was also a fast-paced disco version and about three octaves higher than the usual pitch. I didn't even attempt it and sat straight down. I decided to give it one more try with Billy Joel's 'You May Be Right'. It wasn't a disco version, but it was a hip-hop version and at the start of the song the backing music kept repeating the lyrics, 'You may be right, right, right,' over and over again. While I tried to keep up, Beth laughed so much that she actually did fall off her chair.

Back at Je T'Aime, it wasn't 'quiet' as the old guidebook promised. While we were lying in bed, there was a particularly bad band playing nearby, the dogs were barking and snarling (looking for me, I guessed) and the toilet was making funny noises (and none that involved flushing because we couldn't get it to flush).

In the morning, I hired a scooter for my last chance to try to injure (or kill) Beth. It was easy to hire a scooter because every third shop in Chiang Mai hired out bikes. According to the old guidebook, we were heading up '12 kms of hairpin turns' to Doi Suthep, which had 'fantastic views from the hill top temple of Wat Prathat'. A map was way too expensive (equivalent to one night at the New Cathay Hotel), so instead we got directions from the guy in the scooter hire shop.

'Did you get that?' I asked Beth, when the guy finished giving us the directions.

'No. Did you?'

Not really. It was something like left, and then right, left, straight ahead, then left after a quick right.

'Yeah, I got it,' I said.

This should be fun, I thought.

It actually turned out to be quite easy. The mountains loomed over the town, so I just headed towards them. The roads were also well signposted and even the road itself was entirely pothole-free. And, even better, one long stretch of the steep and winding mountain road was new. It was so new, in fact, that they were still painting the lines in the middle of the road. Beth was also more relaxed this time and wasn't trying to squeeze the life out of me as much. Although some of the tight bends were scary, particularly when practised Thai drivers – their faith in reincarnation apparently replenished by their visit to the temple – executed harrowing passes and almost sent us flying off the mountain.

We pulled into the temple car park, which was dwarfed by a huge market peddling everything from jade jewellery to hill-tribe dolls to fried chicken. The market extended all the way to the front entrance of the temple and continued up the steep steps. The 200 sweat-inducing steps were lined with banisters made up of the rolling, green-scaled snake-like bodies of the *nagas*, with multiple, ferocious dragon-like heads.

The view from the top was outstanding and we sat in the revered temple and watched an ancient and wizened monk give a solemn blessing to a local couple. He finished off the blessing by dipping a branch into some water and spraying their bowed heads and then giving them each a sacred bracelet. 'This is exactly how it would have been thirty years, or even a hundred years, ago,' I whispered to Beth.

'Um . . . look,' said Beth. Our solemn and ancient monk was now taking a break and talking on his mobile phone.

'He's calling his stockbroker,' Beth said.

We made it back to Chiang Mai without crashing, without getting lost and without Beth squeezing me to death.

After our sort-of-hot shower, we headed out to try to find Pat's, a popular open-air restaurant on the east side of the moat. In the old guidebook, Tony wrote that Pat's 'has captured the stomachs of Chiang Mai's travelling population. But don't confuse it with the flashy Pat's on the outside of the moat.'

I flagged down a tuk tuk and asked the driver to take us to Pat's. He hadn't heard of it, so he rang a friend on his mobile phone. 'Yes, I can take you there,' he said, after calling three different friends. His asking price was 150 baht, which I thought was a tad expensive, but he did ring around for us.

We headed towards the east side of the moat – then crossed over it.

'Is this where Pat's is?' I asked.

'Yes.'

He must have been taking us to 'flashy Pat's', but that was probably a better idea anyway. It was our last night together (that's me and Beth, not me and the driver) and somewhere flashy would be nice. The flashy Pat's must have been a fair distance outside of the moat because we kept driving further out of town. As in way outside the moat and way out of town. Then we got on to a freeway. 'This is an adventure,' I said to Beth. But I was getting worried. We had passed the airport and were on our way to the Laos border.

We finally turned off the freeway down a dark and nondescript street. Beth was now looking worried. I tried to lighten the mood. 'This is the part where we get kidnapped and sold for white slavery,' I said. That didn't help.

A few minutes later, we pulled up in front of what looked like a restaurant, but there weren't any other houses or buildings nearby. 'Um, is this Pat's restaurant?' I asked the driver.

He turned around with a big smile. 'Yes.'

It didn't look that flashy. The restaurant itself was upstairs on the open roof with fairy lights strung up around the low brick wall. In the distance, beyond green rice fields, the sun was setting over the mountains. The view was certainly flashy. 'Is this Pat's?' I asked the young giggling waitress.

'Yes,' she said as she handed us a menu.

On the top of the menu was the name of the restaurant. It was called Pat Restaurant.

'Oh, well,' I said to Beth. 'Close enough, and we're here now.'

The menu was somewhat eclectic. There was snail curry, fried pig's brain dipped in flower (no mention of what flower), spicy chicken feet and an even more extensive frog menu than Aroon Rai's, including spicy frog with lab chilli soup (whatever that is) and stir-fried spicy frog with a sauce. Even more unnerving than the frogs was that there were ten dishes with snakeheads, including deep-fried whole snake's head with a sauce. We chose the rather more mundane baby coconut with prawns – which was delicious and there wasn't a snake's head or frog in sight.

As we were eating our dinner, a young guy was playing melodic Thai folk songs on an acoustic guitar and I commented to Beth that it was a lovely mistake ending up at Pat Restaurant. Beth agreed that it was wonderful. That was until we tried to get back to town. There were no taxis or tuk tuks anywhere to be seen, so we started walking along the side of the road. Twenty minutes later, we were back at the freeway where cars were zooming past at close to the speed of sound. Even if a taxi did go by, the driver couldn't stop anyway (or see us, for that matter). It was so dark we could barely see where we were going as we stepped over piles of rubbish then almost stood on a dog. The dog was as stiff as a board with its back legs in the air, looking as if it was playing dead. Except that it was dead.

What a great way to spend our last night together, I thought. Then just as I was thinking that we might have to kip down by the side of the freeway for the night with only a dead dog as company, we saw lights up ahead. Our beacon of hope was a huge Tesco supermarket. But it may as well have been the Shangri-La because we couldn't get to it. We had to cross the freeway, which was a constant stream of traffic. After ten minutes, there was suddenly a brief gap and I screamed out, 'Go, go, go!'

'Jesus Christ Almighty,' Beth squealed as we bolted in between cars.

We walked through the car park (or more like a scooter park) and right next to the entrance of the supermarket was a taxi. I was so happy that I ran up to the driver and hugged him.

*

We were both quiet in the taxi on the way to the airport the next day. Neither of us wanted to talk about where our future would take us. We did know that we wanted to be together. That we would be together. Not only was I going to miss travelling with Beth, I was going to miss Beth. Our time together was spontaneous, adventurous, carefree, romantic and fun. I sat there wishing that she could have continued travelling with me – although my guess was that the sheets in Laos and Burma would probably send her running home screaming. I grabbed Beth's hand and looked into her big, sad blue eyes. 'Would you like to come live with me in Australia one day?' I asked.

Beth smiled. 'Yes, I would.'

Laos

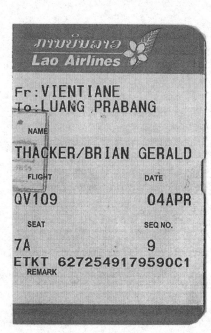

14

Vientiane

Vientiane is more of a laze around, enjoy yourself and
eat well place.
South east Asia on a shoestring, 1st edition, 1975

Vientiane is full of things to see.
Southeast Asia on a Shoestring, 15th edition, 2010

My flight from Chiang Mai to Bangkok arrived late
and I missed my connecting flight to Luang Prabang.
Bangkok Airways tried to charge me $US185 to issue a
new ticket for a flight the next day, so I told them politely
to shove it. I then tried the Thai Airways counter, but I'd
just missed the 12.15 flight. The next flight was at 9.30,
but that was sold out. Like an episode of *The Amazing
Race*, I ran from counter to counter trying to get on a
flight. The Lao Airlines desk had tickets to Vientiane,
but they could only sell them to travel agents. They
told me to look for a 'roaming' travel agent. I found one
roaming around the entrance to the toilets. The young

fellow, who was wearing a rather snazzy and shiny suit, called his travel agent office on his mobile phone. 'There is a flight at six o'clock,' he said.

'Perfect,' I beamed.

'But there is only first class left.'

'First class?' I gasped. 'I can't afford that. I'm a back-packer.'

'It's business class,' he said. 'Same thing.'

The ticket was $190, which was still cheap in the scheme of things. He then dragged out a credit card machine from his bag, connected it to the airport's free wi-fi and printed out a receipt. 'That's all you need,' he said.

The first-class (or business-class) seat was not that much different to the economy seats. I just got a glass of orange juice when I boarded. I was in shorts and most of the other folk in business class were in suits. Back in the 1970s, people often would dress up in their Sunday best for a flight – men wore suits with ties and women would don their best dresses. Air travel was still a novelty back then and in 1974, only 207 million well-dressed folks took to the skies. That might sound like a lot, but compare that to today when more than 2.5 billion passengers jump on a plane each year.

Back then, there was no point in shopping around for the best deal, either, because governments regulated airfares and all the prices were the same. If a return ticket between Sydney and Singapore was $327 on one airline, it was $327 on all the airlines. Airlines needed a point of difference to attract customers, so stewardesses began wearing miniskirts and hotpants to appeal to the predominantly male business passenger. The airlines then tried to outdo each other by advertising the fact that they had 'the sexiest stewardesses'. They even went as far as to design skirts that would 'accidentally' ride up when the stewardesses reached up (there must have been a lot of, 'Excuse me, can you get my bag from the overhead locker?'). One airline, Braniff International Airways, went all out (so to speak), promoting an 'Air Strip' campaign. And yes, it was as bad as it sounds: stewardesses would change uniforms mid-flight.

Another way for airlines to distinguish themselves from the competition was the food and service. I found a menu from a 1974 first-class flight with Swiss Air, and on the menu were real turtle soup, imported Malossol caviar with melba toast, slices of foie gras de Strasbourg with pumpernickel, fresh cold lobster bellevue and roast pheasant en cocotte with Mascotte potatoes and leaf spinach salad. Passengers often adjourned to separate dining rooms, with accompanying piano bar, and tables were set with crisp linens and fine silverware (back when we could be trusted with cutlery).

That same sort of luxury has only recently returned to the skies. Some airlines have gone so far as to model their first-class section as suites. After I returned from this trip, I was lucky enough – as in incredibly lucky enough – to get an upgrade to international business (V Australia's version of first class) from Melbourne to

Los Angeles (yes, I was on my way to visit Beth) and, besides hostesses in miniskirts, it was just as salubriously opulent as first-class air travel was in the '70s. I was welcomed aboard with a splash of 2003 Vintage Moët in sparkling Riedel glassware, which magically appeared the second that I was seated among the rest of the plum passengers who were all mostly in suits. (I was dressed up: I had jeans on instead of shorts.) Without trying to make you too jealous, my plushy and pampered flight included a totally flat bed with a big fluffy doona, complimentary Bulgari pyjamas, noise-cancelling headsets and a Bulgari 'amenity kit' that included the best quality amenities that I'd ever owned. The meals were 'created' by Australian celebrity chef Luke Mangan (although there was no real turtle soup or pumpernickel on the menu) and it was served on beautiful Narumi china. There was a 'bar in the sky'. There was even a limousine pick-up from my house.

Business class on Lao Airlines wasn't quite up to that standard – although I was given an 'Invocation Card'. I wasn't quite sure what 'invocation' actually meant (I had to look it up in the dictionary when I got home: it's the 'act of invoking or calling upon a deity, spirit, etc., for aid, protection and inspiration'), but I figured it had something to do with praying, which perhaps wasn't a good sign. On the card were Islam, Protestant, Catholic, Hindu and Buddhist prayers. The Islamic prayer asked to 'seek the help of Allah, the most Gracious, the Most Merciful, who has bestowed upon us the will and ability to use this aircraft', while the Catholic prayer begged the Holy Spirit for 'a safe trip with good weather and bless us with guidance from your angels, so that the crew of this aircraft will lead us to our destination safely'. The Protestants asked the Lord to 'accompany us on our journey', the Hindus asked to 'keep our minds and manners pure' and the Buddhists simply asked that 'may all beings be well and happy'.

The immigration officials at Vientiane Airport, on the other hand, weren't very happy and their manners were certainly not very pure. The dour-faced official grunted at me then tried to charge me more for the visa. Tony warned in the old guidebook that this would happen: 'If the border officials try to charge you for weekend overtime tell them to get lost. You already pay enough for a visa.' It was the weekend. And they were still charging for overtime. Except I wasn't about to tell the grunting and grumpy official to get lost – he had a very up-to-date, large gun. Mind you, if I was Canadian I'd definitely tell them to get lost. For some crazy reason, Canadians have to pay $42 for a visa. Just about every other country listed on the board paid only $25.

The old guidebook described Laos as a small, lightly populated landlocked country, torn by internal conflicts almost continually since World War II but which 'has finally found a semblance of peace'. That semblance of peace lasted only a few months after the original guidebook came out. In 1975, with the war in Vietnam finally over, the Communist Pathet Lao stormed into power and, in the process, ended the 600-year-old monarchy. Laos became a tourist no-go zone and the country was dropped from the *South east Asia on a shoestring* guidebook after the first edition and didn't make a reappearance until 18 years later in the seventh edition.

Back in 1975, however, Laos was well rated in the old book. In the Rated Features list, Laos won accolades for the Touchiest Photographic Subjects in South-East Asia (the Pathet Lao army); the Classiest Food (Le Paix Restaurant in Vientiane); the Nicest Airline Flight (from Luang Prabang to Ban Houei Sai); and the Craziest Currency. In fact, Tony described Laotian money as 'kind of a joke' and advised: 'Never change more than $US 20 at a time unless you have very big pockets – $US20 in Laotian bank notes is one hell of a thick wad.' The biggest banknote then was 1000 kip. That wouldn't even buy you a packet of chewing gum today. At the time of my trip, the exchange rate was 7000 kip to the dollar and the largest note was 100,000 kip. I got a big wad of cash out of the ATM at the airport (travelling, and life in general, is so much easier with ATMs).

There were three places listed to stay in the old guidebook and I got three definite nos from the taxi driver when I asked if they were still around. 'I take you to a good guesthouse,' he said. It was only a short drive into town from the airport through spookily quiet, sleepy streets until we turned off into a street that was filled with guesthouses. Sitting out the front of the guesthouses was a bevy of backpackers 'lazing around' and 'enjoying themselves', just as Tony had described. And drinking lots of beer, which I suppose is the same thing. 'This place is best for you,' my driver said, as we stopped in front of one of the guesthouses. 'I wait here.' Yeah, so he could go in after I check in to pick up his commission. I jumped out and walked into the guesthouse next door. The taxi driver started waving frantically at me to go back to his one. He wasn't happy at all.

I had to trudge up five floors of hot, sweaty stairs, so I was desperate for a shower when I got to my room. The old guidebook had warned:

> Beware the Laotian Sink. You may have grown accustomed to sinks where the drainpipe dumps the water straight on the floor – usually on your feet. Well in Laos they have a refinement on this – no drainpipe at all. The water pours straight out of the bottom of the sink and down your legs.

The shower sprayed water all over the bathroom – so much so, in fact, that I had to take the toilet paper out of the room. But when I cleaned my teeth, thankfully my feet stayed nice and dry.

*

'The food budget tends to get thrown out the window in Laos,' the old guidebook noted. 'Not because it's more expensive, but can you resist the call for breakfast time croissants?' Tony suggested starting the day at Bouen Khaam for 'croissants and marmalade, naturally'. Or you could start your day with a natural massage: Bouen Khaam was now Champa Spa – For Natural Body and Soul Massage. The Scandinavian Bakery was across the road, so I had my croissants and marmalade there, instead.

I spent most of the morning wandering the dusty streets of Vientiane in search of the three hotels listed in the old guidebook (I had a sneaking suspicion that my taxi driver from the airport claimed they weren't there anymore because he wanted his commission). The French-influenced tree-lined boulevards were quiet and relaxed. Even the tuk tuk drivers were relaxed – some had hammocks strung up inside their vehicles. One driver politely called out to ask if I wanted a ride, and when I said, 'No, thanks,' he looked relieved because it saved him the effort of rousing himself from his stupor.

The first hotel recommended in the old guidebook was Samboun Inthavong, which was described as a 'vast rambling, decrepit, dirty, derelict rabbit warren in the final stages of complete collapse'. Not the best write-up, but they did add: 'It's also very central and has bags of character.' I discovered the hotel had completely collapsed a long time ago and had been replaced with a modern glass building, which housed the customer service centre for Lao Telecom.

Next on the list was the Vieng Vilay Hotel, but I couldn't find it. I asked a tuk tuk driver who pointed directly across the road. The building looked like a vast, rambling, decrepit, dirty, derelict rabbit warren in the final stages of complete collapse. 'Lao people live there,' he said. 'No good for tourists, so government closed.'

I was just about to walk off when he leant in and whispered, 'Do you want some marijuana or some opium?' It could have been 1974: he was the third person that day to ask me if I wanted to buy marijuana or opium.

'No, thanks,' I said to my new friend. 'I'm okay for opium at the moment.'

'You want nice girl? Boom, boom.'

I asked him if they used dynamite to make the nice girls go boom, boom.

It turned out the taxi driver from the night before was right. The last hotel listed in the book was now an internet cafe: 'Come in and Burn CDs and Download music,' the sign read. They also hired out bicycles, so I picked up one for the rest of the day. And the hire cost was only one dollar more than it was in 1974.

I'd had no luck finding any of the old hotels, but maybe I'd have better luck with the restaurants. There really must not have been much to see in Laos back in '74 because Tony wrote: 'French food, if not the only, is certainly one of the good reasons for visiting Laos.' Top of the list was Le Paix Restaurant, which had the Classiest

Food in South-East Asia. Finding addresses in Vientiane wasn't easy. I couldn't locate the street because quite a few of the street names had been changed since 1974. I found the right address eventually, after asking half the population of Vientiane, but sadly Le Paix wasn't there anymore. It was now the Classiest High Speed Internet Cafe in South-East Asia.

The other French restaurant recommended was La Bonne Fourchette in Place Nam Phoo. I asked pretty much everyone in the square, but no one knew where the restaurant was or even where it used to be. There was another French restaurant in the square, so perhaps it had changed names. I asked the manager at Le Provençal, but he wasn't even sure how long his own restaurant had been there.

I wasn't having much luck in Vientiane. I thought that Laos would be one place that wouldn't have changed much since 1974, but I'd found absolutely nothing so far. I asked one of the dozing tuk tuk drivers if he knew of an old, classy French restaurant and he reluctantly told me to hop in. 'I take you,' he sighed.

Le Vendôme looked suitably old with a wide enclosed verandah and faded wooden shutters on the windows. It was also suitably French with Edith Piaf playing and French chablis by the glass. I ordered the very classy chateaubriand avec pommes frites (for under three dollars), and then asked the waitress if the restaurant was old. 'Yes, it is *very* old,' she said.

'When did it open?'

'Oh, it opened in 1985.'

I had better luck with the 'Sights' section of the book. At least the city's most famous and revered wat hadn't been torn down and turned into an internet cafe. The massive gilded stupa of Pha That Luang is the most important national monument in Laos and the gleaming gold monument was accordingly impressive. While I was admiring the sacrosanct stupa, a solemn-looking monk in bright orange robes shuffled past listening to his iPod. And by the thumping noise and the way he was nodding his head, my guess was that he was listening to Metallica.

Next up was the Monument aux Morts (or the Monument to the Dead), but no one had heard of it. After following the map, I did eventually find it and realised that no one knew what it was because its name had changed in 1975 to Patuxai. The old guidebook described the monument as a 'bizarre baroque Arc de Triomphe', and it was indeed quite a pimped-up pastiche of the Arc de Triomphe (and yet, ironically, it is dedicated to those who fought for independence from France). And like the Arc de Triomphe, the monument sat in the middle of a traffic circle – but without the traffic and leading nowhere in particular.

I spent the rest of the afternoon riding along a dirt road by the banks of the mighty Mekong River, except that it wasn't that mighty: it was at the end of the dry season and the wide river was down to a trickle. The sun was low and the whole city seemed to be congregating down by the river: couples and families were strolling along the banks while teenagers played soccer in the sand and old men fished on the shore. After clambering down the bank and dipping my toes into the Mekong, I went to visit a bomb museum.

The Mine Advisory Group (MAG) Visitors Centre was in the middle of a row of family homes right on the waterfront. MAG had been clearing landmines in Laos since 1994 and inside the small museum were displays of landmines and a whole bunch of frightening facts. One of the most frightening of these was that Laos is the most heavily bombed nation in the world per capita. This was because between 1964 and 1973, more than two tonnes of bombs were dumped on Laos and, worst of all, about a third of those did not detonate. Today the country is still full of unexploded landmines and people are still being killed and injured more than 30 years later.

After that rather sombre respite, I decided to stop for a stiff drink. The old guidebook recommended trying one of the open-air places beside the Mekong to catch the sunset. I picked the appropriately named Sala Sunset Bar, which was a rustic wooden platform made of old boat timbers hanging precariously over the river's edge, and had a very cheap and tasty meal and a couple of Beerlaos as the sun dropped into the Mekong. I asked the manager how long the bar had been open. 'We are the oldest bar on the river,' he said. 'We have been here for almost ten years.' It was the oldest bar on the river because it was the only bar to survive the government's riverfront-bar demolition program two years before.

After returning my bike (or more like leaving it out the front of the shop because it was closed), I was propositioned by a very tall woman with muscular arms and a deep voice. Even in the dim light, I could tell that she was a he. 'You want some fun?' he/she said. Back in the early '70s, the debauchery in Vientiane bars was celebrated throughout South-East Asia. Catering for servicemen on furlough, the city was full of whores, sex shows and naked waitresses. Paul Theroux, who travelled through Vientiane in 1973, described the city in *The Great Railway Bazaar* as 'the most corrupt and dissolute place' he'd ever travelled to. 'Drugs were easy to buy and so was porno.'

I stopped for a nightcap at one of the happening nightspots in town where there was definitely no debauchery going on. Well, none at that moment at least because the bar was totally empty and the barman was asleep at one of the tables. On the way back to the guesthouse, another lady-man propositioned me, but I couldn't help laughing because he had a beard. I later read in the current *Southeast Asia on a Shoestring* that you must: 'Smile and keep walking, but in no event laugh; last year a man was admitted to hospital after being attacked with a handbag.'

15

Luang Prabang

In Luang Prabang market you can buy pre-rolled
joints from the tobacco stalls.
South east Asia on a shoestring, 1st edition, 1975

In Luang Prabang possession of a joint may cost you
$US500 in fines.
Southeast Asia on a Shoestring, 15th edition, 2010

'Although the Pathet Lao no longer shoot up buses the
occasional bandits still do,' the old guidebook warned.
In another guidebook from the same era, *Student Guide to
Asia*, author David Jenkins warned that: 'the Royal Road,
which links Vientianne and Luang Prabang is NOT safe'.
He described an ambush that took place north of Kasin in
July 1974, in which an elderly Australian couple and two
locals were killed when bandits opened fire on their bus.
'You may get through unscathed if you travel down this
mountain road by bus, but make no mistake you will be
playing Russian roulette if you try,' he wrote.

Just in case the bandits were feeling particularly trigger-happy, I decided to fly to Luang Prabang instead. And to tell you the truth, I quite liked the idea of a 40-minute flight compared to nine hours in a bumpy bus.

I fell in love with Luang Prabang the minute I walked out of the airport. No one hassled me at all and I had to approach a tuk tuk driver to take me into town. And my driver even knew the first hotel listed in the book. The Gold River Villa was described in the old guidebook as the nicest place to stay and 'very pleasant'.

It was very pleasant indeed, and I was shown to a neat and clean room with teak floors and a private balcony overlooking the Nam Khan River. I was feeling quite chuffed with myself until I asked the lady at reception when the guesthouse rooms were built. 'They were built in 1999,' she said.

'Oh, do you have any older rooms?'

'Um, yes, but they are not very nice.'

'Can I see one?'

The room was small and cramped with no windows and looked as if it hadn't been used for a while. I thanked the lady and told her that I was happy to stick with my updated room with a view.

On the way out for a walk, I took a photo of the sign on the front fence that read: 'Welcome to all good people at the Cold River Inn.' Wait a minute, I thought. Cold River Inn? I checked the old book and there it was – the Gold River Inn. Had Tony smoked too many joints and got the name wrong – or was the signwriter smoking opium when he painted the sign? I marched back to reception and asked about the discrepancy and the lady just shrugged. She told me that she wasn't even born in 1974. That's the problem with Laos: no one is over 30.

Luang Prabang was described in the old guidebook as a quiet backwater of a town. It wasn't quite a quiet backwater town anymore. The UNESCO-protected World Heritage city, which is regarded as the best preserved colonial town in former Indochina, is now one of the compulsory stops on the Banana Pancake Trail. The cobbled tree-lined streets of Luang Prabang, where French colonial architecture coexists with the gilded and teak points of traditional Laotian buildings, were jam-packed with snap-happy tourists.

The first thing on my agenda was to check out the other three hotels listed in the book. (I must admit it was becoming a bit of an obsession to see what was still there.) Without boring you with names, one was a fancy gym, another a spa and relaxation centre and the third had been torn down and turned into an upmarket housing estate.

I really wasn't having much luck in Laos at all. And finding a restaurant from the old book turned out to be just as difficult. I tried Pakhane first, which served up 'French and Vietnamese food in a very attractive riverside setting'. The first local person I asked said, 'Yes, I know Pakhane,' and pointed down the road along the river. I walked the entire length and couldn't find it, so I asked someone else. 'Yes, it's that way,' she said, pointing in the direction from which I'd just come. I trudged back up the road, but I still couldn't see it. I asked again and was directed back the same way again. What the . . .? When the next person said, 'Yes, of course it is here,' I made them escort me to the actual restaurant. 'There it is!' he said.

No wonder I couldn't find it. Pakhane was Wat Pakhane. It was a temple.

The next restaurant on the list was a bit further out, so I jumped on the back of a motorcycle taxi. In the old book, Tony noted that 'all the riders look like Marlon Brando in the *Wild One*, cap over the eyes and sultry looks'. Mine looked more like Eminem with the whole gangster rap look going on. 'Nice bling,' I said as I jumped on the back.

We tried two of the places that were listed in the book and were both gone, or at least I think they were gone: the map had no street names and the restaurants listed in the book had no street numbers. My last chance was the Phousi Bungalows, although it was a 'more expensive option'. The Phousi Bungalows was still there, but they'd gone for the more expensive option and changed the name to the Phousi Hotel. I asked at reception when the hotel was built. 'It was built in 1988,' the fellow said.

'Where are the Phousi Bungalows?' I asked.

'They were torn down to build this,' he answered with a big smile.

My shoulders slumped. 'What about the restaurant?'

'The restaurant in the hotel is new, but the outdoor restaurant is still the same.'

Bingo. The Beer Garden Bar B-Q Terrace was in a pleasant spot underneath the shade of an enormous tamarind tree. The restaurant was empty – as in no customers, waiting staff or bar staff in the grass hut bar. I sat down at a table for 15 minutes then got up and returned to reception. No one was manning the desk, but there were a couple of guys, who looked suspiciously like waiters, asleep in big comfy chairs. When I woke one of them up, he seemed quite surprised. 'Can I get a menu?' I asked.

He rubbed his eyes like a little baby. 'Yes,' he huffed.

I went back to my table and waited another ten minutes. When I stormed back into the lobby, he had gone, but the other waiter was still slumped in the chair fast asleep. 'I'm not a waiter,' he said when I woke him up from his slumber. 'Wait here. I get a waiter for you.' I stood at the reception desk for another ten minutes and no one showed. I was now getting very hungry and very grumpy. Sod this, I thought. I turned around and walked out – but not before leaving a note at reception: 'I'll have the fried chicken and rice. I'll be back in 15 minutes.'

I had a delicious lemongrass chicken at a restaurant in town that was open and had waiting staff that were awake.

Afterwards, I walked off my lunch with a steep climb to the top of Phousi Hill, because the old guidebook said that I should. From the summit, I was afforded sweeping views across the encircling forest-covered mountains, the snaking Mekong and Nam Khan rivers, golden temple roofs that rose above flowering trees and a bird's-eye view of the Royal Palace and its gardens. The Royal Palace was listed in the old book, but Tony noted that, 'You can't go in, so the view from the top is the best you will get.' From my lofty height, I could see that the palace grounds were full of tourists – unless the royal family wears Hawaiian shirts and baseball caps and likes taking hundreds of photos of each other posing in front of their front door.

The palace was built in 1904 as a residence for King Sisavangvong and his family. When the king died in 1959, his son Savang Vattana (or his official, and somewhat long-winded, full name of Samdach Brhat Chao Mavattaha Sri Vitha Lan Xang Hom Khao Phra Rajanachakra Lao Parama Sidha Khattiya Suriya Varman Brhat Maha Sri Savangsa Vadhana) inherited the throne. He no longer resided in the palace, because not long after the guidebook came out in 1975 the royal family was exiled by the Pathet Lao to northern Laos and imprisoned in caves. The palace was then converted into a national museum.

Now you can wander around their private rooms, including nosing about in the king and queen's bedrooms which had been preserved as they were in 1975 when the royals departed. They had separate bedrooms with a door connecting the rooms in case the king wanted a bit of rumpy-pumpy in the night. Underneath the queen's bed was a very nice porcelain potty. I bet she didn't get a potty under her bed in the cave.

I perused the restaurants in the charming main street for dinner and stopped in front of Yongkhoune Restaurant. A sign by the entrance read: 'Since 1960 – Yongkhoune is the oldest family restaurant in Luang Prabang.' The restaurant wasn't in the old guidebook, but it was old enough to be. I grabbed a table on the footpath and had a tasty dish of chicken with basil and chilli and sticky rice and watched the large groups of German and French package tourists wandering down the street behind their tour leaders like camera-happy rats following the Pied Piper.

My waiter told me that he was the longest serving staff member. 'I've been here three years!' he said. He was 19.

'Is the owner here?' I asked.

The owner's name was Aiy. He was 32 and wasn't even born when the original guidebook hit the shelves.

After dinner, I moseyed on down to the night market where Tony promised that you could buy 'pre-rolled joints from the tobacco stalls'. Now you could buy novelty T-shirts, mulberry-leaf paper, tribal jewellery, embroidered quilts and lots of stuffed cats (not real cats, I should add). It was possibly the neatest and most organised market I'd ever seen.

I stopped for a drink on the way back to the guesthouse at the very modern and hip Hive Bar and procured a stool at the bar – the solo traveller's favourite spot. Another solo traveller was also sitting at the bar. His name was Charlie and he was from Ireland. 'I was travellin' with me mate and his girlfriend, but I couldn't foockin' stand it,' he told me. 'So I left them in Ko Samui.'

Another solo traveller, a New Zealander, joined us. 'Welcome to the Lonely Solo Travellers' Club,' Charlie said, reaching for his hand. Ten minutes later, we had five members – with the addition of a Finn and a Dutchman (it's very international, this club). At our first meeting of the Lonely Solo Travellers' Club, we sat around drinking beer and talking about where we'd been, where we were heading to and the cheapest country to drink beer in.

Charlie had just come from Vang Vieng (which the old book devoted all of nine words to: 'Vang Vieng is a nice rest and relax place'). According to the current *Southeast Asia on a Shoestring*, it is as if 'a section of Bang-kok's Khao San Road . . . has been transplanted to this once sleepy retreat'. And according to Charlie, Vang Vieng was 'fookin' mental' and 'everyone gets fookin' blind drunk and has sex'. Although Charlie admitted that he did so well on the blind-drunk part, that he wasn't capable of having sex.

I woke up with my first real hangover since Kuta and was in desperate need of a banana pancake. I had to get up early, too, because I was going on a boat trip up the Mekong River. The old guidebook recommended that the one trip definitely to make from Luang Prabang was the 30-kilometre upriver jaunt to the Pak Ou Caves. The book also advised that 'both travel agencies' could sell you a boat tour. I passed 20 or so travel agents before I even got to the river.

I booked a 'Cave and Waterfall Tour' and joined the throng of tourists waiting at a boat ramp on the bank of the Mekong. It was all very efficient and we were each given a ticket with a number on it, like a queue for a deli, and a well-dressed lady with a megaphone called a series of numbers as each of the long, narrow brightly painted boats was ready. There were only six in our boat: an American girl, Carly, and a family from Thailand. (Thais make up more than 50 per cent of tourists to Laos, I later read.)

Carly was what I dubbed a JAB (Jet-About Backpacker). JABs plan their itineraries around must-see spots then fly between them all without catching a single bus or train. This was certainly a noticeable shift from travellers in the 1970s who tended to use surface transport, and the odd ferry, within the region. The main backpacker routes in South-East Asia had clearly evolved since then. Backpackers now have the luxury (but without the actual luxury) of using low-cost carriers such as Air Asia and Tiger to hop, skip and jump around. I was one of them. Why pay $20 for a ten-hour bus ride when you can fly there for $25, or sometimes even less?

Carly was one of the new breed of 'flashpackers'

who took that to the extreme. She had flown into Hanoi, hopped across to Siem Riep in Cambodia, skipped on over to Luang Prabang and was then jumping over to Bangkok and Phuket. She was spending a few days in each place then flying home to America. And she didn't have a guidebook: she just downloaded the Lonely Planet city guides onto her iPhone. (Incidentally, Lonely Planet mobile apps have been downloaded more than 8.5 million times in the first two years since they launched in 2008.)

She was also staying in 'nice' guesthouses. The flashpacker market is now huge and many destinations are targeting these cashed-up backpackers. They like to think that they are doing it 'on the cheap', but they prefer to splurge on clean, comfortable accommodation and good food. Not far from where I live in Melbourne there is a Base Backpackers Hostel (they are all over Australia), which promotes itself as being 'specially designed for you, the modern day global travellers, with state of the art facilities, superior comfort and friendly services'. These flashpacker hostels come with clean rooms, made-up beds, bars and restaurants. There are no 27-bed dorm rooms and there are definitely no stained sheets and ants around the hole-in-the-ground toilet.

The boat was a bit of a comedown for Carly. There was no in-flight service or TV screens on the back of the seats. Mind you, we didn't need TVs: we were treated to a perfectly photogenic moving picture show of lush jungle, tiny wooden villages, smiling locals splashing in the shallows – and even a smiling elephant splashing in the shallows. In '74, it wasn't quite as tranquil. Tony told me back in Bali that when you got a boat, you didn't ask what time the boat was leaving or how much it cost; instead you asked, 'Is it safe?' Most of the time it wasn't safe, he explained. 'Travellers were getting killed. And there was a pretty good chance that bandits or communist insurgents would take a shot at you.'

As our boat motored gently upriver, the only people taking shots were the German package tourists snapping hundreds of photos in the boat next to us.

We passed a family doing their laundry on the river's edge and everyone, including me, took a photo. Which really isn't very nice when you think about it – imagine people coming into your home to take photos while you're sorting through your smalls.

The river tour was similar to the one described in the old guidebook: we also stopped at a 'rustic' village for some 'local firewater whiskey'. Except that the first local firewater whiskey stall that we came to after getting off the boat was now sponsored by 'Pop Skincare – We enhance the loveliness of women'. The small rustic house behind it had a big advertising banner hanging over the door. Most houses had tables out the front selling something: most often, silk scarves, wooden elephants and lots of local firewater whiskey. I passed on the firewater. Besides the fact that it was ten in the morning, most of the bottles of firewater whiskey also contained snakes, lizards and scary-looking black scorpions.

After two hours of cruising up the river, we docked at the base of a sheer limestone cliff where steep steps led up to the Pak Ou Caves that were punched into the side of the cliff like the aftermath of a bomb blast. There was only one other small boat docked and a gaggle of tourists were halfway up the steps at a booth paying the entrance fee. There was no mention of an entrance fee in the old book, nor did it warn you to look out for kids trying to sell you birds and moles. Loitering on the steps were young local children – as in very young, maybe five or six years old – selling tiny birds in even tinier thatched cages. 'Free the bird. Buy it, free the bird, good,' they chorused. 'One dollar to set them free.' Older kids, of perhaps seven or eight, had squirming moles, hanging upside down with string tied around their hind legs, around their necks. 'For you, mister, two dollars to set him free,' a bedraggled girl begged. I felt so sorry for the mole, but I knew that if I set it free the kids would undoubtedly just catch it and tie it up again.

While I was standing in the main cave, which was filled with rows of wooden Buddhas, a swarm of German tourists swarmed in. I looked down to the river and a massive boat, four times bigger than ours, had docked with another two equally as large pulling in behind it. I had to fight my way through the crowd to get to the cave further up the cliff face. The old guidebook noted that your guide will supply candles, so you can explore the cave. Our guide was having a nap in the boat, so the cave was dark. Well, until the army of German tourists all turned up with torches. Then it was lit up like the Griswolds' house at Christmas.

When we got back to Luang Prabang, the Thai family left and Carly and I were taken to the tour office to wait for the minibus for the afternoon trip to Kuang Si Falls. While we waited, we were given lunch – a humungous baguette filled with cucumber, tomato and some sort of meat with grey, sludgy bits in it. I told Carly that it's always best not to ask.

The falls weren't in the old book, but they were certainly popular now: the car park was full of mini-vans, buses and tuk tuks. To get to the main falls, you had to trek up a steep hillside through thick jungle, past a multitude of multi-tiered waterfalls tumbling over limestone formations into turquoise-green swimming holes. The swimming holes weren't too crowded, but that was because there was a legion of Japanese tourists in nice slacks and sensible shoes, not swimming, but taking hundreds of photos of people swimming. They were quite sensible, actually – the water was ice-cold.

On the way back, our tour included a stop at a 'local' village, but I told everyone on the bus that it would be full of tourist shops, so we talked the driver into giving it a miss. One of the great things about back-packing is that it is so easy to make instant friends. The seven of us from the bus trip all decided to meet up for dinner. It was a very international group, too. There was an Australian, an American, a Belgian, a Canadian, a Dane, a Dutchman and a fellow who said, 'I'm from Hawaii, which I suppose is sort of part of America.'

We all met up at Lao Lao Garden Restaurant, which is recommended by Lonely Planet. I knew that because there was a huge sign out front that read: 'It's about as much fun as dinner gets – Lonely Planet Laos 2007.' Admittedly it was a stunning setting inside with the tables set up in a terraced, candlelit garden with exotic lanterns strung up in trees. Talk about Lonely Planet influencing where people stay and eat. The Lao Lao Garden Restaurant was positively heaving with back- packers. I witnessed the opposite effect, of not being in Lonely Planet, in Hue, Vietnam when I went out for dinner with a bunch of backpackers whom I met on a boat cruise (which was, of course, recommended by Lonely Planet). We walked past a restaurant and I said, 'What about this place? It looks nice.' A girl in the group responded, 'No, it's not in Lonely Planet.'

Most of the Lao Lao Garden Restaurant menu was given over to their drink specials: two-for-one Lao Lao cocktails, Red Bull and vodka buckets and three big Beer Laos in an ice bucket for 30,000 kip. There were lots of buckets of beer going around and the waiters were handing out free shots of Loa Lao whiskey (minus the black scorpions). I even had a few – it was my last night in Laos, after all.

We all ordered the Lao-style barbecue because Lonely Planet told us to. Our barbecue was a domed metal hotplate, which was like a giant orange juicer with hot coals underneath. Shared between two people, each hotplate was accompanied by a basket of raw meat and vegetables. You start with a huge blob of pig fat then add thin slices of chicken, beef, pork and water buffalo. As the meat cooks, the juices drip down into the water at the base into which you add piles of fresh vegetables, garlic, chilli and coriander to make the best soup I have ever tasted. 'Why is this just so amazingly delicious?' Carly said.

Just as the patrons were all fired up, the restaurant closed (there is an 11.30 curfew in Laos). So what do you do in a small Laotian town late at night with a belly full of beer? Why go bowling, of course. We all jumped in tuk tuks and rode 15 minutes out of town to a bowling alley, which was chock-full of drunk backpackers. A local man approached me when we were dropped off and whispered, 'Do you want some opium?' I turned around and said loudly to the group, 'This kind gentleman has just offered to sell me some opium. Does anyone want any?' He slunk off rather quickly.

Inside the bowling alley, there was lots of drinking and lots of low scores going on. The Danish guy in our group didn't hit a single pin. I concluded there must not be many bowling alleys in Denmark. Although the four buckets of beer he'd drunk may have had something to do with it.

Laos

When I got back to the Cold River Inn, I had to climb over the fence, because they'd locked the gate. I then fell headfirst into the flowerbed. Although the two buckets of beer I'd drunk may have had something to do with that.

Burma

16

Rangoon

Locally made Burmese soft drinks are not very good.
South east Asia on a shoestring, 1st edition, 1975

Locally made Burmese soft drinks are good.
Southeast Asia on a Shoestring, 15th edition, 2010

'For the visitor Burma is a fascinating glimpse of a culturally unique country rapidly going off the rails,' the old guidebook noted. 'Only recently have foreigners been allowed once more to visit Burma and meet the very friendly, but currently very demoralized Burmese.' Burma had well and truly gone off the rails since 1974 and the Burmese today are still very much demoralised under the military dictatorship of Senior General Than Shwe. And I don't know if I'd still be friendly after almost 50 years of oppressive rule and poverty.

When the Wheelers first rolled into Burma, the country was under another maniacal general who stormed into power in 1962 after a military takeover. In the old guidebook, Tony commented:

> Ne Win set the country on the 'Burmese Way to Socialism'. A downhill path. Nationalising everything in sight, including retail shops, soon crippled the country and the Burmese saw their naturally well endowed economy stumbling as exports of everything plummeted.

Some things hadn't changed, however: 'Today Burmese exports are virtually nil, official exports that is, although there is still a thriving unofficial opium trade.' And still thriving – the nation is the world's second largest poppy producer, after Afghanistan.

The entire country looked on the brink of an uprising in late 1974. 'Riots gave the repressive government another hard shake,' Tony wrote, 'but can it take too many more?' Yes, it can, it seems. Not even famine, floods or international pressure and condemnation appears to sway them.

Lonely Planet gets quite a bit of condemnation itself for producing a Burma guidebook, with human rights groups urging foreigners not to visit, saying travel to Burma is unethical and helps prop up the military government. Lonely Planet argues that tourism remains one of the few industries which gives ordinary locals access to income and communication. In reality, the vast majority of a careful independent traveller's expenses will go into the locals' pockets. It's the package tourists who are throwing money into the government's coffers by using 'official' travel companies and staying in expensive hotels owned by the government.

And it's not like the tourists are flooding in, anyway. The queue for 'foreigner nationals' at Rangoon Airport had only ten people in it. The rest of the folks on the plane from Bangkok were Burmese nationals. I'd organised my visa for Burma with the Myanmar Embassy in Canberra before I left, but according to the old guidebook, back in '74 you could get a visa in Bangkok with 'same day service if you smile'. Although back then you could only get a 24-hour or a seven-day visa. I had the option of a four-day or a 28-day visa, so I got the 28-day visa even though I planned to stay for only a week and follow the same recommended seven-day itinerary in the old guidebook.

The airport had certainly been updated and it was modern, clean and efficient – even passport control was surprisingly prompt. In Bangkok, it took 40 minutes to get through immigration while at Rangoon Airport I was through in just four minutes. As I stepped into the arrivals hall, I noticed a large sign welcoming passengers to 'Rangoon Airport'. Make up your mind: Are you Rangoon or Yangon? As well as changing the name of the country in 1989 from Burma to Myanmar, the government also changed Rangoon to Yangon and Pagan to Bagan.

I knew that because I did do a little bit of research on Burma before I left. And I'm so glad that I did. One of the things that I checked was the money situation. I discovered that the country had no ATMs, no credit card facilities and nowhere to change traveller's cheques. It was US cash only for exchange. The old guidebook also noted that there were two exchange rates: an official rate and a black-market rate (the official rate was three times the black-market rate). It even went as far as to say that at the black-market rate of exchange Burma was one of the cheapest countries in South-East Asia, while at the official rate it was the most expensive – although it did warn that changing money on the black market was unwise.

I decided not to change money at the airport and instead paid for my taxi into town with US dollars. And I saved even more by employing an old trick that works in many airports around the world. I was quoted a price of ten dollars for a taxi at the terminal, eight dollars in the car park, seven dollars at the entrance and, by the time I got to the road out of the airport, the price had come down to five dollars. What got me more excited than saving a buck on a taxi fare, however, was that the YMCA was still open.

The government tried to hoodwink tourists into believing that the country was modern and progressive with a very nice, clean, modern airport and a kilometre of very nice, clean, modern roads – then suddenly revealing broken roads, broken buildings and rubbish piled everywhere. On the small strip of modern highway was a massive billboard in English, although I wasn't too sure what it actually meant: 'HAPPY WORLD – We create change for your happiness.' When we hit the road of ruin, the billboards were all in Burmese – which I have to say looked exactly like the language that aliens use in movies.

The oppressive heat, which sapped every bit of moisture from your body, was unbearable (it was so much hotter than Laos or Thailand) and it was even worse in the taxi which had no air conditioning. There was a lovely breeze coming up from the floor, however. That was because the floor was rusted through forming a gaping big hole, so you could see the road zooming by. There was something else odd about the car, but it took me a little while to figure out what it was. And then it dawned on me: even though the car, and most of the other cars on the road, was right-hand drive, everyone was driving on the right-hand side of the road.

Rangoon was described in the old guidebook as a city of wide streets and spacious architecture that looked run-down, worn out and thoroughly neglected. It was still the same – it just had another 35 years of soot and grime on top. The city was also described as having an air of seedy decay. There was more than just decayed air now: there were decayed cars, decayed roads, decayed buildings and downtrodden locals who looked like they'd rather be decayed.

The YMCA, which had a sprinkling of decay and a generous dollop of soot and grime, had 'fairly grubby rooms', according to the old guidebook – but it wasn't the grubbiness that bothered me. An entire floor of the Rangoon YMCA was now occupied by the Myanmar Christian Leprosy Mission. I was worried that if I stayed too long my body parts would start falling off.

The YMCA's reception, a bare concrete room, was up two flights of stairs. I arrived puffing and panting, and two smiling girls in nice grey uniforms greeted me – their uniforms used to be white, but they were now grey with age and covered in stains. Just like the walls. It's fun to stay at the YMCA, but it's a lot more fun with air conditioning. I paid two dollars extra for an air-conditioned room (for the total and princely sum of ten dollars).

One of the girls showed me to my room, which was one level up from the Myanmar Christian Leprosy Mission. I felt a twinge in my ear as I walked past. The corridor on my floor was dark and gloomy and it was hotter than the hinges of Hades. My room was even gloomier and it was so hot that you could roast a marsh-mallow on the windowsill. The room was basic with two old beds, torn lace curtains, a cold-water shower in a scarily stained bathroom and a wide-screen plasma TV with cable. Okay, I made that last bit up. I tried to turn the air conditioning on, but the girl told me that the power didn't come on until five o'clock. That was still more than two hours away.

I asked the girl where I could change some money – wink, wink. 'We can organise it for you,' she whispered. She told me that the exchange rate was 1200 kyats to the dollar. I was happy that I didn't change money at the airport: the official rate was 450 kyats to the dollar. 'You wait here and rest,' she said. I attempted to have a rest on the bed, but it was like lying in a sauna and I was drenched in sweat in only a few minutes. It would have been more than 40 degrees outside and at least 50 degrees in the room.

Fifteen minutes later, there was a knock at the door. I gave the girl $US100 and in return she handed me three massive wads of notes tied up in elastic bands. In 1974, the kyat was divided into pyas and 'a collection of confusing coins'. There were no longer pyas or coins, just bundles and bundles of notes.

I went out for an exploratory amble and as soon as I hit the street, I was struck by sensory overload. The footpaths were bustling with life – although it was hard to see all that life because I was too busy watching the footpath that was broken up and full of gaping holes revealing sewerage drains. Most of the footpath was taken up with makeshift stalls with vendors selling second-hand books (or more like eighth-hand), tatty clothes, badly made shoes and one-dollar T-shirts (but not a single novelty T-shirt in sight). One old man had a stall piled high with an impressive collection of rusty spanners. Entrepreneurial locals in business shirts had set up tables and were writing on envelopes in nice handwriting or typing letters on typewriters that were older than the guidebook I was carrying. The locals were a mix of Burmese, Muslims and Indians, but I didn't see a single foreign tourist. Most of the locals – whether they were young or old, rich or poor, or male or female – were wearing *longyis,* which were like sarongs that were knotted at the waist. Many of the women had thick yellow paint smeared all over their cheeks.

People were also eating on the street, with an eclectic assortment of food on sale, including oranges and mangoes, sad-looking donuts, raw meat covered in flies (and remember it was about 40 degrees) and indefinable parts of animals on sticks that were being cooked in pots like Capital Satay in Malacca – although this wasn't satay; it was a scary-looking black oil. And on every corner was a teashop with adults squeezed into children's plastic furniture.

Above all the nattering and hollering from the stallholders was the constant noise of trucks, buses, cars and scooters – and pretty much all of them with loud clapped-out engines. And over the engine noise mini-van drivers were screaming out at the top of their lungs for more passengers to fill buses that were already overflowing. There was also the constant drone of huge generators on the street that filled the air with the pungent smell of fuel – as there was no electricity until five o'clock, this was the only way that shops and buildings could supplement the fickle power supply.

This was one place that sadly really hadn't changed since 1974 (except the street vendors now also sold pirated DVDs and mobile phones).

In the middle of all this chaos, I suddenly, and quite surprisingly, stumbled across a brightly lit, air-conditioned and well-stocked supermarket. (They must have had a damn good generator.) The old guide-book noted that Burma was 'one of the least western influenced countries in the non-communist world – there aren't many countries where you can't get a Coke these days'. In the supermarket, however, there was an entire aisle devoted to Coke, Sprite, Fanta, Pepsi and 7-Up. And for a third of the price of those well-known brands, there were Burma's own brands, including Fantastic, which looked very much like Fanta, and Star Cola, which advertised itself as 'Fresh and floating . . . it's like flying'.

Back out on the street, I noticed the buildings for the first time. Almost hidden behind this shambling streetscape were the colonial buildings (the British ruled Burma until 1948) that were in such a sad state of disrepair, they were being preserved simply because they were being ignored.

I headed towards Sule Pagoda, a religious site more than 2000 years old. According to the old guidebook, it 'is right in the centre of town'. And it was: it was right in the centre of the town's busiest roundabout. The whole city may have been falling apart, but no expense was spared with the upkeep of the pagoda as the slanting late-afternoon sun illuminated the enormous, perfectly gilded stupa. I made my way up to a walkway that spanned the main road to take some photos and as I was clicking away, a petite girl with a big smile said hello. May Oo was a 21-year-old student who was studying English at Dagon University.

'Are you Christian?' May Oo asked.

'Um, yes,' I said. (I'm actually a very lapsed Catholic who doesn't believe in God, but technically, yes.)

'You must come to church with me on Sunday.'

'Oh, I'm sorry; I won't be here,' I said, trying not to sound too happy. 'Are there many Christians in Burma?'

'Some,' May Oo said.

May Oo then told me that her parents were Buddhist and that they were not happy when she 'turned to being a Christian'.

'Why did you become a Christian?' I asked.

May Oo smiled. 'Other religions are too noisy.'

I asked May Oo about the yellow paint on the women's cheeks. 'Is it a religious thing?' I asked.

'No, it is for beauty,' May Oo said.

I later read that it is called *thanaka* and not only does it give a cooling sensation and provide protection from sunburn, it is also believed to help remove acne and promote smooth skin.

I continued up the main street and May Oo tagged along as we strolled past side streets full of barbecue grills cooking lots of food on sticks. The old guidebook recommended the side streets where 'numerous bbq food stalls can be found, some of very dubious cleanliness'.

'Are you hungry?' I asked May Oo.

At least a local would know where to eat with passable cleanliness.

We sauntered down one of the side streets and the first barbecue food stall we came to was grilling graphic, sliced-up pigs' parts. We passed on those and sat down at another stall with sticks of chicken, beef, potatoes, mushrooms and something that resembled a penis (although I was assured that it was pork) on display. With the help of May Oo, I picked out a selection of things on sticks and grabbed a cold Mandalay beer – which back in '74 was 'generally out of stock since the "Peoples Beer Brewery" can't match production to demand'.

The food was tasty and of passable cleanliness and all up, including my beer, it came to under three dollars. As I was finishing my beer, a man wandered past carrying a large plastic bowl full of grasshoppers. As in cooked grasshoppers. Tony wrote: 'You will probably see some less appetizing Burmese cuisine. A popular favourite are crunchy grasshopper kebabs. Give them a try if you dare.'

'Are they nice?' I asked May Oo.

'Yes, very good. You must try.'

May Oo called the grasshopper seller over and he gave me one to try. It was burnt to a cinder and its little eyes were staring at me. I shoved the whole thing in my mouth and bit into it. It was dry and crunchy. Except for the gooey and slimy bit in the middle.

'Mmm, nice,' I said, being polite.

May Oo said something in Burmese to the grass-hopper seller and she handed him some money. He then filled a tin with blackened roasted grasshoppers. 'These are for you,' May Oo said with a sweet smile. I felt guilty because May Oo obviously didn't have a lot of money, so I ate them slowly, one at a time, wishing desperately that I hadn't finished my beer. I couldn't eat the last two, though. They were burnt to a crisp and their heads had exploded.

May Oo offered to walk me down to the Rangoon River to watch the sunset. We made our way down Pansodan Street, which was like walking down Pall Mall in London after an apocalypse. I marvelled at the massive Victorian buildings with their long colon-nades, tall windows and balconies – and all crumbling apart. When we got to the river, a huge orange sun was dropping into the water. It would have been idyllic, if not for all the rubbish piled on the banks of the river. As we walked along the shore, May Oo said, 'Don't fall in. You will get very sick.'

Overlooking the river was a very grand colonial building that wasn't crumbling apart and even had paint on the walls. It was the Strand Hotel. The old book noted that the bar at The Strand, 'is a good place to drink up those last night kyats'. It was only my first night in Burma, but the air-conditioned bar looked too inviting. Built in 1901 by the Sarkies Brothers (of Raffles Hotel in Singapore fame), The Strand was one of the most luxurious hotels in the British Empire. After Burma achieved independence in 1948, postcolonial governments neglected the hotel and it wasn't until 1989, when the hotel was sold to Burmese businessman Bernard Pe Win, that renovations took place. The Strand reopened in 1995 as an upmarket boutique hotel.

The doorman, in his immaculate frock coat and white gloves, welcomed us into the spruced-up hotel lobby with teak and marble floors, high ceilings and large comfy mahogany chairs. Tony Wheeler told me that when he and Maureen stayed at The Strand in 1974, the hotel was very run-down. They would sit in the lobby drinking beer when the bar closed and watch all the rats leaping around the furniture and occasionally across their laps.

The bar, which was rat-free, looked like it belonged in the era of pith helmets and tweed jackets. The only other patrons were two old fellows who wouldn't have looked out of place in tweed jackets. We sat on rattan chairs around a teak table and I almost fell off my chair when I saw the prices on the drinks menu. A bottle of Mandalay beer was four US dollars – eight times the price for exactly the same beer I had at dinner – and they didn't have grasshoppers on the bar snack menu. Luckily for my wallet, however, it was a Friday night and all drinks were half-price.

As I sipped my not-quite-as-expensive-as-I-first-thought-but-still-too-expensive beer, May Oo told me about the cyclone that struck Burma in May 2008, which left over 150,000 people dead. 'My dad tied us four children together to the furniture and our whole house was shaking and the roof flew off,' May Oo said. 'Rain was pouring in all night and we had no sleep, just got rained on.' And this was in Rangoon. The countryside was worst hit. 'Many rice crops were destroyed and a cup of rice went up from 100 to 400 kyat,' May Oo said. 'People couldn't eat and many were starving. The US, Australia, Germany and Thailand gave rice, but not enough.' At least they gave rice. May Oo told me that Malaysia gave headache tablets, because 'if you give them to children they stop the hunger'.

When I stood to go to the bar for another beer, May Oo told me that she was worried that I was going to 'go crazy drunk' after my three beers. 'My brother has two drinks and he goes crazy drunk,' she explained. At the bar, I chatted to the amiable and talkative barman who told me that when the Japanese occupied the hotel during the war, they converted the bar into stables for their horses. When I asked him if the bar was always empty, he nodded. 'The occupancy of the hotel is normally only ten per cent,' he explained. 'We have many tour groups who visit and have tea, but they do not stay,' he lamented. I wondered if the published rates for the various types of suites might be a factor. Superior Suites went for $US550 a night, Deluxe Suites were $630 a night, and the hotel's special suite, The Strand Suite, cost $1100 per night. That's more than a schoolteacher in Burma earns in a year.

After I finished my beer, I offered to walk May Oo to the bus station. 'No, I'm not drunk,' I told her when she asked if I could walk. On the way, we passed a sign to the train station and I told May Oo that I was planning on catching the overnight train to Mandalay. 'You be very careful,' she said. 'You will be robbed.'

I dropped May Oo off at the crowded bus station – although it was quite late at night, the streets were still full of people (I'm guessing because it would be just too hot inside). I watched as May Oo jumped on a bus that was already bursting at the seams with people.

A wedding reception was taking place in the former restaurant on the second floor of the YMCA when I got back. I think the dress code was shabby chic. These folk were in their nicest clothes, but the men's white shirts were grey and threadbare and the women's brightly coloured dresses were faded. At least the plastic chairs were still brightly coloured. A DJ was playing 'I Saw Her Standing There' by the Beatles in Burmese. May Oo told me that local bands re-record hits in Burmese, so they can get away without paying royalty fees and record whatever they want.

Back in my room, the bed was like a picnic table and the pillow was like a sack of potatoes, but I was probably the happiest person in Rangoon. The air conditioner was on and the room was cool. It was heavenly.

*

I was up and out of bed by 7.30. I had no choice. The power went off at seven o'clock and the room was a sauna ten minutes later. I had breakfast on the fourth floor, but it wasn't quite a floor. It was a big open space that had large windows with no glass and most of the floor was taken up by laundry flapping in the breeze. There was only one table set up for breakfast, which was for me. (The lepers must eat in their rooms, I thought.) A large lady was frying eggs in the corner on the floor while an older woman was cutting up vegetables and kids were running around the billowing bedsheets. I scoffed down my fried eggs and toast (and banana for dessert) because I wanted to get to Shwe Dagon Pagoda, the most sacred Buddhist temple in Burma. The old book recommended visiting the pagoda in the early morning when the 'gold spire gleams in the sun'.

There were already big crowds of locals at the entrance when I arrived. And what an entrance it was, with a grand, ornate passageway guarded by two gargantuan, dazzling-white statues that were a cross between proud lions, ferocious dragons and, from the way they were sitting up so straight, very obedient puppies. The dark passageway that just kept going and going was one long shopping strip of stalls selling gold Buddhas and wooden elephants (as in just about every single stall sold gold Buddhas and wooden elephants). When I finally ascended the passageway up a very un-1974 new escalator, I was blinded by the bright sun and the shimmering kaleidoscope of temples and stupas.

One of the greatest joys of travelling for me is when I am wowed. And now and again, like that very moment when I stepped out into this mesmerising sight, I was totally and utterly wowed. The main pagoda, which was positively beaming in the morning light as it soaked up and reflected the intense glare of the sun like an enormous mirror, was certainly the most impressive Buddhist pagoda I'd ever seen (and boy, had I seen a few). And it wasn't just the main pagoda that was extraordinary: the whole compound was full of intricate pagodas with glittering architecture, magnificent gold Buddha images, statues, shrines, bells, deities, temples and palm trees. There were over 82 structures and each building and pagoda was as unique and spectacular as the next one. As Tony summed it up: 'It is the sheer mass of buildings that gives the place its awesome appeal.' The magnificent central stupa, which stood over 100 metres high, was clad with enough gold and jewels, including sapphires, rubies and diamonds, to finance the rebuilding of a country (hang on a sec . . .). Except that would never happen because this most revered and sacred stupa is considered the heart of Burma.

I wandered around in a daze and as I was standing by an incredibly large bell, a smiling monk befriended me. He told me that the British dropped the bell into the Rangoon River while trying to take it back to England and when they couldn't recover it, they gave it back to the Burmese who refloated it by tying vast numbers of lengths of bamboo to it. I sat down and he sat with me and asked what day I was born. 'July the eighth,' I said.

'No, what day?'

'I have no idea,' I shrugged.

He looked shocked. 'The day you were born is *very* important to Buddhists,' he said.

I looked it up when I got home and the day on which you are born determines your character, optimum profession and your colour. I was born on a Sunday, so my colour is red, my character is respectable, carefree and wise and I am beloved by both friends and relatives. My optimum profession is a manager, doctor, trader or craftsman – even though I'm none of them and have never aspired to be any of them. Oh, and yes I am probably too carefree, but I'm certainly not wise.

I wisely left the monk after he asked for some money and spent the rest of the morning wandering in awe from one spectacularly ornate pagoda to the next. It was like a Buddhist Disneyland: perfectly clean and oh, so bright and cheerful. Some of the pagodas had even gone for the addition of '70s disco lights around the Buddhas – which wouldn't have looked out of place in Patong.

By noon, I was dazzled out and went to check out the market near the pagoda. The old guidebook recommended buying 'opium weights, which are cheaper than in Thailand'. The markets were also a good place to sell your wares as 'any western goods from radio batteries to cheap make-up have an amazing demand in Burma'. But I was out of radio batteries and the market seemed to have plenty of cheap make-up on sale, anyway. I had lunch in the market at a busy stall where customers, bent double on their tiny stools, wolfed down their food. 'Burmese food is basically curry and rice,' the old book noted. I had the curry and rice and indeed it was very basic.

After lunch, I rushed back to the YMCA for my kickboxing class. The class was taking place on the ground floor and hostel guests got a discount for lessons. I joined a class of fit young guys who all had their shirts off, all had tattoos and were all half my size but had double the amount of muscles.

The instructor didn't have much English, but that was okay – I didn't have much skill. Everyone warmed up by pairing off and kicking bits of plastic held up way too high for my limited flexibility. There was lots of grunting going on and, after two minutes, I was a sweaty mess. I consider myself reasonably fit, but I was lucky to get my foot as high as the instructor's hip – while his foot was swinging nonchalantly past my earlobe. The local boys were very polite, though, and didn't laugh at me once. It was a two-hour lesson, but I only lasted an hour. I was way too hot and way too uncoordinated. Oh, and I got kicked in the head twice, I punched some poor fellow in the stomach once and almost kicked the instructor in the balls.

'If the Y fails to satisfy, there is a nice Indian open air place in the park across from the Strand Hotel,' the old guidebook noted. Or in this case, if the Y fails to have a restaurant anymore. I made my way to the open-air place, but it was so dark, I couldn't quite make out exactly what food was for sale. Most of the stalls seemed to be selling oranges and that was it. I did find one place that at least had a light and a sign for 'Special Myanmar Fried Rice'. I asked what was in it and the proprietor said 'possibly chicken'. I couldn't see what was in my container of food and I had no idea what I was eating but it tasted like a cross between the fried frog in Indonesia and the grasshopper guts I'd had the day before. I ate a couple of mouthfuls then tossed it in the bin and headed to the air-conditioned 50th Street Bar & Grill near the YMCA for a cheeseburger and fries.

17

Mandalay

Mandalay was founded in 1857.
South east Asia on a shoestring, 1st edition, 1975

Mandalay was founded in 1861.
Southeast Asia on a Shoestring, 15th edition, 2010

At first I wasn't sure if my taxi driver was taking me to the central train station. We'd turned off the main road down a pot-holed and rutted dirt track and were heading towards a large run-down old building. But it turned out that the shabby building was the central train station. The trains inside didn't look much better. Thankfully I hadn't got an 'ordinary-class' ticket, I thought. It would have been very ordinary, indeed. And it was: the ordinary-class carriages had wooden seats and folks were piled in on top of each other. Even first class looked very ordinary: there were no bunk beds, just dusty-looking seats. I had an upper-class ticket (I'd purchased it the day before through the YMCA) and my somewhat scruffy compartment had four bunk beds and a small old fan whirring in the corner (that was the 'air conditioning'). The pillow on my seat-cum-bed hadn't been changed since 1974.

If I'd read the current *Southeast Asia on a Shoestring* guidebook, I might have reconsidered catching the train:

> Trains are government operated and foreigners pay about six times (or more) the local rate, meaning a wad of US dollars for the government coffers. On top of this, trains are much slower than buses (the Yangon-Mandalay Express ought to take 15 hours, but often takes double that), and derail quite frequently.

Okay, more expensive and slower I might have been able to put up with, but derailing 'quite frequently' was a concern. Not to mention that I was adding more cash to the fat General's wallet.

After just five minutes in my compartment, I was drenched in sweat. My YMCA room was like a cooler compared to this. I thought I might have the carriage to myself until a man, who was wearing a traditional Burmese longyi and carrying a laptop computer, entered the compartment. We nodded hello as he took a seat. No one else joined us by the time the train was ready to leave, so we had two spare beds (and two spare ratty pillows).

The train left exactly on time at 12.15. I was actually hoping it would be running late. Very late. The train was due to arrive at Mandalay Railway Station at three in the morning and I wasn't looking forward to wandering around in the dark trying to track down a guesthouse that may or may not exist anymore.

As the train rattled through the rubbish-strewn suburbs stacked with apartments made of papier-mâché, I started to doze off. Which was a rather impressive feat considering that the train was throwing me around so dramatically, it was like sitting in a popcorn machine. I wasn't necessarily tired – I think I had heat stroke as I drifted in and out of consciousness. The heat in the compartment was so bad that the other fellow had passed out even though he too was getting tossed around like a ragdoll.

After rattling my bones for a time, I sat up and looked out the window. We had left the dusty city and were now trundling through the dusty countryside. Out of all the places that I'd been on the trip so far, this looked like it had changed the least since 1974 – or even 1874. For the next hour, I didn't see a single car on the dirt roads, although there were plenty of ox-drawn carts and old bicycles laden with hay. The houses we passed were mostly thatched grass huts and the dry flat plains were dotted with folk tending fields. Then suddenly the train would clatter through a tangle of thick jungle with tall glistening gold stupas rising up from the trees.

I wasn't sure if there would be any food on the train, so I grabbed the only thing I could find at the station – a cold packaged 'hamburger' with a use-by date in two weeks' time. I opened it and took one bite and then threw it back in the package. What I'd do for a bowl of grasshoppers right now, I thought. My compartment mate managed to procure some sustenance, however. He'd ordered something from a fellow wearing a jacket and tie. Well, that's what I figured he'd done when the dapper young chap returned with two polystyrene containers filled with rice and vegetables. I thought it a little odd that my travelling companion kept his feet up on the seat the entire time, even when he was eating his lunch. That was until a massive cockroach crawled across my bare feet.

When he finished his meal, he tossed both polystyrene packs and a large plastic bottle straight out the window. I looked down at the tracks, which were littered with polystyrene packs and plastic bottles. I glanced at my watch and three hours had passed. There were at least another 12 hours to go and my back was killing me. I hoped they had good chiropractors in Mandalay.

My very quiet companion must have been very hungry because not long after he'd finished eating his lunch, he dragged out a huge bag of oranges. He had four and gave me two and kept insisting that I have more. I was still hungry, so I went for a wander up the carriage to find the man in the jacket and tie. On the way, I passed the toilets, and the strong smell of urine wafting out was so horrific that I had to run past with my nose blocked. At least I wouldn't need to go to the toilet for the rest of the trip, because even though I'd drunk a big bottle of water I'd already sweated it out in the heat. I didn't find the man in the jacket and tie, but I did find the grubby restaurant car, which had the same grubby furniture from 1974 (and which I'm pretty sure wouldn't pass Workplace Health and Safety Regulations). The restaurant car was full of men, half of whom were drunk and glassy-eyed. I sat at the one vacant table and ordered chicken and vegetables and a beer. When the waiter came back with a large bottle of beer, it took him ten attempts to pour the beer into my glass because the train was rattling around so much. I then had to take a big gulp straightaway, so it wouldn't spill everywhere. Eating the food, or more like trying to eat the food, was even more difficult. Using chopsticks while the train was shaking around was like trying to play pick-up sticks in an earthquake. The food was actually quite tasty – well, the bits of it that didn't end up on the floor or on my lap. But at least I knew the cockroaches would clean up after me.

When I got back to my compartment, it was dark. The window was open to let in cool air, but the only problem was that every bug in Burma was flying through the window and into my hair. I tried to sleep, with a big emphasis on *tried*, but I was getting thrown around and the flying bugs were now flying up my nose. Oh, and the giant cockroaches crawling all over the walls were a little disconcerting as well. After a spell, I was just about to doze off when the train hit a huge bump (When do train tracks have bumps?) and I got thrown in the air and hit my head on the bunk above me.

I finally fell asleep then there was a loud bang on the door. 'Mandalay!' the attendant hollered. The train was only seven minutes late, even though the girl at the YMCA told me that the train is always late. The platform was certainly alive at 3.07 in the morning. It was alive because people were living on the platform: there were rows of bodies lying on thin mats with all their possessions bundled up around them.

I picked out a trishaw driver in the dark. 'Do you have reservation?' he said. 'I take you nice hotel.'

'I have a reservation at this hotel,' I said, showing him the old guidebook.

'That no hotel.'

'Must be this one, then.'

'No hotel no more.'

The third hotel on the list was still a hotel. The Sabai Hotel had 'spartan but quite clean rooms', according to the old guidebook.

'Yes, that is the one I have a reservation for,' I said. 'I'm just a little confused at this time of the morning.'

The trishaw driver rode silently through the dark streets then turned off into an even darker side street down a narrow dirt track. The hotel was suspiciously dark inside as well. 'It's okay,' he said, as he dropped me off. I rang the bell, but there was no answer. Then I tried again. And again. It wasn't until I held the buzzer down for about two minutes that someone finally came to the door.

The very groggy, and somewhat grumpy, manager showed me to my room. Even though I was exhausted, I couldn't take the room. Out of all the cheap run-down hotels that I'd stayed in on this trip, this was the most disgusting room I'd seen. The room was dim and dirty, with splintered wooden furniture and the walls and floor were covered in thick grime. And so were the sheets on the bed. The stains in the bathroom looked like the crime scene from a triple murder-suicide that involved machetes. 'Can I change rooms?' I asked.

'There is no other room tonight.'

'Can I get a discount then? It's pretty . . . grimy.'

'No, we clean room.'

Two teenage boys, who had been undoubtedly woken up from their slumber, came up to clean the room. This involved throwing a bucket of water around the entire bathroom and trying to remove 30 years of grime and dust with a feather duster. Mind you, they did also spray the room with air freshener.

I laid out all my T-shirts and my towel on the bed because there was no way I was touching those sheets. It was like one giant Petri dish full of bacteria. Beth would have freaked out. Amazingly I slept until eight o'clock. It was amazing because there was no air conditioner or fan. And it was amazing because I didn't get any skin lesions or boils.

*

I decided to move from the Hotel Grime. I skipped breakfast (grime on toast, I was guessing) and jumped in a trishaw to check out the 'upmarket' Tun Hla Hotel, which had a 'nice swimming pool and air conditioning', according to the old guidebook. I liked the sound of that – even though it was only nine in the morning it would have been close to 40 degrees.

Fifteen minutes later, we pulled up in front of the MYA Mandalay Hotel. 'The hotel change name,' my driver said. I walked enviously past a family splashing in the pool to the very nice and grime-free hotel reception. A room was $US20, which was four times the price of the Sabai Hotel, but I would have happily paid ten times the price for a lovely, cool air conditioner and a lovely, cool pool.

I told the girl at reception that I needed to pick up my bags from the other hotel, but she asked me to fill out a registration form to hold the room.

'So, when did the hotel change its name?' I asked.

'The government bought the hotel four years ago and changed the name.'

'The government owns the hotel?'

'Yes.'

Oh, now I had a moral dilemma. The money I would spend would go straight into General Arsehole's pocket.

'I won't stay, thank you,' I said sadly. I'd already given the General my train money and I didn't want to give him any more.

I had a tear in my eye as I walked past the pool on the way out.

There were a couple more hotels in the old book to check out anyway, so on the way back into town I jumped out of the trishaw and hired a bicycle. It was a clunky old thing, but it was nice to get around the city on my own steam. The first hotel I tried was the Ava, which was at least easy to find with the old map because it was just up the road from the Hotel Grime. The Hotel Ava was now a cement shop. My final option was the Man Shwe Myo Hotel and I found the street, but I couldn't find the hotel. I asked a man in the street and he pointed to a decrepit building that looked as if it was about to fall down. 'Is the hotel open?' I asked a well-dressed man standing out the front of the hotel.

'Yes, but not for tourists,' he said. Mr Lin was the son of the original owner. 'The hotel opened in 1969,' he told me. 'But in 1988 we had our permit taken away, because the hotel is not good enough for tourists.'

'Is it still a hotel?'

'Oh, yes, it is okay for Burmese people to stay here.'

I asked Mr Lin if I could see a room. 'Yes, of course,' he said. Creaky narrow stairs led up to a hallway with beautiful polished teak floors. The room itself was not quite as polished. It was even more basic than the Hotel Grime. An incredibly narrow bed, which looked as if it would collapse if you sat on it, took up most of the room. There was a mosquito net over the bed, but it was full of gaping holes and stained brown – from age,

I supposed. There was no other furniture. No ensuite. No cable. 'There are lots of nice hotels now for foreign people,' Mr Lin said with a big smile. The Hotel Grime wasn't one of those nice hotels for foreign people, but it looked as if I would be spending another night there (and it actually looked quite nice in comparison).

I asked Mr Lin if Shwe Wah Restaurant, which was just around the corner, was still open. 'Yes,' he said. 'It's very nice for foreigners.' Shwe Wah was the only restaurant listed in the old guidebook: 'Plenty of restaurants around but the travelling fraternity generally patronise Shwe Wah.'

There was no travelling fraternity patronising the restaurant when I arrived. There were only two other diners in the simply furnished (as in starkly furnished) restaurant. My waiter turned out to be the owner, Kyin Ngwe Chan, who was the nephew of the original manager, Li Chit Win. 'He is now seventy-four years old,' Kyin told me.

'Does he still work at the restaurant?' I asked.

'No, my uncle opened the restaurant in 1972 and he handed over the business to me in 1981. He wanted to drive a taxi instead, but now he can't drive anymore, so he retired last year.'

Kyin insisted that I look at the menu, which had such tasty treats on offer as cold pig's stomach and special pig's feet. Was the pig special? I wondered. Not special enough, it seemed, as Kyin recommended the fried chicken with mushrooms. I asked Kyin if many tourists came to the restaurant. 'There were many tourists here years ago,' Kyin said. 'But now we have no tourists.'

I showed Kyin the restaurant entry in the old guidebook.

'Ah, Tony Wheeler!' Kyin beamed. 'I remember him. He nice man.'

Kyin rushed off and returned with a few faded photocopied pages from the *Burma* Lonely Planet guidebook from 1982 (second edition). The first page was the inside cover with a black-and-white picture of Tony, Maureen and baby Tashi with white blonde hair. Tony had long hair and Maureen looked just like the English '70s singer Lulu. Tashi had come full circle and was the commissioning editor of the 15th edition of *Southeast Asia on a Shoestring*. The other pages included a long and detailed review of the restaurant from the 1982 *Burma* guidebook:

It's hard to find real Burmese food apart from at street stalls. Shwe Wah, a grubby looking little Chinese restaurant has long been popular with shoestring travellers. The quality of food turned out far exceeds the visual expectations, in my opinion, the food in this little place is of better quality from that in the big tourist Burma Mandalay Hotel. The menu includes nice sweet and sour pork, fresh lime juice a very good fruit salad.

'Our restaurant has not been in a Lonely Planet book in over twenty years,' Kyin said with a sad shrug.

My meal came out and the plate was piled high with chicken and mushrooms. Kyin suddenly rushed off again and came back ten minutes later with another plate heaped with sweet and sour pork, a glass of lime juice and a big bowl of fruit salad. 'You must try,' he said. 'The food is still the same.' I'm glad Tony didn't recommend the cold pig's stomach or the special pig's feet.

Not that I could possibly fit anything in after all this food, but I asked Kyin if the Rangoon Milk Bar, which had 'fairly healthy milk shakes' was still around. Kyin laughed. 'No, the family packed up and moved to America years ago.'

'Has Mandalay changed much since the 1970s?'

'There are lots more Chinese people now,' Kyin said. 'That's all.'

While I tried to put a dent in the massive piles of food, we talked about our families. Kyin was just as interested in my family and my life in Australia as I was in his. Kyin had three children and the oldest was 25. 'He will take over the business when I have finished,' he said.

When I went to pay the bill, Kyin grabbed my hand. 'No, no! I would like to give it to you,' he insisted.

Kyin came out onto the street to wave me goodbye – and to point me in the right direction. It didn't help. I got hopelessly and irretrievably lost but loved every minute of it. I spent most of the afternoon trundling down dirt roads watching locals at work and play. I rode past gaggles of monks strolling down shaded lanes, children playing football on dusty streets, women with bags of shopping on their heads and scrawny dogs lazing under trees (I steered clear of the dogs, of course). On some of the streets, a mountain bike might have been more appropriate – they were so rutted and bumpy, my poor bum took a beating on the hard saddle.

I did find some sights eventually. I rode around the moat filled with lilies and the high ramparts that surrounded the Royal Palace, which had been burned-out during the closing stages of World War II, but I didn't go in. There were only the foundations to see anyway and back in 1974 all you needed was 'permission to entry from the South gate'. They now charged ten US dollars to enter.

Arakan Pagoda, which had a gold-leafed pagoda containing a huge gong and statues of legendary warriors, was interesting – even if I did upset the worshippers. I stood in a tiny space taking photos and watching men applying layers of gold leaf onto the Maha Muni statue for a long time before I realised that there was a sea of worshippers sitting on the ground behind me through an arched doorway. I was standing right in the middle of their view of the sacred monument.

Lined up outside in the courtyard were statues of the six survivors of the 30 magic images of Ayutthaya. It is believed that afflictions can be cured by rubbing the parts of the statues that correspond with whatever ailment you might have. It was obvious where people had afflictions from the worn-away brass: there were lots of problems with the stomach and knees and quite a few had some sort of affliction with their little toe. It was comforting to know that there didn't seem to be many afflictions of the groin area.

It took me about 30 minutes to ride back to the Grime Hotel – although I allowed two hours in case I got lost. In the hotel lobby, I had a chat to Thuya, the lady at reception, who spoke good English and had been working at the hotel for 15 years. And I mean 15 years straight. She told me that she worked 12 hours a day, seven days a week and didn't even take days off when she was sick. 'I get no pay then,' she shrugged. Thuya was paid 15,000 kyat ($US15) a month. She had ten children (Where did she find the time – or energy, for that matter?) and had sent them all to a Catholic Monastery school in Rangoon. Thuya didn't see some of her children for seven years, because she couldn't afford the train ticket. A one-way fare from Mandalay to Rangoon was 3000 kyat. I paid 40,000 kyat for my ticket, which meant 37,000 went into the fat General's fat wallet.

I went to my room and had a cold shower – even though I felt dirtier when I got out – and headed out to dinner. I rode my bike to the main drag, where I thought I'd have a better chance of finding a restaurant that wasn't full of bacteria, and stopped in front of a restaurant with a sign saying 'air conditioning'. I was so sick of the constant draining heat that I went inside, even though a main meal cost more than a night in my hotel. It was very flash inside and full of cashed-up locals. There didn't seem to be any tourists – in fact, the only tourists I'd seen so far in Burma were the two old fellows in the bar at the Strand Hotel. A five-piece live band was playing 'I've Been to Paradise, But I've Never Been to Me' when I walked in and followed that up with 'I Want to Hold Your Hand' in Burmese. (The Beatles sure were popular in Burma.)

The menu, which was a mix of western and Chinese food, really wasn't cheap, but the restaurant was oh, so cool inside. I checked my finances (I usually only go out with the money that I think I need) and I could only afford the cheapest thing on the menu – well, with enough left over for an ice-cold beer, of course. My spicy chicken curry was so spicy that my nose kept dripping into my beer.

After dinner, I went to see the Moustache Brothers who had been sentenced to seven years in a labour camp for telling a joke about the government. Kyim suggested that I go see this famous comedy trio perform as they had been doing in Mandalay since the 1970s. Although the dusty back streets were dark, the Moustache Brothers were easy to find. Everyone seemed to know where they lived – and performed, because their shows were held in the lounge room. I asked for directions a few times and people would say, 'Ah, the Moustache Brothers,' and point me in the right direction.

I arrived early and the family was sitting out on the street. I was escorted inside by one of the brothers,

Lu Maw, who had a very impressive bushy handlebar moustache. In the lounge room was a small stage with a few faded red plastic chairs. 'This is the West End of Mandalay,' Lu Maw said with a cheeky grin. The walls were covered in marionettes and posters of Aung San Suu Kyi. 'They are banned,' he said with a smile.

Aung San Suu Kyi's face is known around the world. For 15 of the past 20 years, Aung San Suu Kyi had been under house arrest after her National League for Democracy party won the majority of the national votes and seats in parliament in 1989. That's what you get for winning an election in Burma. And in that time she only saw her husband Aris five times before he died in 1999. (One year after I visited Burma, Aung San Suu Kyi was finally released on 13 November 2010.)

Aung San Suu Kyi was one of thousands of Burmese locked up by the military junta. Two of the three Moustache Brothers, Par Par Lay and Lu Zaw, were sentenced to seven years of forced labour after criticising the junta during a performance at the home of Aung San Suu Kyi in 1996 (at one of the brief times when the Nobel Peace Prize winner was not under house arrest). 'They did hard labour breaking rocks chained at the ankles,' Lu Maw told me. Lu Maw missed out on being locked up, because only two of them had to go to jail and he flipped a coin with his brother Par Par Lay (Lu Zaw is not a brother, but actually a cousin). 'One of us had to stay to carry the name and keep performing,' Lu Maw said.

In 1997, ten Hollywood comedians wrote to the government urging for their release and they were finally released after five years on 13 July 2001. Two days later, they had their first performance of the original troupe. 'Over two hundred people filled the streets to watch us,' Lu Maw said proudly. Soon they were back to a two-man troupe, because the oldest brother Par Par Lay was back in jail. 'The police dragged him down the street,' Lu Maw observed cheerfully. 'Now he is up the river, in the clink, in the slammer, behind bars. He's a jailbird!'

'When did you start performing?' I asked.

'We started performing sometime in the sixties, but began performing to tourists in 1972. We would buy cigarettes and whiskey from tourists and they would ask, "Is this your job?" and I would say, "No, we are moonlighting. My real job is a comedian." Some of them asked to see us, so we started performing for them.'

Before their arrest, the troupe performed all around the country. 'We built a stage and slept on it at night,' Lu Maw recollected. 'If it rained, we slept underneath.' They were now forced to stay in Mandalay and only performed for the smattering of tourists that turned up. Lu Maw made his feelings clear; while they were fierce supporters of Aung San Suu Kyi, who is often quoted in the West as opposing tourism, they are wholly in favour of tourism. 'Tourists are our Trojan horses,' Lu Maw said. 'Through tourists, the rest of the world can learn of our plight. If there are tourists, there will be no more forced labour; no more killings.'

While we were talking, the rest of the audience showed up – two Germans and an English woman. The show opened with Lu Maw having an informal chat with the audience using technology straight out of the 1970s. The sound system consisted of a single tape deck with a rather squeaky tape and an antique microphone. The slim and jovial Lu Maw started by lighting up a cigarette and saying, 'I am fifty-nine years old and I smoke twenty-four hours a day and look how much good health I have.'

The show was an odd mix of Burmese classical dance, 'take my wife . . .' jokes and a steady stream of English slang. Quite a bit of the show, however, was also taken up with sharply satirical criticism aimed at the totalitarian Burmese military regime and digs at the General and his wealth, corruption and violence. 'Nobody wants them and everyone hates them,' Lu Maw squealed into the microphone. There were many jokes about the regime, such as: 'I went to Thailand to go to the dentist and he said to me, "Why do you come all the way to Thailand to go to the dentist?" and I said, "There are no dentists in Burma because we are not allowed to open our mouths."'

Lu Maw didn't look too worried about being caught again and thrown in jail. 'If the KGB come,' as he dubbed the Burmese police, 'we all run and the police will take you tourists away and lock you up.' His 84-year-old mother was on 'guard' out the front.

As part of the show, his wife, whom he called 'the slave driver', came out in traditional dress and Lu Maw said, 'Okay, you dance.' She gave him a gentle slap on the cheek for his efforts. 'We have been together for three years, but we are not married. We are shacked up!' His de facto wife danced along to some kooky music that sounded like *Looney Tunes* cartoon music on speed.

At the end of the performance, Lu Maw showed us a clip on an old television set from Hugh Grant's film *About A Boy* that mentions the most famous brother of the outfit, Par Par Lay. 'We are even on YouTube and have a Facebook page,' Lu Maw said excitedly.

Burma needs folks like the Moustache Brothers. As I shook Lu Maw's hand, he leant in and whispered, 'Burma needs tourists. Make sure you write that.'

The English woman had her guide/motorcycle rider waiting for her outside while the Germans had a car waiting for them. They all gave me shocked looks when I jumped on my rickety bicycle and rode off into the darkness. And when I say dark, I mean it was pretty much pitch black. There were hardly any streetlights or even car headlights to light the way.

When I turned into 78th Street (which is as close enough as you can get to a main street), at least there were some streetlights and some shops and restaurants with lights. Then suddenly the power cut off and the street was plunged into darkness. I could barely make out the road. There was one good thing, however: no one took any notice of the skinny foreigner on a bike because no one could see me. More amazing still, I made it back to the Grime Hotel without getting lost once. Or crashing into a parked car.

I woke up early because I accidentally touched the sheets and had to get straight into the shower. After breakfast at the Hotel Grime (which wasn't that bad actually and there wasn't a bit of grime in sight), I hopped on my bicycle to Mandalay Hill, which the old guidebook noted was a couple of hours' climb up sheltered steps past traditional shops to a wide view over Mandalay. I tried to follow the old map and ended up down a dirt road. I was sure I was lost until I suddenly happened upon the entrance, which was flanked by two massive white stone lions. Inside, the traditional shops now sold traditional Nike bags and traditional Disney Princess dolls.

It was a long, hot sticky climb in bare feet (you had to leave your shoes at the entrance) past a mini step city. Folks had set up their homes next to their little hawker stalls or souvenir stands. They were cooking food, painting pictures on black silk, carving wooden elephants, washing clothes and scrubbing grubby children with buckets of soapy water right on the steps. I staggered to the top, where I was greeted by a large pagoda housing a gold Buddha inside. Except that it wasn't the top and the steps continued on. As I climbed higher, there were more pagodas and Buddhas with more hidden steps behind them. Two hours later, I reached the top where there was only a small Buddha – even though it did have the best disco lights. The Buddha was pointing towards Mandalay, where legend has it that Buddha once stood and prophesised a great city would be built in 1857 (or 1861, depending on which edition of the guidebook you're reading).

By the time I trudged back down the hill and rode my bike back to the Hotel Grime, I desperately needed a shower before I headed off to the airport. It took me ten minutes to clean the dirt off my feet and 20 minutes to wash away the eight or so diseases that I'd picked up from the sheets.

18

Pagan

There are over 5000 temples in Bagan.
South east Asia on a shoestring, 1st edition, 1975

There are 4400 temples in Bagan.
Southeast Asia on a Shoestring, 15th edition, 2010

The train from Rangoon to Pagan was noted in the back of the old guidebook as the Most Uncomfortable Train in South-East Asia. The train was described as a dirty, uncomfortable, unlit, slow, crowded, tedious, unpleasant cattle train. Not surprisingly, Tony recommended that you avoid it. So I did. I flew instead.

It was more than an hour's drive to the new Mandalay Airport, which was in the middle of nowhere and nowhere near Mandalay. Even from a few kilometres away, you could spot the monolithic ornate Burmese-style building glistening white in the sun. Or more like a big white elephant. Not a single person was milling about outside and it was even eerier inside. There was not a soul about and the duty-free shops were all empty – as in empty of people and empty of wares for sale. The lone security guard pointed towards the entrance to 'check in' when he noticed me standing there looking totally dumbfounded. The check-in counter was in a huge hall, but only half the lights were on and there was one counter open for the Bagan Air flight. There were five airline staff manning the counter and no other passengers. The customs counter was in another massive hall with a long bank of counters and one man stamping passports. He stamped mine just for the hell of it, even though I wasn't leaving the country.

It was then a long walk down a dark corridor and finally down an escalator until I found the 40 or so people waiting at the gate. They were all locals except for one westerner.

We were escorted onto the empty tarmac to a small modern(ish) plane where a mechanic was standing by an open engine panel scratching his head. That was not a good sign, I thought. There was no problem with dodgy engines, however, and before I had time even to settle in for the flight, we were preparing to land on a flat featureless landscape that looked like the Australian outback.

Only the other westerner and I got off the plane in Pagan (the rest continued on to Rangoon). We had to pay a ten-US-dollar entrance fee to the city, but that was because the whole of Pagan was a historical site with a 42-square-kilometre designated Archaeological

Zone. At passport control (even though, as I said earlier, I hadn't left the country), the officer asked me what hotel I was staying in. The first of two hotels listed in the old guidebook was the Moe Moe Inn, which was 'the in place' and was 'very pleasant and clean but the beds are just wooden boards'.

'I not know this,' he grunted, when I showed him the entry in the book.

He asked the woman next to him and she shook her head. He then asked six other people and no one had heard of it. He shrugged and scribbled Moe Moe Inn down on the form and waved me through.

I shared a taxi with the other westerner, Johann, who was Austrian and in Burma on business for the Yangon Teak Import Company. 'People keep buying Burmese teak,' he shrugged.

When I asked the taxi driver if he knew the Moe Moe Inn, he cackled with laughter. 'The hotel closed thirty years ago and the owners are dead,' he said, still chuckling. There was another hotel, the Soe Soe Inn, but it wasn't quite as pleasant: 'Alternative for the impecunious,' I had to look it up: it means 'penniless and poor', 'it is rather primitive.' There was more hysterical laughter when I asked about the Soe Soe Inn. 'They are dead too, and both the hotels were torn down.'

They weren't the only things that had been torn down. Finding the city of Old Pagan from 1974 would have been very difficult. Johann told me that the government moved the town a few kilometres away across the river. As in they razed the entire town and planted everyone in a patch of undeveloped land and dubbed it New Bagan.

'Where do the backpackers stay?' I asked the driver.

'Not in New Bagan,' he said. 'That is where the nice hotels are.'

We drove off the main road into the 'town' of Nyaung U, which was made up of only a few streets – or dirt roads, actually. We pulled up in front of the New Park Hotel. 'This is the favourite backpacker hotel,' he said. It certainly was: I later discovered that the New Park Hotel was the 'Top Pick' in the current guidebook.

The hotel had clean and air-conditioned rooms for eight US dollars a night, but Johann said, 'I'm not a backpacker anymore.' He was heading to the flash hotels in New Bagan.

It was dark by the time I'd taken a nice long hot shower and the friendly chap at reception pointed me in the direction of restaurant row, which was a dirt road lined with restaurants geared towards backpackers. There was Thai, Italian, Indian and a place called 'A Little Bit of Bagan', which served Indian and Italian food – fettuccine vindaloo, anyone? – although there weren't many backpackers around at all.

One of the restaurants had a huge sign out the front claiming: 'Aroma 2 restaurant – REAL RECOM-MENDED BY LONELY PLANETS and voted as one of the top five restaurants in Myanmar by the Lonely Planet Guidebook.' The old guidebook didn't have any recommended restaurants, so this was close enough. I took a seat in the empty but delightful candlelit garden area out the front and the owner Mr Raju served me. 'We are the first Indian restaurant in Pagan,' he told me. 'Then local people come here and order lots of takeaway then try to copy food. There are now five Indian restaurants in Pagan, but we are the only one with an Indian chef.'

I chowed down a delicious pea soup, chapattis and chicken tikka masala and was back at the hotel and snuggled up in my bed by nine o'clock. I needed an early night too. In the old guidebook, Tony recommended hiring a horse and cart as a 'convenient and cheap way' to see Pagan, and the fellow at the hotel reception recommended that I book one for 5.30 am. 'You must see the temples at sunrise,' he said. 'It is very special.'

My horse and cart (with driver) turned up at 5.30 on the dot. My driver's name was Myu Myu and he was 30 years old. He was born in Pagan and his father and grandfather were both horse and cart drivers. He told me all this before we'd even set off. And all the while he kept smiling with teeth that were black-red like clotted blood from chewing betel nuts. When we eventually did get going, and Myu Myu stopped talking, the only sound was the soft clip clop of hooves on the sand road. The old guidebook had quite detailed descriptions of some of the more interesting temples out of the 5000 temples dotted around the countryside. In the current *Southeast Asia on a Shoestring*, the temple count had dropped to 4400. 'Did Pagan lose some temples?' I asked Myu Myu.

It certainly had. On 8 July 1975, and only two months after the publication of the original guidebook, a massive earthquake rocked the ancient site. 'Many temples were destroyed,' Myu Myu told me. 'But some they have fixed.' The temples had lasted a long time before that. Pagan's period of grandeur started in 1057 when King Anuradha conquered Thaton, believed to be Nakhon Pathom in Thailand, and brought back artists, craftsmen, monks and 30 elephant-loads of Buddhist scriptures. Over the next two centuries, an enormous number of magnificent buildings were erected.

Myu Myu suggested that I climb to the top of one of the temples to watch the sunrise and I suggested Thatbyinnyu, which the old guidebook noted was the highest temple in Pagan with magnificent views from the top. Myu Myu shook his head sadly. 'It is now closed for tourists, because a few years ago two French tourists fell off the top and died.' The old guidebook also suggested Gawdawpalin Temple for sunset, but that had been destroyed in the 1975 earthquake and the 'impressive' gold spire had broken off. It had since been rebuilt, but you were no longer allowed to climb it. Instead, we headed to a temple that wasn't on the list in the old book, but Myu Myu assured me that it was 'very beautiful and very quiet'.

It was certainly quiet on the roads of Pagan. We'd been trotting along for half an hour and hadn't seen any other traffic – four-legged or otherwise. The sky revealed the first traces of pink as we arrived and by the time I climbed to the top of the stone temple, the sun appeared as a huge orange hazy ball. As far as the eye could see and in every direction were temples sprinkled around the dusty plains. This was another one of those wow moments. I sat for a time watching the misty landscape and temples change colour, while Myu Myu dozed off in the cart – he would have seen this spectacular sight almost every day of his life.

A couple of hot air balloons sailed overhead, which would have been an out-of-this-world experience (quite literally) but the $US250 ticket was a bit above my budget. (That's 42 nights at the New Park Hotel or, in old money, 420 nights at the Soe Soe Inn.)

The first temple listed in the old guidebook that we checked out was Thatbyinnyu Temple, which was impressive, but not as impressively insistent as the touts who were hanging around the temple. The persistent touts, who were mostly kids, were selling T-shirts, perfume, US flags and postcards. I'd never seen so many postcards. Or so many kids selling postcards.

We stopped for breakfast at nine o'clock and, having already been up three and a half hours, I was starving. The small tin shed-cum-cafe was short on staff, so Myu Myu took over the waiter duties. I had a banana pancake (Why is it that when I travel I eat banana pancakes, but I've never had one back at home?) and a mixed fruit juice. As I was scoffing down my pancake, a troop of orange-robed monks shuffled past carrying pots to collect their morning alms. I offered them some of my banana pancake, but they weren't interested – they must prefer pineapple ones.

We spent the rest of the morning clip-clopping down dirt tracks through the countryside past grazing cattle, bullock carts, goat herds strolling through peanut fields and beaming villagers with yokes on their shoulders. And more temples than you could point an alms bowl at.

Mingalezedi Temple, which was another from the recommended temple list in the old guidebook, was closed. 'Why is it closed?' I asked Myu Myu.

'The government.'

'Why?'

'It's very old,' he said, shaking his head.

'But all the rest are old, too?'

Myu Myu shrugged.

I got out to have a look anyway. A wire fence had been put up around the temple and there was a very official sign, in English, on the fence explaining that the Minister of Culture had closed the temple three years earlier. The temple's custodian was eyeing me off and I thought he was going to tell me off, but he unlocked the gate and let me in. Myu Myu was right: it was old – and falling apart. But it did still have 'fine terracotta tiles around the base', just like the old guide-book described.

We stopped for lunch at a small cluster of outdoor restaurants and souvenir shops in the middle of nowhere and grabbed a table at Golden Myanmar 2 (although there was no sign of Golden Myanmar 1 anywhere). Myu Myu took a nap while the waiter brought out seven bowls of food – just for me. I smelt each bowl of food and put aside any that smelt questionable. By the time I'd finished my smelling test, I had set aside six bowls and was left with one bowl of an only somewhat questionable chicken curry and rice. I pretty much just ate the rice. After lunch, or more like tiny snack, I joined Myu Myu for a nap under the shade of a tree. The waiter kindly brought out a sun chair and I crashed out for an hour.

I had a strawberry lassi to wake me up while Myu Myu chewed on some betel nuts. 'You must try,' he said, handing me a large black nut. It had a bitter taste and I tried chewing it for five minutes then gave up and spat out a blood-red glob that made me look as if I'd been punched in the mouth. The nuts are supposed to be a stimulant, much like coffee, but I didn't feel anything and just ended up with bits of betel nut stuck in my teeth.

We eventually stopped at two of the temples on the list: Manuha, where Buddhas were impossibly squeezed into tiny enclaves and Ananda, which was known as the finest, largest, best preserved and most revered of the

Pagan temples. The temple was fine and large, but its greatest claim to fame was its two Buddha footprints. I had 22 touts watching me look at the two impressive footprints. The old guidebook noted that there was an excellent lacquerware shop near Manuha. I counted 23 lacquerware shops on the road before we even got near to the temple.

As we plodded down tranquil dusty lanes in the blazing afternoon sun, it often felt as though we were the only people around. That was until we got to New Bagan, which was full of flash hotels and package tourists (the ones who were generously lining the General's pockets). We stopped for a drink and I said hello to an American in leisure pants and a safari vest with lots of pockets who told me that he was on a government-run tour, staying in government-run hotels and flying on government-run airlines. I had to bite my tongue.

Back on board the cart, I asked Myu Myu about New Bagan. He told me that on 1 May 1990 everyone got a letter from the government telling them that they had to move to New Bagan. 'They turned off the water and electricity and we had to pay to knock down our houses and rebuild ourselves.' The government didn't finish there. Pagan has not got a UNESCO heritage listing, which is incredible really, because the mad General had done a quick fix on the restoration of temples and stupas and hadn't even bothered to follow the original archi-tectural plans. The junta had also put in a golf course, a paved highway, and built a 60-metre concrete watch-tower smack in the middle of the temples.

We could see the tower looming over the land-scape when we made our way to our last temple for the day, the Shwezigon Pagoda, which was lit up like a giant gold beacon in the late-afternoon sun. In our 12 hours hoofing it around Pagan, I had seen 18 temples, 573 Buddhas and 127 touts.

When we got back to the hotel, I paid my genial and gregarious (well, when he wasn't sleeping) guide double the fee he quoted – and even then it was only $16.

I was so hungry that I skipped a shower, even though I was covered in dust, and headed out down restau-rant row to San Kabar (Italian Specialists since 1998). This was the 'oldest' restaurant in town, according to the receptionist. And for my last night in Burma (I was flying to Rangoon then on to Singapore via Bangkok), I had a traditional Burmese pepperoni pizza.

When I got back to the hotel, I was so tired that I collapsed into bed, even though I was still covered in dust. But that was okay – I was used to grimy sheets.

Singapore

Image: Sentosa

19

Singapore

Trishaws are fading out.
South east Asia on a shoestring, 1st edition, 1975

You can find trishaws around all the popular
tourist places.
Southeast Asia on a Shoestring, 15th edition, 2010

There were two young men with long hair on the plane.
They were lucky it wasn't 1974 or they might not have
been allowed into Singapore. 'In the government's
strange view, having long hair has become a criminal
offence,' the old guidebook noted. And if you did get
into Singapore with long hair, then you would have been
treated somewhat as a pariah, with most government
buildings and banks enforcing strict rules with large
signs stating that 'Males with long hair will be attended
to last'. The government even started a campaign – and
I'm not making this up – to measure the width of bell-
bottomed pants. The government certainly didn't like

hippies and, according to Tony, they didn't like any type of tourists: 'Tourists should please come in, spend as much as possible in the shortest time possible and get out.'

The Wheelers liked Singapore, even if Tony was served last at the bank. This was where they finished their trip around South-East Asia and this was where Tony and Maureen put together the first *South east Asia on a shoestring* guidebook. On the back cover of that book, Tony wrote:

> This book was entirely put together, typed, proof-read, designed, laid out, and pasted up in room two of the Palace Hotel in Singapore. Any mistakes I blame on the noise from the motorcycle repair shop downstairs and the less than ideal working conditions.

Tony had told me that the Palace Hotel was still around, or at least he thought it was, which was why I also wanted to finish my trip in Singapore and hopefully in room two of the hotel. Tony and Maureen spent a lot of time in Singapore, so the accommodation and eating section in the old guidebook was very detailed. The Palace Hotel was obviously their favourite and was described as being 'a little far from the centre' but 'cheap, absolutely spotlessly clean and not having that "lean against the wall and it will fall down" feeling of some of the other cheapies'.

My taxi driver didn't know the Palace Hotel, but at least the book had the full address of 407 Jalan Besar. I showed the driver the old map in the book and he burst into laughter. 'Singapore has changed,' he said. But Jalan Besar didn't look as if it had changed that much compared to the rest of slick, modern Singapore. There were still lots of old Chinese shophouses with faded shuttered windows. The taxi driver got a little confused with the street numbers and when he spotted number 320 he reversed back up the one-way street with cars frantically honking at him. 'This is it,' he said as we pulled up in front of Chip Yew Co (Pte) Ltd. It wasn't a hotel – it was a store selling car parts. 'No, wait,' my driver cried. 'That's it, next door.' Next door was the Madras Hotel Eminence.

'Did this used to be the Palace Hotel?' I asked the man at reception.

'Yes, the name was changed last year.'

And so had the rooms, apparently. A few years before the name change, the hotel had been renovated and all the rooms had been divided into two smaller rooms. The old room number two was now rooms three and four. And room number two was now in the old room number one. Confusing? I was just as confused. I took room number two. It may not have been the same old room two, but it was room number two, nonetheless.

Room number two really was now room half-of-number-two. The room was so small, there was only just enough space to squeeze in a double bed and small writing desk in the corner. Sadly, it wasn't the same desk from 1974. Tony had showed me a photo of Maureen sitting at a round desk that was covered in papers. Even the tiny rectangular desk was half the size and didn't have enough room for two pieces of paper. Incidentally, it was in this same room (or the old room two, at least) and at this desk that Bill Dalton wrote the second edition of the popular *Indonesia Handbook* guide.

There was one nice addition to the new room two, however. When the Wheelers called the Palace Hotel home, there was only a sink on the wall. Now there was an ensuite – as well as cable TV and a iron and hairdryer 'available free upon request'.

Mind you, I couldn't afford to write the entire book here. Back then, it was four dollars a night. It was now $55 a night – and you didn't even get the 'free soft drink upon your hot and sweaty arrival'.

The Singapore chapter in the old guidebook had the largest restaurant section out of any city in the book with 15 places listed. I figured that I must have a decent chance to find at least one out of 15. In the 'Personal Favourites' section, Tony had recommended the nameless restaurant near the New World Amusement Park for really good mee (noodle soup). Jalan Besar may have had lots of old Chinese shophouses, but a long strip of them were now karaoke bars. Not far past the karaoke bars, I came to the entrance gate for the New World Amusement Park, but that's all it was: a gate. Rising up behind it were two colossal glass towers. The New World Amusement Park was Singapore's first amusement park (the second was Gay World – and no, not that type of gay) and was already in decline in the '70s. It was closed in 1987 and was turned into a 910-unit apartment block and eight-storey shopping mall.

Next door was the nameless restaurant, which now had a name. It was called Kingslight. They didn't sell any food, however. But they did sell very nice lamp-shades. It was now a lighting store. Next on the long list was Hai Guan, which was Tony's personal favourite for Hainan chicken rice. The restaurant was only about 500 metres up the road from the former nameless restaurant and was still there – I think. All the signs were in Chinese. I asked the waiter if I was in the right place, but he wasn't sure. Or more like he wasn't sure if he spoke English.

Everyone was eating Hainan chicken rice, so I thought I must be in the right place and ordered a serving of 'very nice Hainan chicken rice', as my waiter called it. There were a couple of very old Chinese fellows sitting next to me, so I thought I'd take a punt and asked if they spoke English. 'Why, of course,' one of the chaps said in a perfect clipped English accent.

I showed him the restaurant name in the book. 'Is this it?' I asked.

He laughed hysterically, but after 12 weeks and seven countries, I was used to the laughter. He pointed directly across the road. What were the chances? Hai Guan was now The Design Light Store. It was another lighting shop. They must really like lamps in Singapore.

On the way back to the hotel, I wandered in to one of the many karaoke bars. (I can't help myself; it's like a disease.) The bar was full – although the room was so dark, it took my eyes a while to adjust before I could actually see the crowd. I was escorted to a table and given a drinks menu. It was then that I almost fell off my stool: a small glass of beer was $13. 'I'll wait a bit,' I said to the waitress. I wasn't buying a beer – I could fly to Kuala Lumpur for less than that (and I could: I just checked the price on the Air Asia website and a one-way flight was $11.25).

Picking a song is very high-tech in Singapore karaoke bars. Around the room were computer screens where you simply scrolled through the song list on the touch screen and picked your song and put in your table number. When your table number flashed up on the TV screens, the waiter handed you a microphone. I did get a little confused with the song list, but a friendly local girl in a very tiny miniskirt helped me (very friendly, in fact – she put her hand on my knee while she helped me). On the way back to my seat, I noticed lots of very friendly local girls in tiny miniskirts with their hands on men's knees. Men who were probably double their age. Ah, I was in a hostess bar. These girls were flirting with these men and laughing at their bad jokes, so the men would buy them very expensive drinks (and the girls took a cut from the bar).

I left after an hour. I waited to sing, but my song was way down the list. Plus the waiter was getting a bit peeved with me saying that I hadn't made up my mind about what drink I wanted. But most of all, my ears couldn't take the men singing soppy wailing Mandarin love songs to their 'dates' any longer.

In 1974, there was a frequent bus service to shuttle you around Singapore. Now there's a super-duper frequent MRT service crisscrossing the island. I headed first down to the harbour front. The old book recommended starting at Raffles Place for a good view over the 'teeming harbour'. Signs in the MRT ticket concourse indicated no smoking, eating or drinking and, seemingly, no hedgehogs. The latter actually applied to durian, a stinky, spiky fruit. The train station was spotless, the train was spotless and even the bins at the train station were spotlessly clean. Back in '74, Singapore was just as spotless, according to the old guidebook: 'Mr Lee's somewhat ironhanded government turned Singapore into a green, tidy garden city where no one dares litter the streets, or even carelessly drop cigarette ash. The water is drinkable from taps and smoking in public places is forbidden.' Lee Kuan Yew was the Prime Minister of Singapore from 1965 until 1990 and his son Lee Hsien Loong now has the reins. And no one still dares to litter the streets or drop cigarette ash. It's an $800 fine for littering and a $600 fine for smoking on the street. And heaven forbid that you dance in public. That's a $4000 fine.

The harbour wasn't very teeming and the good view was mostly of the rampant construction of apartment blocks across the harbour. I couldn't find the next attraction in the old book, either. The book advised walking along the waterfront to Merlion Park, where the great symbol of Singapore spouts water over the Singapore River. I asked a local what had happened to the great symbol of Singapore and he pointed further up the river to the statue of a bizarre hybrid lion/fish creature sitting next to a bland, concrete bridge. 'They moved it a few years ago,' he said.

'Why?'

He shrugged. 'No one knows why they do things in Singapore.'

There was quite a list of temples in the old book, but frankly I was templed out. The book also recommended visiting Chinatown, but I'd been there before on another trip to Singapore and it was now so clean and sterile that it had lost any charm. There was one place that I hadn't been to before. The old guidebook recommended catching a cable car to Sentosa Island. Back then, Sentosa was being developed as a resort island and it had a coralarium, a swimming lagoon and pushbikes for hire.

The cable car, which opened in 1974, departed from the 15th floor of an office building on the harbour front. Sentosa Island was originally called Pulau Blakang

Mati, which in Malay means the 'Island of Death from Behind'. The name came from Blakang Mati Fever, which in the late 1840s almost wiped out everyone on the island. In a 1972 contest organised by the Singapore Tourist Board, the island was renamed Sentosa, a Malay word meaning peace and tranquillity – which sounds a bit more enticing than Death from Behind.

I asked at the cable car office but they hadn't even heard of the coralarium or the swimming lagoon. The girl did say, however, that there were now three man-made beaches and that they still had pushbikes for hire. There may not have been a coralarium, but the five-square-kilometre island is now jam-packed with attractions, hotels and restaurants. From the cable car, it wasn't hard to spot the latest addition to the island. Construction was just finishing on Resorts World Sentosa, housing a massive casino (that cost a world record $US4.93 billion to build), six hotels (including the Hard Rock Hotel) with over 1800 rooms, a Universal Studios theme park and a Marine Life Park with the world's largest ocean-arium (which I suppose is just like a coralarium).

The cable car stopped at Tiger Sky Tower, which was a tall frothy tower of Tiger Beer with a rotating Tiger Beer viewing platform. The whole place was surprisingly quiet and the only other person on the wide open plaza at the top was a female staff member having a break. I walked down via the 'nature trail', which was suitably nature-like, but it was totally fabricated. The waterfall maintenance man was cleaning out the waterfall trying to make it look 'natural', while another fellow in green overalls was sweeping the nature trail then placing leaves, perfectly art directed, onto the track. And the Bose speakers hidden under the bushes everywhere playing 'Octopus's Garden' weren't very natural, either. There were lots of birds tweeting, but I couldn't see any and I had a sneaking suspicion that it was probably piped bird noises.

The first raked man-made beach at the bottom of the hill was perfectly spotless and had spotlessly perfect palm trees. There was a lifeguard on patrol sitting in his tower, but there wasn't a single person on the beach. The bike trail running along the beach was so clean that you could eat your dinner off it. Maybe it was because it was only ten in the morning, and a weekday, but even all the restaurants on the beach were empty.

I went for a swim in the clear, warm water then laid on a sun bed in front of one of the restaurants. And like any good backpacker, I pretended to be asleep when the waiter came, so I could use their sun beds without having to buy anything. The restaurants were too expensive for my shoestring tastes, so I went to the immaculately gleaming hawkers' market for lunch. I had a deliciously spicy curry laksa, but halfway through I got up to get some napkins and when I came back my bowl was gone. 'You're kidding,' I said loudly to no one in particular. Singapore was just a little bit too efficient and tidy.

I took advantage of the free bus around the island. Not intentionally. I was just trying to get back up to the cable car and I got on the wrong bus, which circumnavigated the entire island and ended up exactly where it started.

By the time I got back to my hotel, it was time for my final restaurant hunt for the entire trip. Tony recommended heading to Serangoon Road where 'there is always a spicy smell wafting out of shop fronts'. This was Singapore's Little India, except unlike India it was clean, had no cows roaming the streets and there were no people hassling to be your guide or take you to a 'good shop for you'. The street was full of sari shops, gold shops, tandoori restaurants, Bank of India branches and lots of God-awful distorted Bollywood music blaring out from large speakers in front of music shops.

Another of Tony's 'Personal Favourites' was Komala Vilas where the masala dosa was 'the best 35¢ meal to be had in Singapore' or you could 'go upstairs in the evening and for $1.50 eat (off a banana leaf with your fingers) your fill of rice, dahl and vegetable curries'. Komala Vilas was easy to find: the restaurant was in a large bright yellow building. I was happy to be ending my trip in one of Tony's favourite restaurants. When Tony and Maureen first came here, the restaurant was already old. A sign out the front read: 'Open Since 1947.'

The upstairs room looked as if it had been renovated. Well, they had added an electronic till. It was full of Indian families: women in brightly coloured saris and men in nice slacks and nice shirts. I couldn't see any western tourists (the restaurant is not in the current guidebook).

The masala dosa was still on the menu and so was the rice meal, which was exactly the same as it was described in the old guidebook – although it had gone up in price to $6.50. I ate off the banana leaf with my fingers and worked my way through piles of rice, vegetable curries and . . . I had no idea what half of the stuff was. One of the greatest joys of travelling for me is food and this restaurant, like many of the restaurants that I'd tracked down on this trip, gave me a chance to eat authentic local food – even if I didn't know what I was eating a lot of the time. I also got to try things that I probably wouldn't serve up for dinner at home, like fried frog, indefinable animal parts smothered with hot chilli, and crispy grasshoppers. I think that in many cases it was a good thing that a lot of these old restaurants had been dropped from the guidebook because it kept them authentic. You'll never find a banana pancake or cheeseburger on the menu at Komala Vilas. You just get lovely piles of things that you have no idea what they are.

My waiter kept refilling my leaf with those lovely things, so by the time I was ready to leave, I was absolutely stuffed. But before going back to the hotel, I had to have one final farewell drink. I somehow ended up in the 'backpacker' street at the Prince of Wales Pub, which had Foster's on tap.

I sat outside on the street and raised my glass in cheers to Tony and Maureen. Yes, Lonely Planet had almost single-handedly created the Banana Pancake Trail through South-East Asia, but as Canadian travel writer Rory MacLean puts it so well: their 'work has taught a generation how to move through the world alone and with confidence'. I certainly have had some of my most memorable experiences and meals throughout my travels because of the advice from Lonely Planet guidebooks.

This journey turned out better than I had ever imagined. I managed to get both a good glimpse of the past and a look into the future. Places had of course changed a lot in the years since then – as has the technology that helps us travel there – but when it came to the way people travelled, the community of backpackers, cultural traditions and the fruit salad at the Hotel Carolina, it was refreshing and even gratifying to see that nothing had really changed at all. And as I sat at my half-desk in my half-room writing these notes I felt for a minute just like Tony Wheeler – but without the bell-bottoms.

Bibliography

Books

Dalton, Bill, *Indonesia Handbook*, Moon Publications, 1977

Jenkins, David, *Student Guide to Asia*, AUS Student Travel, 1975

Martinkus, John, *A Dirty Little War*, Random House, 2001

Theroux, Paul, *The Great Railway Bazaar: By Train Through Asia*, Hamish Hamilton, 1975

Wheeler, Tony, *Burma: a travel survival kit*, Lonely Planet, 2nd edition, 1982

Wheeler, Tony, *South east Asia on a shoestring*, Lonely Planet, 1st edition, 1975

Wheeler, Tony, *South-east Asia on a shoestring*, Lonely Planet, revised edition, 1979

Williams, China, *Lonely Planet Thailand*, Lonely Planet, 13th edition, 2009

Williams, China [et al], *Southeast Asia on a Shoestring*, Lonely Planet, 15th edition, 2010

Yamashita, Shinji, *Bali and Beyond: Explorations in the Anthropology of Tourism*, trans. J. S. Eades, Berghahn Books, 2003

Articles

MacLean, Rory, 'The Pariah Countries', *The Guardian*, 24 April 2007

Shenon, Philip, 'The End of the World on 10 Tugriks a Day', *The New York Times*, 30 June 1996

Sobocinska, Agnieszka, 'Hippies Blazed a Trail to Those Far-Out Reaches', *The Australian*, 4 October 2006

Websites

Thorn Tree Travel Forum

www.lonelyplanet.com/thorntree

Thanks

Yeah man, first I owe a huge debt of thanks to those cool cats Tony and Maureen Wheeler. Not only did they show righteous love towards my book (and actually give me the old guidebook itself), they have inspired me, and millions more, to set out and hang loose around the world.

A big thankyou to the hip gang at Lonely Planet for allowing me to use all that way-out material from their books. And thanks to those cool cats at Poppies, YTL hotels and Sentosa Island for the use of their cool images.

To my fab chick Beth, who showed me what true love is – and also put her red pen all throughout my manuscript. (It's handy having a babe with a Master's degree in writing.) By the way, Beth did move to Australia and a few months later we went back to Ubud where I proposed to her. She said yes.

Peace and love to all the far-out folks during the trip who gave me their time and awesome stories:

Joaquim Calluto, José Maria Borges, Nino Borges (East Timor); Rai Yasa, Agus Yasa, Jenik Sukenny, Oka Wati, Ibu Canderi, Wayan Balik, Dewa Gede, Jahja Lawalata, Bernard (Indonesia); Captain Ho Singong, Mr Lai, Syed Aliar (Malaysia); Panchan Noimeecharoen, Somkuan the Doorman, Charles Henn (Thailand); May Oo, Mr Lin, Kyin Ngwe Chan, Lu Maw, Mr Raju and Myu Myu (Burma).

I would also dearly like to thank all the neat-o chicks at Random House for their funkadelic enthusiasm and support, in particular Nikki Christer, who sent me a lovely email after seeing me talk at the Byron Bay Writers Festival to which I promptly wrote back and told her that I just happened to be looking for a new publisher. Much thanks to my editor Virginia Grant for your good vibes and for keeping me honest. And right on to Larissa Edwards for being a real trip, baby.

And to my hip agent Pippa, who is way cool and outta sight.

Can you dig it? If slide shows are your bag, you can check out the groovy photos from my trip, including lots of pics of stained sheets and me eating grasshoppers, at www.brianthacker.tv.

Peace, dudes.

Brian Thacker, St Kilda East, June 2011